MODERN SOUTHEAST ASIA SERIES

James R. Reckner, *General Editor*

VIETNAM AND BEYOND

Vietnam and Beyond

A DIPLOMAT'S COLD WAR EDUCATION

Robert Hopkins Miller

An ADST-DACOR Diplomats and Diplomacy Book

TEXAS TECH UNIVERSITY PRESS

FIRST EDITION

This book is typeset in Bitstream Caslon 540. The paper used in this book meets the minimum requirements of ANSI/NISO Z39.48-1992 (R1997). ∞

Designed by Barbara Werden

Printed in the United States of America

LIBRARY OF CONGRESS CATALOGING-IN-PUBLICATION DATA

Miller, Robert Hopkins.
Vietnam and beyond : a diplomat's cold war education / Robert Hopkins Miller.
p. cm.—(Modern Southeast Asia series)
"An ADST-DACOR diplomats and diplomacy book."
Includes bibliographical references and index.
ISBN 0-89672-491-3 (cloth : alk. paper)
1. Miller, Robert Hopkins. 2. Diplomats—United States—Biography. 3. United States—Foreign relations—1945–1989. 4. Vietnamese Conflict, 1961–1975—Diplomatic history. 5. Cold War. I. Title. II.Series.

E840.8.M53 M55 2002
327.73'0092—dc211 2002004202

02 03 04 05 06 07 08 09 10 / 9 8 7 6 5 4 3 2 1

Texas Tech University Press
Box 41037
Lubbock, Texas 79409-1037 USA
1-800-832-4042
ttup@ttu.edu
www.ttup.ttu.edu

To

PHIL HABIB

Truly a giant of the U.S. Foreign Service

Contents

Illustrations

FIGURES

MAPS

Modern Southeast Asia Series Foreword

FEW EPISODES in American history have generated as much emotion, as much division, and as many long-term consequences for America and American society as our nation's involvement in Vietnam, Laos, and Cambodia in the latter half of the twentieth century. With this volume, Texas Tech University Press launches its Modern Southeast Asia Series, intended to facilitate an open dialogue about the Vietnam War and its lessons, with contributions reflecting all points of view.

It seems appropriate that the first volume in this series—in a sense, Texas Tech University Press's new exploration of Vietnam and related Cold War aspects—should recount the journey of a diplomat whose working life with the U.S. Department of State essentially encompassed the entire Cold War, from its early days through to its promising, and yet in many respects illusory, conclusion. "Victory" in the Cold War, a goal two full generations of Americans who served their nation in the diplomatic as well as the military sphere strove to achieve, rather than opening a bright new world, simply unleashed a dizzying array of new problems that had long been submerged or contained because of the overarching concerns of the superpower confrontation.

Ambassador Robert H. Miller's career involved him in many of America's foreign policy issues of the day, but his central, defining experience was Vietnam, which he first encountered as first secretary, political officer and deputy chief of the political section of the American Embassy in Saigon, 1962–65. Thus, he was on the scene during the final year of the Ngo Dinh Diem government. He notes presciently that "Diem's political strategy and our acquiescence in it ensured that effective, alternative, noncommunist leadership in the country could come only from within its own military establishment." In a sense, this was the American dilemma: how to support stabilization of the South Vietnamese government and at the same time develop a cohesive and functional body politic. After the United States condoned Diem's overthrow in 1963, Miller reports, "the United States accepted responsibility for a war that, without Diem, became an increasingly losing struggle."

Later, in Washington as director of the State Department's Vietnam Working Group, Miller, harboring growing doubts about American policy in

Vietnam, submitted numerous reports questioning America's deepening involvement in Vietnam and offering approaches that sought to limit that involvement and bring it into greater balance with underlying American interests in the region. But, as Miller acknowledges, his views, like those put forward by many others at many levels, had no impact on the U.S. government's apparent inability to change course and, in effect, fell on deaf ears.

In some ways, America's failure in Vietnam was an organizational one. In 1903, Secretary of the Navy William H. Moody reported that in the existing fragmented Navy Department organization there was "power without knowledge in one place and knowledge without power in another place. The knowledge," Moody advised, "should be available to those who have the power to act so that the power may be exercised with intelligence."[1] Six decades later, a similar situation prevailed which, combined with vincible ignorance, led to a misguided exercise of American power.

Following the fall of Saigon, Miller served as Ambassador to Malaysia, in which position he dealt with one of the many after-effects of the failure of American policy in Indochina: the flood of Vietnamese escaping the "reunified" communist state by sea, who reached Malaysian shores and there encountered a generally less than friendly welcome.

Finally, like so many Americans who served in Vietnam in one capacity or another during the turbulent decade of heavy American involvement there, Miller in retirement revisited the scenes of his earlier service. Nostalgia drives such visits, and, like so many other returning Americans, Miller feels a certain ambivalence about what he finds: the absence of hostility from the ordinary Vietnamese people, the evident failure of the economic system imposed on the conquered South, and the barren fruit of "victory" enjoyed by the North. As one northern Vietnamese confided to me in one of my visits to Vietnam in recent years, "We sacrificed everything for the Revolution, and we got nothing."

And so Ambassador Miller's journey ends. And Texas Tech University Press's Vietnam journey begins by bringing you this most remarkable account.

JAMES R. RECKNER
Texas Tech University

* "Annual Report of the Secretary of the Navy," *Army & Navy Register* 34 (5 Dec. 1903): 4.

ADST-DACOR Diplomats and Diplomacy Series Foreword

FOR MORE than 225 years, extraordinary men and women have represented the United States abroad under all kinds of circumstances. What they did and how and why they did it remain little known to their compatriots. In 1995, the Association for Diplomatic Studies and Training (ADST) and Diplomatic and Consular Officers, Retired (DACOR) created a book series to increase public knowledge and appreciation of the involvement of American diplomats in world history. As this book exemplifies, the series seeks to demystify diplomacy by telling the story of those who have conducted our foreign relations, as they saw them and lived them.

Robert Hopkins Miller, a former career minister in the Foreign Service of the United States whose service, from 1951 to 1991, spanned virtually the entire Cold War, spent nearly one-third of those years working on Vietnam and Southeast Asia. The Vietnam War of the 1960s and 1970s dominates the book as it dominated U.S. foreign policy at the time. At once personal and historical in tone, this account demonstrates Bob Miller's exceptional "hands-on" knowledge of Vietnam in the pre-Diem and post-Diem periods, when he served at the U.S. Embassy in Saigon. It informs and enlightens us on the policy context and critical debates in the Washington bureaucracy as the war dragged on; the personalities and complex events of the Paris Peace talks; and the war's aftermath in Malaysia, as thousands of Vietnamese "boat people" arrived in neighboring Southeast Asian countries. As the story of these years unfolds, Miller poignantly reveals how his own views on Vietnam evolved over time, from a young officer's enthusiastic acceptance of John F. Kennedy's challenge to "bear any burden, pay any price" in the defense of liberty to a maturing officer's growing doubts and frustrations regarding a policy—and a war—gone awry.

During Bob Miller's diplomatic career, as the book recounts, the "needs of the service" involved him, first, in the NATO buildup in Europe, presidential travel and summitry, and the Congo crisis of the early 1960s. Later, post-Vietnam, he served as ambassador to Malaysia (1977–1980) and to Côte d'Ivoire (1983–1986), in senior policy and management positions in the State Department, and as vice president of the National Defense University. Since retiring from the Foreign Service, Ambassador Miller has served as DACOR's president, taught graduate courses on U.S. diplomatic issues and on Southeast Asia at Georgetown University's School of Foreign Service and senior honors courses at George Washington University, and lectured in a number of East Asian countries under U.S. Information Agency sponsorship. He is the author of *The United States and Vietnam, 1787–1941* (National Defense University Press, 1990), *Inside an Embassy: The Political Role of Diplomats Abroad* (Congressional Quarterly Press, 1992), and articles on Vietnam and Southeast Asia. In *Vietnam and Beyond: A Diplomat's Cold War Education,* he has given us a thoughtful first-hand account of life on the diplomatic front lines.

KENNETH L. BROWN, *President,* ADST
ALAN W. LUKENS, *President,* DACOR

Preface

My career in the Foreign Service of the United States spanned forty years of Cold War, my retirement coinciding with the end of that great struggle between East and West. Today's very different world argues for, indeed compels, the Foreign Service's "Cold War generation" to record their experiences to help succeeding generations better understand the era and American foreign policy at the time.

Each Foreign Service career during the Cold War formed its own, individual perspective on that piece of history; in recording our experiences, we thus resemble the blind men who describe an elephant according to which part of it they touched. Foreign Service memoirs are by no means definitive appraisals of events; rather, they are part of history's raw material. As such, they fill an important niche as primary sources for historians. They are first-hand accounts by "those who were there" that help inform and enrich the scholar's more deliberate and objective work.

Personal recollections are an important part of this story, although I have not relied solely on my own memory to reconstruct this account. The core of the account is based on published and unpublished official records of the State Department, as well as published accounts of historians, journalists, and statesmen, on the events in which I was a participant.

Where it seemed important to supplement published accounts, I have had access, with the cooperation of the State Department, to my own official files. Official published records often do not include the views of middle-ranking, or even senior, officers on what was going on at the time and what they personally thought we should be doing—or not doing. Many such documents are now being systematically declassified after twenty-five years, mine included.

Like most of my Foreign Service colleagues, I was a "generalist," with no previous background in foreign affairs other than what I acquired at university. I was given no specialized training that would have made me a Cold War expert in global strategic or ideological issues, or in colonialism or the emergence of the third world. But it was my lot, as determined by the times and by the "needs of the Service," to become involved in several key phases of the Cold War: the NATO buildup in Europe in the 1950s, presidential travel and summitry at the end of that decade, the initial Congo crisis in central Africa in the early 1960s, and Vietnam in the 1960s and 1970s. I devote some four chapters of this account to my experiences during America's unsuccessful Vietnam venture, on which I spent over a third of my career, and to my views about that U.S. involvement as they evolved from roughly 1962 to 1980.

While I cannot expect readers to be as emotionally caught up as I have been in this account—in effect an account of my entire professional life—I hope that it will enhance their understanding of the mind-set of America during those years, as well as its fears and concerns, and why America responded to a perceived global threat the way it did. For me personally it has been especially important to look back and reexamine my own views about our Vietnam engagement—and my own modest role in it over more than a decade. I have tried to reflect the gradual evolution of my own feelings: at the beginning, outright acceptance of what we were doing as right, good, and in the interest of both the United States and South Vietnam in the face of the global Sino-Soviet Cold War threat as it was perceived at the time; then, emerging doubts and frustrations as we seemed unable to extricate ourselves from that engagement; and, finally, growing conviction that our massive involvement in Vietnam, and our apparent inability to change course there, may have gotten far out of proportion to what I saw as our declining national security interests there.

I hope, too, that this account will increase the reader's appreciation of the work of the Foreign Service—its excitement, its variety, the dedication of its employees, and the dangers, frustrations, and challenges they face.

Acknowledgments

NEEDLESS TO SAY, I could not have brought this work to completion without the help of many people. My wife, Kaity, and my children, George and Margaret, encouraged me to write it—for them if not for others. They also read it and made useful and important comments, and Margaret gave it a first copyediting. I am grateful to ADST for accepting the manuscript for the ADST-DACOR series, and to Margery Boichel Thompson, ADST's publishing director, for her infinite patience and professional skills in guiding me through the entire process of writing, editing, and marketing the manuscript. I also want to thank John Cunningham of the Department of State for working with me to gain access to my official records; colleagues Kenneth N. Rogers, Frederick Z. Brown, and James D. Rosenthal for reading the manuscript, making many insightful comments, and correcting a number of errors of fact and memory; and W. Scott Butcher for reading and commenting on the section on Malaysia. Finally, I must express my deep appreciation to Texas Tech University Press, its director, Noel Parsons, and his colleagues for their decision to publish the manuscript and make it the book I had long envisioned it to be. Nonetheless, I alone bear full responsibility for the content and for any errors that may have crept through. But without the dedicated help of those acknowledged here, the book could not have been realized.

ROBERT HOPKINS MILLER

VIETNAM AND BEYOND

INTRODUCTION

The Setting

I JOINED the State Department in 1951 and retired in 1991. Harry Truman was president and Dean Acheson was his secretary of state when I began my career. When I retired, George H. W. Bush was president and James Baker his secretary of state.

In 1951, I was twenty-four years old. Six years before, in 1945, the United States and the Soviet Union had emerged victorious over Germany and Japan after the most destructive war in history. To end the war more quickly, the United States had unleashed the atom bomb, a new weapon of unprecedented destructive force, against Japan. At the opening of the nuclear era, Europe and Japan lay devastated, and the Axis powers—Germany, Italy, and Japan—were prostrate before the victorious Allied armies. Less than six years later, the wartime alliance between Moscow and Washington had soured and the Cold War between East and West was under way.

Despite the absence of any family background in foreign affairs, I was drawn to the State Department by an American vision of a better world after World War II's devastation. My career was touched by America's greatest postwar foreign policy successes—European recovery and the North Atlantic Treaty Organization (NATO)—and by its greatest excess and failure—Vietnam. My professional experience, like that of my peers, was shaped and defined by the great struggle of the age—America's global effort to contain what it perceived to be a major threat to its national survival: the expansionist policies of the Soviet Union. That effort avoided nuclear war for more than forty years and kept the United States secure throughout. Moreover, the fruits of America's major postwar foreign policies—the rebuilding of Europe and Japan, the dissolution of Europe's colonial empires, and the creation of the United Nations Charter and system—remain manifest today. Can anyone really ask for more in terms of career satisfaction?

If I can discern any common thread—any unifying theme—throughout my career, it is that America's motives in seeking to build a better world have been increasingly seen by those with whom we sought to share its benefits to be directed mainly by its own selfish interests as the dangers of the Cold War receded and former colonies sought to pursue their own destinities.

As with most Foreign Service careers, the "needs of the Service" took me on a seemingly disconnected journey for nearly forty years. It was an odyssey without any apparent logic or central theme or purpose—from Europe to Southeast Asia to Africa; from multilateral to bilateral diplomacy to the frustrating and endless negotiations on Vietnam and on Mutual and Balanced Force Reduction (MBFR) in Europe; from staff secretariat or "paper-pushing" functions to counterinsurgency and third-world development, to arms control, resource management, and professional military education, and on to civilian academia. Much, but not all of this experience, was in the developing, post-colonial world within a few degrees of the equator, much of it, but not all, in the francophone world.

When I joined the State Department, the Foreign Service of the United States was made up in large part of white males educated in Ivy League schools on the East Coast—"the best and the brightest." Over the forty years of my career, the Foreign Service struggled to cope with the democratization of its ranks: first through a conscious effort to widen the geographic distribution of its members, and later through the systematic recruitment of women, blacks, and other minorities by way of aggressive "affirmative action" programs.

I was a product of small public schools in the Pacific Northwest. My three brothers and I had passed our childhood in western Washington state in the comfortable, close world of small, white-collar and blue-collar communities—mostly Protestant and all white—with the values that went with that environment and time. I was fortunate enough to attend Stanford University as an undergraduate and to complete my education with a master's degree at Harvard—thanks to the GI Bill. In the ongoing evolution of the Foreign Service, I saw my own place in it gradually transformed in the 1960s and 1970s from that of a beneficiary of the Service's progressive democratization after World War II into that of a white male Ivy League product, and thus part of the traditional Foreign Service still needing reform.

Along with this social and demographic evolution came other changes that also reflected changes in our society at large. When I joined the Foreign Service, it took its elite nature as a mark of distinction and pride, took its professionalism for granted, and was confident its values were America's values. This gradually gave way to a Foreign Service whose energies were increasingly absorbed by concerns for equal opportunity and fair treatment for its employees, by pressures for adequate compensation for sometimes dangerous and difficult work, and by constant management attention to the concerns of the employees and their families. And as the demographics of the Foreign Service changed, its values came into question from both inside and outside. Its pride in its elite character and professionalism was seen as elitism pure and simple, giving way at least in part to careerism and to charges that the Foreign Service was inadequate or inappropriate to its tasks.

The tasks changed, too. As the Cold War expanded from the center of Europe in 1946 and 1947 to a perceived confrontation between freedom and communism worldwide, traditional U.S. diplomacy gave way to a broader concept of national security that came to include defense, intelligence, information, propaganda, and foreign aid. In this panoply of policies and programs, the diplomatic function of the department and the Foreign Service became only one arrow in America's national security quiver—the one with the fewest resources behind it.

For me, it was a varied and satisfying career in public service. Those who have come after me face the challenges of today's more disorganized and more dangerous world, of an increasingly complex bureaucracy to meet these challenges, and of a more fractious foreign policy process at home. For them, I cannot judge.

PART I

Preparation and Apprenticeship

ONE

Prelude to Service

I ENTERED Stanford University in 1943 in a wartime program that combined the last year of high school with the freshman year of university. Until that moment my world had been confined to western Washington and Oregon, apart from one family visit to Yellowstone Park. San Francisco and Stanford opened new horizons I could not have imagined—wealth, luxury, and sophistication beyond anything I had ever been exposed to, to say nothing of the level of intellectual endeavor. My letters home reflected this new world and my wide-eyed adjustment to it.

After a brief period of homesickness—I was barely sixteen—I came to love the life at Stanford. I relished the mild climate and beautiful surroundings, the academic challenge, fellow students from many walks of life—mostly more prosperous and worldly than my own, it seemed to me—the growing friendships. It was a life that tested my sheltered childhood's values and behavior.

My Stanford experience—inside and outside the classroom—opened my eyes and my mind to a broader, more complex world than I had known, one that my childhood had left me woefully unprepared to deal with but one that I was eager to come to terms with if I could. I thirsted after knowledge and at the same time felt uncertain that I would be able to compete in the larger and more unfriendly world of knowledge and affairs beyond my university cocoon.

Two happy years went by. I passed my eighteenth birthday three weeks after V-J ("Victory over Japan") Day. Still subject to the draft, I enlisted in the army for eighteen months. The army was an eye-opener of a different sort. Although I remained at Fort Lewis, Washington, close to home, for my entire army tour, I went in at the bottom and was thrown in with those who make up the bottom ranks of the service at any time—uneducated, rough young men, and in those days just a few similar women, who caroused during their free time and did as little as possible while on duty. I was immediately assigned to the Fort Lewis Separation Center as a clerk-typist to help process thousands of wartime GIs out of the army and was told I would be sent to basic training after six months.

Instead, after six months I was assigned to a rifle company in the 2nd Infantry Division, which in the meantime had been transferred from Fort

Hood, Texas, to Fort Lewis. Without basic training I was totally useless to the rifle company, and I quickly sought refuge from it as the division chaplain's assistant. In that assignment I eventually rose to the exalted rank of buck sergeant at which I finished my tour.

In the fall of 1947, I returned to Stanford under the GI Bill to complete my bachelor's degree in political science, accomplished in the spring of 1949. Still feeling inadequately prepared to compete in the possible careers open to me, I had enough GI Bill eligibility left to entertain the idea of working for a graduate degree. By then, I had become interested in international relations and a possible career in the State Department. I had followed the momentous developments of the war and its aftermath with growing attention, and the idea of public service and foreign affairs attracted me. The world of business did not.

My parents made no effort to deflect me from my path, even though in their world a civil service career was looked down upon as reserved for those too lazy or afraid to work. I never gave a thought to the possibility that I might pursue a career in the private sector and, at an appropriate moment, seek a high government job through the political appointment route. My horizons were too limited for such ideas. Moreover, my grandfather Miller had worked for the Department of Interior in Alaska and a cousin of my father had a mid-ranking civil service job as an engineer with the Department of Interior in Washington. On the other side of the equation, my father's uncle by marriage, who had made a fortune in apple orchards in central Washington state without a college education, had great disdain for those who sought education instead of entering the real world of free enterprise, to say nothing of those who took shelter in the federal bureaucracy.

The Allied invasion of Normandy had occurred during my first two years at Stanford, followed in dizzying succession by Franklin Roosevelt's reelection to a fourth term, his death a few months later, the United Nations' founding conference in nearby San Francisco, Nazi Germany's unconditional surrender in Europe, Truman's decision to use the atomic bomb against Japan, and Japan's unconditional surrender days later. Suddenly a bright, new, hopeful world emerged in which the United States—and the United Nations—would play leading roles for lasting world peace, stability, and international justice. I wanted to be a part of that great endeavor.

By the time I returned to Stanford, however, the Cold War had already begun. During my two final years at Stanford, the Soviet Union consolidated its occupation of Eastern Europe, and the United States responded: the massive U.S. airlift broke the Soviet blockade of Berlin. The Truman Doctrine brought economic and military aid to Greece, embroiled in a civil war with communist elements, and to Turkey, vulnerable to a hostile Soviet Union across the Black Sea. Subsequently, the Marshall Plan and the historic North Atlantic Treaty transformed the course of European history. Events in Europe and elsewhere in those two years, and Washington policymakers' debates on how to respond, led Harry Truman, Franklin Roosevelt's modest but feisty and determined successor, to make decisions that for two generations formed the basis of America's foreign policy and strategic posture. The result was the policy of "containment" of the Soviet Union by diplomacy and, if necessary, by military force wherever and whenever it threatened small powers—or perceived U.S. interests.

In the fall of 1949, I entered Harvard University to work for a master's degree in international relations—an opportunity that I and millions of my contemporaries could never have even considered without the generosity of the post–World War II GI Bill for veterans. My program was one designed for young men and women interested in government service in foreign affairs. Like me, many of my classmates in this program actually entered public service—the State Department, the Economic Cooperation Administration (ECA), which administered "Marshall Plan" economic aid funds to Western Europe, the Central Intelligence Agency (CIA), and the U.S. Information Agency (USIA).[1]

At Harvard, I devoted my studies to filling in some of the gaps in my education, principally in international economics. One of the hotly debated issues of the day in that field was whether the "dollar gap" between Europe and the United States would be permanent, thereby requiring the United States to give aid to Europe indefinitely. Politically, the burning issues were the fall of China to Mao Zedong's communist forces, whom in the American government to blame for this diplomatic and strategic defeat, and the outbreak of the Korean War. In Washington, Senator Joseph McCarthy's disgraceful communist witch-hunt gathered momentum, focused largely on the State Department. In Europe the Cold War deepened and became institutionalized. The young NATO alliance, under U.S. prodding, established permanent structures, both civilian and military. Wartime hero General Dwight D. Eisenhower was appointed Supreme Allied Commander for Europe (SACEUR), and NATO members were asked to commit at least some of their forces to his command even in peacetime.

Despite my initial qualms about being able to scale Harvard's vaunted intellectual heights, I found that Stanford had prepared me well. After surviving a first bleak and depressing Christmas holiday far from home, during which I was writing several term papers and preparing for my first set of final exams, I settled in and found little difference in the quality of education at the two institutions, or between Stanford's undergraduate and Harvard's graduate programs. With my studies at Harvard focused on international affairs, and more particularly on international economics, I became a strong supporter of the Truman Doctrine, the Marshall Plan, NATO, and our forthright response to North Korea's attack on South Korea.

By the time I left Harvard for the State Department in 1951, I was firmly separated from my father's Republican orientation (my mother had consistently voted for Norman Thomas, the perennial Socialist candidate for president) and had become a Democrat, at least in foreign affairs. In my "conversion," in addition to my support for the Truman-Acheson foreign policy, I shared with my fellow Harvard students a strong revulsion at Senator McCarthy's communist witch-hunt against the State Department and Foreign Service.

I was fortunate to be nominated by Harvard and accepted by the State Department for an internship that offered the prospect of a permanent civil service career appointment after a probationary period. I received my master's degree from Harvard in June 1951 and began as an intern trainee on September 17, 1951.

Apprenticeship

Washington, D.C., opened yet another new horizon to me: the world of politics, power, ambition, and foreign policy. It was heady stuff. I loved my new adventure, but feared it as well. Everyone I came in contact with seemed so knowledgeable and self assured. In my own mind, I was far from being either. My starting annual salary was thirty-three hundred dollars.

Jobs abounded in Washington in 1951. Government in general, and foreign affairs in particular, were growth industries in the brave new postwar world. The deepening Cold War had spawned a plethora of new government agencies and bureaucracies: the Marshall Plan, the U.S. Information Agency, a rapidly expanding State Department, the Central Intelligence Agency, military intelligence agencies, and, eventually, the Arms Control and Disarmament Agency. International agencies also proliferated, notably the United Nations and its specialized agencies, the World Bank and International Monetary Fund, and NATO. All one had to do to be part of the great struggle for a better world was to find one's niche, obtain medical and security clearances, and go to work.

My fellow interns and I were about twenty-five in number, all picked from different universities and colleges.[2] After two weeks of orientation classes at the Foreign Service Institute, we were to be given three assignments of three months each in different parts of the State Department to vary our experience and prepare us for our future careers. These brief on-the-job assignments were worked out partly on our own initiative and partly with the help of the intern program's organizers. It soon became apparent that the promise of permanent employment in the department after three temporary assignments was no guarantee at all that we would land jobs that interested us or that had good career prospects.

Toward the end of my first assignment in the Office of International Conferences, the office that administratively supported U.S. delegations to a wide variety of international conferences, I began to look around for greener pastures. I was in luck: The Office of European Regional Affairs was looking for a warm, young body eager to do "pick-and-shovel" work in the exciting new arena of NATO, that historic departure in U.S. foreign policy—an "entangling alliance" in peacetime. I leapt at the chance!

TWO

From NATO to the Congo

IT IS HARD to convey today the intense atmosphere of participation in and commitment to history in the making that radiated at the time from the Office of European Regional Affairs. The North Atlantic Treaty had been signed less than three years earlier. The Cold War had deepened. The broad lines of a global U.S. containment policy had been set, and the United States and its new partners were busy strengthening the young NATO alliance and institutionalizing its structure.[1]

NATO: Cold War Frontline

When I joined the office in January 1952, feverish preparations were under way for the NATO meeting of foreign ministers to be held in Lisbon the following month. Analyses were being made to establish U.S. views on what would constitute reasonable military contributions from each NATO ally, including the United States. We were also developing plans for a major military assistance program for European allies that would supplement Marshall Plan economic assistance. Testimony had to be prepared to persuade the Congress of these new departures in U.S. foreign policy.

Electricity was in the air—or so it seemed to an inexperienced newcomer to the State Department. Secretary of State Dean Acheson was to head the large U.S. delegation to Lisbon. The director of the office, Edwin McCammon Martin, a brilliant, tough, unyielding taskmaster, imposed the highest professional standards on himself and on all those who worked for him. In those days Ed Martin was a distant and forbidding figure. In the much smaller, more simply organized State Department of the 1950s, office directors were fewer in number and had greater responsibilities and far greater direct access to the secretary of state than is the case today. Happily for me, as the most junior of professional staff in the office, there were several layers of protective bureaucracy between Ed Martin and me. I had little firsthand knowledge of him but saw and heard plenty of evidence around me that he kept all personnel on their toes and producing at top speed and top quality.[2] This, then, was the office I wanted to work in, and my immediate supervisor, Laurence (Larry)

Vass, offered me a permanent job after my three-month internship. I had pangs of conscience about bolting the intern program. Nevertheless, if I stayed with the program, I had no assurance that I would end up with something as interesting as the NATO job or that held so much career potential. So I made my decision and never looked back.

The Lisbon meeting came and went, and I settled into my new responsibilities. Spring changed to summer and summer to fall. In early September 1952, on my first trip outside the United States (apart from short hops to Canada), I was married in Athens, Greece, to Catherine Antoniades. She had gotten her master's degree in government from Radcliffe College, also in June 1951. Kaity and I spent the first three months of our married life in Paris, where, thanks to Larry Vass's understanding intervention, I was temporarily attached to the secretariat of the U.S. delegation to NATO. The delegation secretariat had been augmented to support the preparation of papers and positions on the results of NATO's annual review of its members' defense programs, to be considered by foreign and defense ministers in December.[3]

While we were enjoying our "work/honeymoon" in Paris, Dwight Eisenhower, the American standard-bearer in war and again in peace, defeated Adlai Stevenson to succeed Truman as president. Eisenhower had declined Truman's offer of the Democratic Party's mantle and instead accepted the Republican Party's call to run for the presidency. After his election, Eisenhower named John Foster Dulles to be his secretary of state.

On January 16, 1953, Acheson said farewell to State Department employees gathered in the department's parking lot. He had been a strong secretary of state and personally popular with his staff. Having returned from Paris a few weeks before, I was in the audience. With barely fifteen months' experience in my new career, I shared what was an emotional farewell ceremony.[4]

On Inauguration Day, January 20, 1953, Kaity and I had gathered with some close friends to watch the festivities on television. When the announcer informed us that the outgoing cabinet, including President and Mrs. Truman, were going to lunch at Dean Acheson's house in Georgetown, we all jumped in our cars and raced to Acheson's house. Sure enough, the Trumans drove up, as did a number of departing cabinet members. The two hundred or so people who had gathered with the same impulse applauded the departing presidential couple. The Trumans were clearly touched by this gesture of loyalty and affection.[5]

Several days later, on January 28, 1953, the new secretary of state, John Foster Dulles, gathered all employees in the same parking lot where Acheson had spoken to us a few days earlier and addressed us from the same back steps.

Dulles was a different personality, and his remarks carried a far different message. The Republicans had not held the White House since Roosevelt defeated Hoover in 1932—twenty years earlier; they were hungry for power and ready to make their mark on the federal government. And twenty years of loyal service to Democratic administrations made the career civil (and foreign) service suspect in the eyes of our new political leaders. Nowhere was this more evident than in the State Department.

In his "inaugural address" to State Department employees, Dulles told us all how he had always aspired to be secretary of state, and he called for his new team to give him and the new Republican administration "positive loyalty." It was suddenly a very different atmosphere in the department.[6] The Republicans saw themselves surrounded by an unsympathetic, even disloyal, and swollen workforce that for twenty years had fed at the public trough of profligate Democratic spending. Moreover, Senator Joseph McCarthy's baleful witch-hunt against alleged Communists in the State Department was in full swing, and neither Eisenhower nor Dulles seemed willing to stand up to McCarthy. Instead, they merged the department's Office of Security and the Bureau of Consular Affairs into one Bureau of Security and Consular Affairs. The new bureau was placed under the direction of Scott McLeod, a conservative Republican who met with Senator McCarthy's approval. Combining security and consular affairs in one office was designed to protect the American people from subversion from within and without.[7]

The new administration's decision to subject the State Department's civil service employees to a massive reduction-in-force had a more immediate impact on me personally. In order to be eligible for the State Department's intern program, in addition to being nominated by a university, one had to have passed the civil service's Junior Management Assistant (JMA) examination. At the time, only those hired from the JMA register could receive permanent civil service tenure after a year's probation. All other new civil service employees at the time received "temporary-indefinite" appointments. When the reduction-in-force was announced, I had completed my probationary period and received permanent tenure.

Nevertheless, within months I received notice that I was being "bumped" out of my job by someone who after many years of service as a secretary had reached my exalted rank as a junior officer. I was to be transferred to what I considered then to be the department's "graveyard" for junior officers—the office of international exchange programs for foreign visitors and for Americans studying or teaching abroad under U.S. government auspices. The office was staffed with many junior positions and some years later was transferred to the

U.S. Information Agency (USIA) in one of the U.S. government's periodic reorganizations. In any case, in my eyes it could not be compared with the Office of NATO Affairs, which was at the center of the most critical American foreign policy initiative of the time.

This was my first unsettling experience with personnel changes brought about by the vagaries of domestic politics on the one hand, and the ingrained American penchant to reorganize on the other. Fortunately for me, my boss, Larry Vass, appealed my case, less for reasons of my indispensability than on the grounds that the person "bumping" me out was not professionally qualified for the job. The appeal carried the day and I stayed where I was. Such changes, which can be personally devastating when they occur, usually end up proving the old French adage *plus ça change, plus c'est la même chose* (the more things change, the more they stay the same). In this case, a number of my former intern colleagues ended up in USIA through this process and had successful and rewarding careers in public diplomacy.

For the next year I worked contentedly as a junior professional analyzing all NATO countries' defense programs, developing recommendations for the U.S. representatives to make during the NATO annual review of those programs, and drafting background and talking papers for department witnesses to use in hearings before the appropriate congressional committees in support of our growing military assistance programs for our NATO partners. I was certainly not making policy personally, nor was I anywhere near the policymaking process, but the office was intimately involved in that process. For my part, I had the great satisfaction of feeling that I was making a small contribution to our top-priority foreign policy objective of forging an effective alliance to defend the West against an apparently menacing Soviet threat.

Those around me in the office, all senior to me, were working on other aspects of this great effort. I shared the office with Russell Fessenden, ten years my senior. Fessenden followed on a day-to-day basis the steps being taken by the six nations that were already linked in the European Coal and Steel Community (CSC) and EURATOM, the European nuclear community, to create a European Defense Community (EDC) in order to integrate the former German enemy permanently into the Western defense structure. To reinforce U.S. policy in support of the EDC arrangements, the Congress passed an amendment to the Mutual Security Act of 1953, the so-called Richards Amendment, named for the congressman who put it forward, requiring that 50 percent of the military equipment and materiel procured for European countries from fiscal year 1954 appropriations be delivered directly to the EDC or to its member countries. I was asked to prepare a memorandum for Secretary Dulles alerting him to the possible consequences of the Richards Amendment. I was thrilled when the memorandum came back to me with the noncommittal notation "Secretary saw."[8]

In the summer of 1954, I sought and received a transfer to the U.S. mission to NATO and European Regional Organizations (USRO) in Paris. Kaity had become a U.S. citizen, and we had had a baby boy that spring. I was assigned as a second secretary in the Political Section of the U.S. NATO delegation, with responsibility for following the work of the NATO Annual Review Committee. So I continued to develop my expertise in this area and was now exposed to the arcane domain of multilateral diplomacy. (Even the Foreign Service inspectors who inspected our delegation were puzzled by our explanations of what we did, which was so different from the traditional work of bilateral diplomacy. Ambassador Bernard Gufler, the senior inspector who interviewed me about my work, said at the end of our discussion—much to my concern—"I wish I could understand what all of you do here!")

As a new second secretary, I was the junior member of the office. For much of my assignment I shared an office suite with Arthur Hartman, who later served as assistant secretary of state for European affairs, ambassador to France, and ambassador to the Soviet Union. Delegation headquarters were in the Hotel Talleyrand, an eighteenth-century *hôtel particulier* once occupied by the famous French foreign minister. My work was not of great moment. It was the "grunt" work of the Foreign Service—in this case, analyzing NATO governments' defense programs in light of their professed commitments to NATO. These analyses provided the basis for policy recommendations to Washington as to whether a country's programs should be approved or amended. I also drafted reports to interested Washington agencies (primarily the State and Defense Departments) on the proceedings of the NATO Annual Review Committee meetings. This committee was the forum under the North Atlantic Council where the United States and its allies exchanged views on each other's defense plans and proposed increases or decreases in their force commitments to NATO and their defense budgets to support those commitments. It was a central aspect of the young alliance's cooperative effort at the time, and it continued to hold excitement for me.

Shortly after we arrived in Paris, the French National Assembly voted to reject the European Defense Community—on August 30, 1954. Two months later, the NATO foreign ministers convened in Paris to endorse alternative arrangements for integrating West Germany into the Western defense structure.[9] NATO foreign and defense ministers also gathered to discuss the major issues of Western defense and to take or ratify decisions about the NATO force buildup. John Foster Dulles came to town and occasionally I attended delegation meetings in his presence. For the rest of the year, when the Permanent NATO Council considered the recommendations of the NATO Annual Review Committee, I was invited to the ambassador's preparatory staff meeting to participate in the discussion of those agenda items, and then to attend the council meeting itself to draft the report to Washington on the discussion there.

The sense of participating in historic events was also enhanced just by living in Paris. France was going through its final agony in Indochina. Dien Bien Phu had fallen to Viet Minh forces in May 1954, and the Geneva Conference to end hostilities and temporarily partition Vietnam ended on July 20 of the same year, a month before we arrived. On November 1, 1954, a major uprising occurred in Algeria that opened the Algerian war for independence, which tore apart the French body politic during our entire stay in France. It seemed clear to everyone but the French that Algeria would one day be independent. But *l'Algérie française* was such a part of the French psyche—especially in the face of the debacle at Dien Bien Phu—that it took several years of bitter, bloody warfare and a political upheaval in France before Algeria was in fact independent. In 1956 came the Suez crisis, which strained relations between the key members of the NATO alliance, the United States, Britain, and France.[10]

We returned to Washington for a new assignment in mid-1957, by now with two children. A girl, Margaret Helen, was born in Paris a year earlier, joining son George Keith, now three years old. On a personal level, our three years in Paris had been pleasurable ones. We had enjoyed our three-month "working honeymoon" there in 1952, and we continued to enjoy it immensely from 1954 to 1957. We explored the chateaux, cathedrals, and restaurants of the Île-de-France; visited Belgium, Holland, and Switzerland; and toured the Haute Savoie—the French Alps—and the Riviera as well. Each summer, we went to Greece for vacation with Kaity's mother, who had been widowed two months after we were married. We lived in a cheerful apartment in the sixteenth *arrondissement* in Paris, which was rented to us by a most amiable, elderly, recently widowed French architect. We made friends among our younger colleagues in our own and other NATO delegations and saw frequently several French friends from our university days. Looking back, our life there was idyllic.

Another important career uncertainty nevertheless arose during this otherwise pleasant period. Based on recommendations in a study by a prestigious commission chaired by Henry Wriston, then president of Brown University, the Eisenhower administration decided to integrate most jobs in the State Department and in its missions abroad into one Foreign Service. Until then, Foreign Service officers served mostly abroad and rarely at home, while the State Department in Washington was staffed principally by civil servants who rarely served abroad. The Wriston commission's argument for change essentially was that policy analysts at home made foreign policy judgments and recommendations with little or no foreign experience; conversely, Foreign Service officers serving only or mostly abroad lost touch with the domestic political and bureaucratic realities at home that directly affected the foreign policy process.

I was confident that I would be accepted permanently into the Foreign Service. Such, indeed, turned out to be the case after several months of uncertainty, and I returned to Washington as a full-fledged career Foreign Service officer. The fact that we so-called Wristonees had been able to achieve the coveted status of career Foreign Service officer without going through the highly competitive written and oral examination process was a bitter pill for the "old-line" Foreign Service. It felt both degraded and threatened—degraded because the floodgates had been opened into their elite service, and threatened because they alleged that civil servants working in Washington had been promoted while the Foreign Service slogged it out abroad, unnoticed and unpromoted. Ironically, some of the most vociferous opponents of the Wriston program had themselves been taken into the Foreign Service without examination in 1946 under the War Manpower Act on the basis of their wartime experience in the Office of Strategic Services (OSS), military intelligence, and other services.

Naturally I sympathized with the Wristonees. Almost all of the professionals I had worked with and admired most at that early stage were career civil servants. These colleagues, unlike the generalists of the Foreign Service, who were schooled more in classical bilateral diplomacy, foreign languages, and foreign cultures, were specialists in political-military, economic, and defense-production issues. Again unlike the Foreign Service officers, who were subject to regular transfers every two to four years or so and whose advancement depended on the wisdom of yearly promotion boards, my civil service colleagues tended to stay in their specialties for longer periods and their promotions depended on openings above them or in other offices. Civil servants thus tended to be less distracted by promotion and assignment considerations than were their Foreign Service colleagues. In any case, I felt the Foreign Service was fortunate to have this new blood injected into it through the Wriston program.

The State Department's and Foreign Service's responsibilities were expanding from traditional bilateral to multilateral diplomacy as well at the

United Nations (UN), NATO, and a growing number of other international bodies. At the same time, the War Manpower Act of 1946 and the Wriston integration program of the mid-1950s were broadening the structure—and the outlook—of the Foreign Service. Most Foreign Service officers preferred the diplomatic lifestyle abroad, where they and their wives circulated prominently in local society and where they were able to sustain such a lifestyle with housing, education, representation—and sometimes hardship—allowances. In contrast, life in Washington, where Foreign Service officers lost their allowances, had to live in the suburbs like everyone else, and got lost in the infighting in the Washington bureaucratic jungle, was much less glamorous and personally less satisfying. With the Wriston program, former civil servants had to face the trials and tribulations of adjusting to life abroad in foreign cultures while Foreign Service officers had to face the trials and tribulations of adjusting to an average life at home. It was an inevitable—and essentially felicitous—evolution in America's diplomatic establishment, and a forerunner of the struggles for even greater diversity benefiting women and minorities that were to come in the 1960s and 1970s. Nevertheless, just as with the Foreign Service Act of 1980 some twenty-five years later, the Wriston program did little to stem the gradual erosion of the department's and Foreign Service's influence within an increasingly powerful national security structure managed more and more directly at the White House under the aegis of the National Security Council (NSC) and the president's national security adviser.

Summitry and Presidential Travel

By the time we returned to Washington in mid-1957, the second Eisenhower term was well under way. Dulles felt by then that the State Department was his and no longer a leftover of twenty years of Democratic stewardship.

The Executive Secretariat, to which I had been assigned, was in a real sense the heartbeat of the State Department. Some, less charitably inclined, called it—and probably still do—the bureaucracy's bureaucracy. Its primary functions were to keep the secretary of state and his principal deputies up to date on latest developments, to review all staff paper going to them for information or decision, and to ensure that decisions taken by the secretary and his deputies were acted on and implemented. The office also coordinated scheduling and paper preparations for the secretary's and, as it turned out, the president's conferences and trips abroad.[11]

It was an exciting place for a junior officer to work. I had emerged from the uncertainty of the Wriston process as a Foreign Service officer with my career intact. However, I had dropped back in rank from level four to level five when the department expanded the number of career ranks from six to eight. I suffered no loss of salary but had to get one more promotion before moving further up the career ladder.

The pressure in the office was intense, the hours long, and the sense of being in the thick of things palpable. Two features of my years in the secretariat stand out: the dominance of the Dulles personality and Eisenhower's precedent-setting trips abroad.

Most of us junior secretariat officers had the experience at one time or another of working in close proximity to Dulles on trips or conferences, and of feeling his powerful presence so keenly that finally each of us had a Dulles dream to recount.

One colleague, Jim Carson, had worked for several days in the Dulles suite at the Waldorf Astoria in New York at the opening of the United Nations General Assembly. The secretary of state normally spent up to two weeks heading the U.S. delegation when the General Assembly opened. During that time he addressed the assembly and met privately with scores of foreign dignitaries, many of whom he did not see for the rest of the year.

Secretariat officers assigned to assist in this period of intense diplomatic activity helped to ensure that the secretary's fast-paced (and often changing) schedule proceeded without mishap; that briefing papers and any support documentation were prepared on time; that participants in the secretary's meetings were named (often not an easy task, as the claimants were many and space was limited) and note-takers assigned; and that records of conversations were promptly prepared, approved, and disseminated appropriately.

On this particular occasion Jim faced the added stress of using as his office the pantry of Dulles's private hotel suite. In the evening, while secretariat officers were feverishly wrapping up the day's work and preparing for the following day's activities, the secretary of state would often pad by in slippers and dressing gown to fix drinks for himself and his wife. After several days of this enforced intimacy with the Dulles couple, Jim one night dreamed he was lying naked in the conjugal bed unable to move when he heard the Dulleses coming to retire for the night!

When Dulles could get away for brief vacations, he escaped to the solitude of Duck Island in upstate New York. Another of my secretariat colleagues, Bob McKinnon, had a "Dulles dream" centered on this locale: Dulles was away at his Duck Island retreat when a state document requiring Dulles's own signature had to be gotten to him immediately—despite his strict standing instructions not to be disturbed there. Bob was chosen to be the courier for this important—and forbidding—mission. He flew to New York City, and from there he took a small commuter plane to Watertown, New York. From Watertown he took a boat to Duck Island.

As the dream went, he arrived at Duck Island, was given directions to the Dulles hideaway, and trudged down the beach to find the great man. As he rounded a bend, he saw Dulles's hulking figure chopping firewood with his back turned.

Bob approached, cleared his throat, and addressed the secretary. Dulles whirled around and glowered. Bob explained the urgency of the business that had caused him to break the secretary's strict rule of privacy, and opened his briefcase—only to discover that it was empty! Needless to say, the shock woke him up.[12]

My own dream was far less dramatic, but perhaps fraught with much deeper significance. I dreamed that I called Dulles "Daddy"!

Barely thirty years of age at the time, I found Dulles to be a forbidding figure indeed—stern, unsmiling, and seemingly oblivious of the young staff officers who were ever-present to do his bidding and to ensure the smooth scheduling of events and prompt implementation of his decisions. Once, in June 1958, sitting in a meeting between Dulles and President Carlos Garcia of the Philippines,[13] my mind wandered a moment while listening to issues with which I was unfamiliar. Suddenly Dulles looked around for a factotum, saw me, and beckoned me to him. He handed me a press statement, directed me to take it to Lincoln White, the department's press spokesperson, for issuance at his daily noon press briefing, and waved me away. Hoping I had heard him aright in my daydreaming, I did his bidding.

This is how I remember John Foster Dulles—a man seemingly oblivious (again I use the term) of the human organization and machinery that worked long hours to smooth his way as he carried out his heavy responsibilities. But I do not recall ever hearing him utter a word of anger or irritation at any of his colleagues, young or old, junior or senior. Dulles was a stern, exacting person who expected all his colleagues to do their jobs well. Nevertheless—at least to my knowledge—he did not allow the pressures of his job to cause him to erupt in anger or vindictiveness at those around him who might not have understood his wishes or whose performance in some way let him down. Dulles was also the first secretary of state—and last, in my experience—into whose home Kaity and I were both invited for a purely social occasion, a Christmas party for his staff and senior associates. Although the Dulleses mingled more with senior associates and their wives, and we juniors mingled with each other across the room, our host and hostess greeted each of us individually and warmly amid festive Christmas decorations and refreshments.

I spent my first six months in the secretariat as an "early morning editor" of the secretary's Top Secret Summary and of the weekly classified publication of "Current Foreign Relations." As the early morning editor, I arrived at the State Department at 3:00 A.M. with a team of writers assigned from policy bureaus in the department. Together we reviewed key telegrams from our embassies around the world for developments that, through the Top Secret Summary, should be brought to the secretary's attention first thing in the morning. As editor, I was responsible for making the decisions as to what items went into the summary, how they were written—grammar and style, and in what order to run them—and what should be the lead story to catch the secretary's attention; in other words, to ensure that he would continue to find the summary useful and to read it on a daily basis.

It was heady stuff for a young officer to know that he was responsible for bringing these developments to the secretary of state's personal attention on his arrival at the office each morning. To be sure, after normal office hours began, my supervisor, crusty old-line Foreign Service officer Eugene MacAuliffe, let me know in no uncertain terms whether in his eyes I had goofed in some way—chosen the wrong lead story, let an awkward or unclear sentence or phrase get by my editorial blue pencil, or worse yet, whether an assistant secretary or some other senior official had complained about how we had handled a story, thereby—in their judgment—misleading the secretary or raising questions about their own judgments on breaking events.

My worst experience in that task was of my own making. The summary writing team was on a tight schedule: The stories had to be written, edited, and ready for the typist (this was well before the computer age) by, say, 6:00 A.M. so that the typing, proofreading, reproduction, and distribution could be completed to get the finished product on the secretary's desk by 8:30 A.M. So editorial decisions effectively had to be made by 5:30 A.M. On the morning in question, a late-breaking story that clearly was the most important development of the day arrived on my desk late in the process. I mistakenly rearranged the summary to give the new story the lead instead of tacking on a "this just in" addendum. As a result, the summary was late by fifteen or twenty minutes, and Under Secretary Douglas Dillon had come in early especially to read it before going to an early morning meeting at the White House. I survived the reverberations from that misjudgment, but it was an uncomfortable morning!

The weekly publication, "Current Foreign Relations," had a wider circulation, including to embassies and consulates abroad. It was a summary of important developments around the world and of official U.S. government views, or at least State Department views, on those developments for the guidance of our diplomats at home and abroad. This publication was less exciting, in fact more drudgery than anything else. Our most important editorial crises with it were stylistic rather than substantive, and some stylistic errors were more political than grammatical or syntactical. The director of regional affairs in the Bureau of Far Eastern Affairs, Ruth Bacon, objected strenuously if we capitalized the "n" in North Korea or North Vietnam, thereby giving those renegade communist regimes a status that implied U.S. recognition. She was equally tenacious in insisting that we refer to the capital of Communist China (Beijing today) as Peiping and not Peking. And in those early days after China had fallen to communism and Chiang Kai-shek's nationalist forces had escaped to Taiwan and established the Republic of China, we had to be especially careful not to use the Communist name for Mainland China—the People's Republic of China. We could refer to Mainland China, or the Chinese Communist regime, or the Chicoms, but not to the People's Republic of China. Nationalist China was the seat of Chinese legitimacy, and that seat was in Taipei on Taiwan. Thus, similarly, we had to refer to Nationalist China as the Republic of China, and not Taiwan.

After six months of dealing with tight editorial deadlines and these finer points of politically correct grammar, spelling, style, and syntax, I was pleased to be given a new assignment within the secretariat—that of department policy briefing officer. The secretariat gave such briefings to public groups seeking to be informed about American foreign policy. It was good experience developing a lecture and learning how to answer questions, all within the framework of established administration policy. I learned much about the world, what was going on in it, and how to defend what the administration thought and was doing about world developments. Most of the time the audiences were friendly, but sometimes not. Anyway, it was good training for later, when I found myself obliged to go around the country explaining—and defending—U.S. policy on Vietnam!

After about a year in the secretariat, I was admitted into its "holy of holies"—the "line." This was the part of the secretariat that everyone in the department knew—and mostly disliked. Under the eagle eyes of Gene MacAuliffe and of Thomas Dunnigan, the "line" supervisor, each line officer was tasked to review staff studies and information memoranda coming up to the secretary and his deputies from a number of bureaus and offices. We were also expected to sit in on meetings and conferences in which the secretary or under secretary participated, in order to record views or decisions they expressed during the meeting and to make sure that those views and decisions were appropriately conveyed to other department officials. It was in such a capacity that I found myself sitting in on Dulles's meeting with Philippine president Garcia in June 1958 (see above).

It was also in that capacity that I often had to convey the secretary's decisions on policy recommendations back to the assistant secretary who had submitted them. One such decision, by Acting Secretary of State Christian Herter (who replaced the dying Dulles in mid-1959), that I conveyed, as department duty officer, to Assistant Secretary of State for Latin American Affairs Roy Rubottom, remains preserved for history: The newly victorious Cuban revolutionary leader, Fidel Castro, had accepted an invitation to speak at the annual meeting of the American Society of Newspaper Editors in Washington on April 17, 1959. After presenting the pros and cons of offering official courtesies to Castro, Assistant Secretary Rubottom recommended to Herter that he invite Castro to lunch at Blair House. Rubottom cited the "long-range aspects of our relationships with Cuba . . . particularly the harm that might be caused if we did not extend courtesies to Castro which would be expected for any leader of a Latin American country."[14] I attached a note for Rubottom's staff aide, Frank Devine, conveying Herter's approval of the recommendation, but with the caveat that, before conveying the invitation, our embassy in Havana should look into a report by Congressman Adam Clayton Powell that Castro was on the verge of a nervous breakdown and that "violent changes" in Cuba were about to take place.[15]

"Line" officers were drawn on to perform two additional demanding functions. As noted above, the first was to serve weekly stints as the department's duty officer—to be available and reachable by phone on a twenty-four-hour basis by the secretary or under secretary, the White House staff, other cabinet officers, ambassadors abroad, and others. The department duty officer stayed in the office until the secretary and under secretaries had left in the evening and until all of the staff paper coming out of their offices had been processed so that the decisions recorded therein would be conveyed to staffs—or transmitted to embassies abroad—and available for implementation first thing the next morning.

Until the Cuban missile crisis in 1962, more than fifteen years into the Cold War, the State Department did not have the Operations Center, with its round-the-clock modern communications facilities that give it nearly instantaneous contact with key national security agencies in Washington—the White House Situation Room, the Pentagon's National Military Command Center, the CIA—and with every U.S. embassy and consulate around the world.[16] Instead, the Executive Secretariat had a roster of eight to ten carefully chosen young officers (men, in those days) who took weekly turns at being the State Department duty officer.

The second demanding—and exciting—function we became eligible for as "line" officers was to travel abroad as staff members of delegations led by the secretary of state or, as it turned out, by the president himself.

My first chance for such travel abroad came as a junior staff member of the last delegation that Dulles headed to the NATO ministerial meeting in Paris in December 1958. He was already ill with the cancer that was to take his life a few months later. For me, it meant returning to the scene of my earlier days at NATO and actually participating—at a low level—in the activity generated by a major international conference. My responsibilities were mundane: keeping track of meeting changes so that an accurate schedule of the next day's events could be distributed to all delegation members in the evening; assuring that delegation members knew who was responsible for recording the content of the meetings in which the secretary participated; assuring proper clearance and authorization for reporting telegrams being sent back to Washington; making sure that late changes in briefing books were placed in the secretary's briefing book and distributed to the other members of the delegation; and, finally, assembling the complete official record of the U.S. delegation's activities during the conference.

One morning I was assigned a task out of the ordinary routine: to stand by at the Palais de Chaillot conference site should the secretary or other senior delegation members need any assistance—errands run or papers fetched. I was outside the conference room where the foreign and defense ministers were meeting, waiting for any sign that I was needed. Suddenly the door of the meeting room swung open and Dulles emerged. I hurried to him and asked if I could be of assistance. He asked me where the men's room was, and I was pleased to be able to point the way.

The day Dulles died I was department duty officer. Dulles had resigned in declining health some months earlier and his under secretary, Christian Herter, had replaced him. At the time of Dulles's death, Herter was in Geneva representing the United States at the latest four-power foreign ministers meeting on Berlin. I had gone into the department that Sunday morning expecting a short, routine stay to review incoming cables. Instead, shortly before 9:00 A.M., I took a call from Martin Agronsky of CBS asking if I could confirm Dulles's death. Agronsky was in a great hurry because he had a 9:00 A.M. broadcast. It was the first I had heard the news, and I told Agronsky I could not confirm it. He hung up. I turned on the radio and received another phone call. This time it was Douglas Dillon, acting secretary of state, informing me that Dulles had indeed died (the news was by then also on the airwaves), and asking me to set the wheels in motion to bring Herter back from Geneva for the funeral. I had no idea what the arrangements were, so from that moment until late that evening my quiet duty day turned into a three-ring circus of phone calls from embassies seeking funeral information, from the Pentagon concerning arrangements for Secretary Herter's return, and so on. I went home exhausted by the day's unforeseen exertions but conscious that the influence of a powerful, ideologically motivated secretary of state was at an end.

Over the next eighteen months I traveled on several historic presidential trips abroad, travel that brought me—briefly—into the presence of Dwight Eisenhower and his close entourage and taught me something about presidential trips, their accompanying tensions, egos, pomp, and circumstance. Before beginning my "presidential" travel, however, I was chosen as a staff member of the U.S. delegation to the second half of the Four-Power Conference on Berlin in July 1959 in Geneva, Switzerland. Secretary Herter, Foreign Minister Andrei Gromyko, and their respective delegations arrived in Geneva on July 12, 1959, for the second half of the Berlin Conference. Herter flew in the first official sortie of one of the White House's newly acquired Boeing 707 presidential jet aircraft. Gromyko and his delegation traveled on a Tupolev 104 jet transport. Both planes were open to public inspection at Geneva's Cointrin Airport, and the events received much public attention as yet another aspect of Cold War competition.

For me, the opportunity to be on this first official Boeing 707 trip was exciting indeed. The jet was a marvel of speed and altitude. It flew some 10,000–15,000 feet higher than the previous propeller-driven Constellations and was remarkably free of noise and especially of vibration.

Our trip to Geneva began with a half-day stopover in Ottawa, where Herter met with his Canadian counterpart. Not being involved in those bilateral talks, I did what every good secretariat officer was supposed to do—I went directly to the embassy to make sure the secretary and his senior advisers were kept abreast of any late-breaking developments around the world, including any events that might affect the resumed conference in Geneva.

Once in Geneva, we secretariat staff officers settled into our conference routine: attending delegation meetings in the morning, chaired by the secretary of state and attended by his senior advisers; following up any of the secretary's decisions or instructions flowing from the meetings; preparing for each day's meeting at the United Nations' Palais des Nations; updating meeting schedules, updating briefing books, and assigning meeting note-takers and reporting officers for each session; distributing telegrams and documents to delegation members; and assembling the permanent records of the conference and delegation activities for the State Department's records and archives.

Aside from the humdrum routine of a conference that lasted from May to August and that achieved no results, the month I spent in Geneva held many attractions, professional and personal. That summer in Geneva was uncharacteristically sun-drenched. The sun shone virtually every day, and the city, surrounded by the snow-capped Swiss Alps, sparkled on the edge of deep blue Lake Geneva. When we were not working long secretariat hours, we were exploring the city's old streets and shops and trying out its many enticing restaurants. On the weekends we went further afield, looking for the picturesque villages and towns—and again restaurants—in France's nearby Jura Mountains.

There were professional interests and satisfactions as well. The four powers had agreed that for the first time at a foreign ministers conference on Berlin they would allow representatives of the two Germanys to be present as "adviser groups." In other words, German representatives could be present at the formal sessions and they could speak, but they could not be part of any decisions. The difficult issue over which the four powers wrangled was how to seat the two adviser groups at the conference table. The Western powers did not recognize any legitimacy in the East German regime; the Soviets did not recognize the legitimacy of the West German government. The final decision was a diplomatic tour de force: It was agreed that the two German delegations would be seated behind tables separated from the main circular conference table by six pencil widths! (I had occasion to be reminded of this solution ten years later during the painfully long "shape-of-the-table" negotiations with the Saigon and North Vietnamese delegations at the Vietnam Peace Talks in Paris, while in Vietnam the war ground on and the casualties mounted on both sides.)

I regularly attended the Geneva conference sessions and absorbed the atmosphere and proceedings of a major East-West international conference. I saw the principal delegates in action at close hand: Christian Herter, the rumpled, courtly New Englander, representing the United States as its new secretary of state; Selwyn Lloyd, the peppery, immaculately dressed British foreign secretary; Maurice Couve de Murville, the suave, soft-spoken French foreign minister; and Andrei Gromyko, the dour personification of the Soviet regime he represented as foreign minister. And there were also Heinrich von Brentano, the West German foreign minister, and Lothar Bolz, the "so-called foreign minister of the so-called German Democratic Republic," whom we lightly dubbed among ourselves "the so-called Dr. Bolz."

In the delegation rooms before and after the formal conference sessions, Secretary Herter would come in and out from his activities, always with a friendly greeting for the staff, always solicitous for our welfare—conscious of the long hours we were working in his support. Perhaps Herter was not a memorable secretary of state, but he was a human being capable of genuine personal warmth and human communication—far more so than Dulles.

Among the other senior members of the U.S. delegation were some stars of the Foreign Service—Martin Hillenbrand, who later became ambassador to Germany and assistant secretary of state for European affairs, and Walter Stoessel, who later served as ambassador to Poland, ambassador to the Soviet Union, and deputy secretary of state. I also met someone on the delegation whom I was to get to know better later—William P. Bundy, Dean Acheson's son-in-law, older brother of McGeorge Bundy, and later assistant secretary of state for Far Eastern affairs. At Geneva, Bundy was the intelligence briefer for the delegation. It amused me later to recall that Bundy had been mildly rebuked by the gentle Herter for mumbling his morning intelligence briefings in an Ivy-Leaguish, super-smooth, "nothing can surprise me" tone. "Speak up, Bill!" Herter would say, with an ever so slight suggestion of impatience.

Later that summer, after the Geneva Conference on Berlin had adjourned yet again with no results,[17] and after a vacation in Greece with my family, I found myself flying to London and on to Paris, attached to President Eisenhower's party as a junior staff member during Eisenhower's visits to London, Bonn, and Paris to reassure Prime Minister Harold Macmillan, Chancellor Konrad Adenauer, and President Charles de Gaulle regarding his intentions in receiving Khrushchev in the United States and in later going to Moscow himself. I do not remember much about this introduction to presidential travel and to summitry. For me it was a high-pressure jumble of briefing books, schedule preparation, cable traffic management, and ensuring that records of meetings were produced, cleared properly, and transmitted.

After Khrushchev's visit to the United States that September, during which he had agreed to lift his ultimatum on Berlin, and while the Congress was in recess, Eisenhower decided to proceed with his goodwill trip to the developing world. In his own words, he wanted to demonstrate, during the height of the Cold War, the desire of the United States for peace. He understood the power of his reputation and felt that the trip should be made toward the end of his presidency when "a President's influence on domestic affairs normally wanes."[18]

The trip took place in November and December 1959. Eleven nations finally ended up on the itinerary, each one added for one reason or another and many more left off because of time constraints or for political reasons. The final list consisted of Italy, Turkey, Pakistan, Afghanistan, India, Iran, Greece, Tunisia, France, Spain, and Morocco.[19]

I was asked to go on the trip to assist Thomas McElhiney, the deputy executive secretary, in the usual secretariat functions of managing schedules, distributing cables and documents, assigning reporting responsibilities, and assembling official records. It was an exhausting trip—the hours were endless across many time zones, and we were constantly "cleaning up" one visit while preparing for the next. Sometimes I traveled with the presidential party (on the second, "backup" Boeing 707), and sometimes I went ahead commercially, skipping the shorter presidential visits in order to prepare for the longer ones. I flew "advance" to Rome commercially. From Karachi to New Delhi, while the president and his closest advisers flew to Kabul for lunch with the Afghan king, I flew with other staff members on the *Columbine,* President Truman's official aircraft, a propeller-driven Constellation that had been kept in the presidential fleet as a backup and taken along on this trip in case the Boeing 707s were unable to get into places like Kabul for such reasons as weather or length of runway. From New Delhi to Athens, while the immediate presidential party flew to Tunis for talks with President Bourguiba, I flew commercially on a British Comet jet, stopping overnight to change planes in Beirut.

In Rome I set up my office in the beautiful old Italian palazzo that houses the American embassy on the Via Veneto. I called on the ambassador, met the embassy personnel I had to work with, established procedures for handling incoming and outgoing cable traffic for the State Department element of the presidential party, and braced myself for the onslaught of the presidential party's arrival, which I watched on television at the embassy.

Eisenhower's plane, the Boeing 707 I had flown in to Geneva that summer, arrived at Rome's Ciampino Airport in a heavy rainstorm. Arrival ceremonies took place under umbrellas. There for the first time I watched the president's remarkable interpreter, Colonel Vernon "Dick" Walters, amaze the Italians present and those watching on television with his impeccable translations of each president's statement, one into English from Italian, the other into Italian from English, without notes and with a perfect Italian accent. It was a bravura performance and one to be repeated several times along the presidential itinerary. Walters went on to a distinguished career as military attaché in Paris, deputy director of the Central Intelligence Agency, ambassador to the United Nations, and ambassador to Germany.

In Rome I experienced the less agreeable side of a presidential road show. I had been charged with ensuring that an urgent and important message, now long forgotten, from one White House assistant to another arrive overnight at the hotel where we were all staying. The message did not arrive at its destination, and the State Department messenger (me) was fixed upon as the culprit. In looking into what went wrong, I quickly discovered that the White House assistant who was to receive the message had been too drunk that evening to know what messages he had or had not received. The whole matter was quickly forgotten (except by me!).

Then on to Ankara, Turkey, this time on the presidential "backup" Boeing 707. We landed at Ankara's airport at dusk. The road from the airport to town was lined with soldiers spaced every hundred yards or so on both sides. Ankara seemed to be a city in development—large impressive buildings, including Ataturk's neoclassical tomb, among dusty unpaved streets. But we were not there long enough to form any valid impression. We were up before dawn the next morning to continue on to Karachi.

Karachi was my first glimpse of the "teeming millions of the Orient." In the Hotel Metropole where we stayed, an old British colonial-style building with open, covered corridors on each floor giving onto an inner courtyard garden, there were people doing partial jobs—a dramatic display of underemployment. One man would be dusting the marble floor of the hotel lobby by shuffling back and forth with a rag under each bare foot. Another would be watering plants. Still another was delivering messages. On the floors above, there were cleaning women and turbaned servants to bring tea. It was a new experience for a young American from a country where even shoeshine boys were disappearing as relics of the past.

The American embassy chancery in Karachi was over a garage in an old, shuttered colonial-style building of shabby appearance. From the office where we were set up for our brief stay to the snack bar where we grabbed something to eat, the United States was indeed housed badly—and pestered by flies around the food to a disgusting degree. Paris was never like that!

On my last morning in Karachi, I looked forward to sleeping in a little longer. Eisenhower and his senior advisers were flying to Kabul for their lunch with King Daud. We junior members of the staff were scheduled to fly directly to New Delhi on the *Columbine,* arriving still two or three hours ahead of the president.

At 6:30 A.M. there was a knock on my door and the cheerful words, "Morning tea, sir!" I groaned, woke up, and opened the door to the smiling, turbaned bearer. I was not ready for this special courtesy left over from the British colonial era—at least not without warning!

Then off to New Delhi on the *Columbine.* En route, we overflew the Taj Mahal at Agra, India. The pilot took the aircraft down several thousand feet and circled that beautiful example of Mogul architecture.

When we arrived in New Delhi, people were already beginning to line the route from the airport to town to catch a glimpse of the famous American president. An estimated one million Indians had massed for the event and almost got out of hand in their enthusiasm. When Eisenhower arrived and he and Prime Minister Jawaharlal Nehru rode together in their cavalcade into the city, Nehru finally had to get down from the vehicle carrying the president to persuade the mass to let them pass. It was a nightmare for the Secret Service and their Indian counterparts, but the only danger Eisenhower was in was that of being crushed by an enthusiastic mob.

I saw none of this, having earlier gotten established in the hotel and then gone to the embassy to set up the secretariat office. We stayed in India four and a half days, and the first night I was so exhausted from the trip so far that I arranged to be off duty until noon the next day. I fell into bed and slept through until morning. I took a brief walk to see a bit of the city and went to the embassy to resume my duties for the next three days.

The one event of the presidential visit to India that I was able to attend was the opening of the New Delhi Agricultural Fair, with a large American exhibit. I have no idea how big the crowd was, but it was many thousands of people, most of whom were kept behind rope barricades manned by police. When Eisenhower appeared on the podium with the Indian president, there arose a crescendoing murmur from the crowd behind the barricades as it surged forward to see the American president better. Ropes and police together strained to hold the crowd back. I wondered if they would be successful, or if we would all be trampled by the apparently friendly crowd. The police held, happily, the crowd subsided, and the opening ceremonies took place more or less on schedule.

I had barely had time either in Karachi or New Delhi to form impressions of the subcontinent, on this, my first trip to Asia, other than of teeming populations—poor, unclean, ill-clothed—mixed with dust, heat, animals, and their carts. But in New Delhi in the early morning, or at sunset, going from the hotel to the embassy or back to the hotel, I caught a sense of the magic and the beauty, the romance and beguiling strangeness and mystery of ancient cultures in tropical settings that I came to experience later in Southeast Asia and still later in West Africa. It was only a foretaste of a major career change in the offing.

Soon, however, I was winging my way westward by BOAC Comet aircraft to Beirut and thence to Athens, where Eisenhower was due, after a brief stop in Tunis to see President Bourguiba.

I arrived in Beirut near midnight and was to depart for Athens at 8:00 A.M. the next morning. The hostess who assisted me through customs and police saw stamped in my passport "The bearer is a member of President Eisenhower's party." She asked me in an awed voice if I knew the president and, happily, without waiting for my disappointing reply, she said admiringly, "You must be very important!" Perhaps she was grateful for Eisenhower's dispatch of the U.S. Marines to Lebanon the year before to maintain order even then in that troubled land. Whatever she had in mind, I succumbed to the temptation not to disabuse her and accordingly was sped through the formalities with uncustomary dispatch.

I made a big hit with our Greek friends in Athens, coming as a member, no matter how junior, of the Eisenhower party. I stayed with my mother-in-law but, as at the other stops, spent most of my time at the embassy screening telegrams, preparing briefing books, collecting detailed records on past stops, mainly schedules and memoranda of conversation.

Eisenhower was to arrive before dark so that he and King Paul could drive in from the airport and be seen—together—by the throngs lining the parade route. The U.S. embassy was toward the end of the route, on Queen Sophia Avenue just a few blocks from the palace where Eisenhower was to stay. Crowds had been massing there, as they had all along the route. Memories of the Truman Doctrine aid to Greece during its civil war were still fresh. Indeed, U.S. military and economic assistance levels were still high. Eisenhower was remembered as the Supreme Allied Commander who had defeated Nazi Germany, which had so brutally occupied Greece for more than four years. The United States got the credit, too, for helping Greece to victory over the communist guerrillas who, in 1944 and early 1945, had virtually occupied all of Greece except the center of Athens.

Perhaps an hour before the president arrived, a concrete fence across Queen Sophia Avenue from the embassy collapsed under the weight of far too many people eager to catch a glimpse of the American war-hero president. There were several injuries and one death. It was a sad footnote to a triumphal visit.

There was a humorous footnote as well. The president's plane was half an hour late. Darkness was falling fast long before the president and King Paul arrived in front of the embassy. American flags—along with Greek flags—seemed to be on every building in sight. Suddenly, the U.S. Marine guard appeared where we were standing looking out past the embassy's Stars and Stripes and onto the excited, expectant masses of people gathered below. In accordance with his normal orders, the marine began lowering the flag for the night. I was startled and pointed out that the president would soon pass by and see an American flag on every building except the American embassy. The marine quite properly would not be moved by argument or by the unusual circumstances. Orders were orders. He was willing to display the flag after dark only on orders from his superior, the embassy security officer, who naturally was at the airport for the arrival. We finally tracked him down by telephone, and he authorized the marine to fly the flag in these extraordinary circumstances. The U.S. embassy stood tall again.

Then on to Paris and a Western summit with de Gaulle and Macmillan. By then it was generally accepted that there would be an East-West summit. Eisenhower, who had resisted the idea of such a summit without progress at Geneva on the Berlin issue, felt he had gotten Khrushchev to back off his ultimatum to force the Western powers' hands on Berlin during his one-on-one chats with the Soviet leader at Camp David. But de Gaulle did not want an East-West summit before the spring of 1960—until after France had exploded an atomic device and had thereby joined the exclusive nuclear club. At the Western summit in Paris that December, it was agreed to follow de Gaulle's timetable. Thus, a four-power summit meeting was set for Paris in May 1960.

It was at this Western summit that I caught a glimpse of Charles de Gaulle and that I almost met President Eisenhower. On the day that de Gaulle was to be Eisenhower's guest at lunch at the American ambassador's residence, I was asked to be the staff officer available at the residence for whatever unforeseen bureaucratic emergency might arise. No such emergency arose. Instead, I spent a rather heady day in the company of senior White House staff members—Ann Whitman, the president's secretary, Colonel Andrew Goodpaster, the president's assistant for national security, and Major John Eisenhower, the president's son and Goodpaster's assistant. We were all squeezed into a small office off the main entrance hall of the ambassador's residence, from whence, with a little ogling and craning of the neck, we could see the comings and goings of the great.

When de Gaulle arrived for lunch, we watched Eisenhower greet him and take him into a reception room for cocktails. During lunch, we fared on the same dishes that had been prepared for the French president. When luncheon was over, again we observed the two presidents' good-byes. Then Eisenhower, whose health remained precarious after ileitis and a heart attack, announced he was going upstairs for a nap.

At four o'clock in the afternoon, Ike descended the staircase, ready for the trip by car to Rambouillet outside Paris, where he was to be de Gaulle's guest. While cars were being loaded with baggage and staff personnel, Eisenhower, like everyone else, milled around in the entrance hall waiting for someone to say "Let's go!" Ann Whitman took the opportunity to present various State Department and residence staff members to the president. After she had made several presentations, she paused, looking around for others. Just as she spied me, Eisenhower, tired of standing around in the general confusion, said, "Well, let's get this show on the road!" My chance to meet President Eisenhower disappeared forever.

I doubt that anyone could attribute a lasting impact to presidential goodwill trips like the one Eisenhower had just completed. Eisenhower was a personality—even an idol—to millions of people around the globe, mostly for his wartime leadership of the massive Allied assault on Nazi-occupied Europe but also undoubtedly for his role as the American president. Despite his "goodwill" and his desire to manifest America's yearning for peace by traveling to the far ends of the earth, there is little evidence that his visit to India, for example, caused that huge democracy of the subcontinent to shift any closer to the United States and further from the Soviet Union in its political alignment. Nor did his luncheon stop in Kabul with the king in any way bolster Afghanistan's ability to fend off Soviet pressures. Nevertheless, in the context of the Cold War and of the Eisenhower presidency, the goodwill trip to eleven countries served at least its immediate purpose of letting millions of people for the first time see America up close in the person of its popular, warmhearted, open president, with his likable grin, his ability to reach out to audiences, and his simple and direct speaking style.

In any case, after what had been for me a remarkable, exciting, eye-opening, and exhausting trip, I returned to Washington thinking it was time to look for a new assignment. I had been in the Executive Secretariat for two and a half years. I had learned the importance of timeliness, accuracy, and thoroughness in the preparation of materials going to the foreign policy decision makers, as well as that of ensuring that their decisions were conveyed downward, followed up, and implemented. No detail was too small for our attention in the secretariat, no error too minuscule, no coordination too tangential to escape our notice. When serving as department duty officer, we junior officers often found ourselves speaking directly to the secretary of state and other top officers of the department or of other government departments or agencies.

All of these responsibilities required great care and attention to detail, long and often odd working hours, and patience on the part of our families. It created a camaraderie among us, and a feeling that we were the elite of the elite. At the same time, one reached the point of longing to deal with substance rather than form, of wanting to write a policy paper oneself or conduct a bilateral talk or negotiation however minor or unimportant the subject, rather than to count the minor imperfections in someone else's efforts.

I sought a country desk assignment, where I would be dealing with U.S. diplomatic relations with one country. This kind of assignment—the country desk—was considered in the Foreign Service to be basic to a career path to the top. It was akin to the platoon leader billet in an infantry company, the basic function in the military career ladder.

But I had six months more to serve in the secretariat and, as it turned out, one more presidential trip to go on—the failed, tension-packed, "U-2 summit" between Khrushchev and Western leaders in Paris in May 1960, which was supposed to have been followed by Eisenhower's trip to Moscow a month later. Two weeks before the summit meeting was to begin, a Soviet missile hit and disabled an American U-2 spy plane. The pilot, Gary Francis Powers, had escaped by parachute and been captured.

In Paris, on the eve of the summit meeting, the drama was palpable. Washington's initial reaction to news that the Soviets had captured the pilot alive was to acknowledge that the United States engaged in aerial reconnaissance but to deny that Powers's flight deep over the Soviet Union had been authorized. Ultimately, however, Eisenhower publicly acknowledged responsibility for authorizing such flights over the Soviet Union. Khrushchev had carefully avoided blaming the president personally on the eve of the summit meeting and did not change his plans to go to Paris. For his part, at a press conference on May 11, Eisenhower defended U.S. intelligence activities as a "distasteful but vital necessity" and said he would renew his 1955 Open Skies proposal at the Paris summit. To a group of congressmen privately, Eisenhower said he would continue to plan to go to Moscow after the summit unless Khrushchev revoked his invitation. To his cabinet he directed that all activities that the Soviets might consider provocative be called off.

Both Eisenhower's and Khrushchev's arrival statements in Paris pledged every effort to make the conference a success. Khrushchev, however, demanded a public apology from Eisenhower—a demand that irritated the president. Khrushchev and Eisenhower called separately on French president de Gaulle, their summit host, and British prime minister Harold Macmillan, but not on each other. Khrushchev was waiting for Eisenhower to make the first gesture; Eisenhower was planning instead how to handle Khrushchev should he bring up the U-2 incident at the first summit meeting.

As a Staff Secretariat officer, I was located in the beautiful paneled library on the second floor of the U.S. embassy at the northwest corner of the Place de la Concorde. Under normal circumstances, at such a conference, the Staff Secretariat served as a delegation command post—the place where telegrams and other communications were received and sent, schedules maintained and updated, briefing books assembled and revised—in short, the central location where all delegation members, high and low, could count on getting the latest information of importance to each one: what meetings they were to attend (and not to attend); who was to do the report on each meeting; positions in cavalcades; lunches, dinners, and receptions to be attended (or not attended), and so on.

At the "U-2 summit," the Staff Secretariat carried out this function in an atmosphere of high drama and tension. In addition to coordinating the activities of the U.S. delegation and its members, we also served as a central point for information on Khrushchev's whereabouts and intentions—whether he would in fact participate in the summit as planned or not.

On Monday, May 16, 1960, the summit was supposed to begin. Macmillan had breakfast with Eisenhower at 8:00 A.M. at the American ambassador's residence. Khrushchev sent word that the first summit session should be delayed from 10:00 to 11:00 A.M., and with two advisers each instead of alone with interpreters. The meeting began at the Elysée Palace as Khrushchev wanted. After brief introductory remarks by de Gaulle, Khrushchev demanded the floor. Speaking in irate tones for forty-five minutes, he blasted the United States, demanded that it apologize for its acts against the Soviet Union, and proposed the conference be put off for eight months (until after Eisenhower was out of office). Khrushchev also stated that Eisenhower's visit to Moscow was off.

Eisenhower responded that the United States had no intention to resume flights over the Soviet Union and offered to meet bilaterally with the Soviets to iron out these matters while the work of the main conference continued. Khrushchev, noting that Eisenhower had not expressed regret for the U-2 incident, referred to the meeting as a preliminary meeting—not as the opening summit session—and hinted he would reflect on the matter of postponement. He also implied that he did not exclude bilateral talks if any other party wanted them. The session thus broke up without agreement on the next meeting.

The next morning at 10:00 A.M., Eisenhower, de Gaulle, and Macmillan met and agreed that de Gaulle would invite Khrushchev to attend a 3:00 P.M. session and ask for a written reply. Eisenhower and Macmillan then went for a ride in the country, visiting the house outside Paris where Eisenhower had lived when he was SACEUR—Supreme Allied Commander, Europe. Khrushchev also went for a ride in the country, where he received de Gaulle's invitation to the 3:00 P.M. session. In the "command post" at the embassy library, we staffers were trying to keep up with events. Phones rang incessantly, with delegation members either seeking or giving information—or rumors—about Khrushchev's whereabouts in the country, whether he was headed back to town or not, whether any word had been received about his intention to attend the 3:00 P.M. session.

At 3:00 P.M., the other three heads of government gathered at the conference table; no reply had yet been received from Khrushchev. At 3:20 P.M., one of Khrushchev's assistants called the Elysée Palace to inquire whether the session was to be an actual summit session or another preliminary meeting. The assistant made clear that Khrushchev would not attend a formal summit session because Eisenhower had not apologized. With that, the "U-2 summit" was over before it began. The Staff Secretariat packed its bags and its footlockers and headed home.[20] And I was ready to begin my next assignment as Belgium-Luxembourg desk officer in the Office of Western European Affairs.

On the Belgian Desk

To be named "desk officer" was the dream assignment for a young Foreign Service officer—the basic "line" function of the career Foreign Service: the conduct of bilateral relations between the United States and another nation. Also, the Belgium-Luxembourg desk kept me pointed toward Western Europe as an area of career specialization. It could not have been more perfect: a country desk assignment in the State Department's oldest and most prestigious regional bureau, the Bureau of European Affairs.

But it turned out very different from what I expected. Shortly before I took over my new functions, Belgium gave full independence, with virtually no preparation, to its huge, sprawling, mineral-rich colony in the center of Africa, the Belgian Congo (later Zaire and now the Congo again). Law and order quickly broke down, Europeans were endangered and occasionally killed by Congolese mobs, and Patrice Lumumba, a radical nationalist, took power. Belgium's precipitate action formed part of Africa's dramatic and disorderly decolonization process, starting with Ghana's independence from Britain in 1957, and continuing with de Gaulle's sweeping offer of independence to all of France's colonies in French West and Equatorial Africa in 1958. Belgium found itself faced with growing and undisciplined pressures within the Belgian Congo to follow Britain's and France's lead. Thus, in January 1960, Belgium, a small European nation saddled by history with a huge colonial preserve in the center of Africa, gave in to the Congolese pressures and set independence for six months later, June 30, 1960.

Belgium was defensive and prickly about its record in its former colony in light of the trouble that held the world spotlight. Its approach to colonization had been largely paternalistic, with little effort devoted to preparing the Congolese people for independence. The most frequently quoted statistic dramatizing Belgian stewardship of its huge colony was that at independence the Congo had a total of sixteen university graduates. Belgium's failure to anticipate the pressures building up in the Congo, the incipient political groupings that were forming, and the impact on these developments of the rapid accession to independence of French and British colonies in Africa all left Belgium dazed, smarting, and sensitive, and ready to blame everyone but itself—especially the United States.

At the same time, Belgium was a NATO ally and a country with which the United States had enjoyed good and productive bilateral relations over many years. The giant Belgian holding company Union Minière du Haut Katanga had supplied the United States with uranium for its first atomic bombs, even when Belgium itself was occupied by Nazi Germany. By 1960, Union Minière supplied 10 percent of the world's copper and 60 percent of the world's cobalt. Truly, the United States had major interests in Belgium and its vast mineral-rich colony.

On July 9, 1960, the Belgian government announced that it was sending an additional twelve hundred soldiers to the Congo as a precaution in light of continuing disorder and attacks against Europeans. Within days Belgian planes attacked the Congolese port of Matadi, and Katanga (Shaba today) declared its independence. Congolese president Joseph Kasavubu and prime minister Patrice Lumumba demanded the immediate withdrawal of all Belgian forces and appealed to the United Nations for assistance in restoring order. Against Soviet and radical third-world pressure (including Lumumba's) to put an immediate end to Belgian "aggression," the United States worked with its NATO allies (including Belgium) to get quick UN Security Council agreement on a UN peacekeeping force for the Congo and on a Belgian troop withdrawal once UN troops were on the scene there.

However, the terms under which the UN Security Council negotiated the dispatch of the UN force required compromise between Western and Soviet positions, which contributed to Belgian irritation at the United States. To avoid charging the Belgians with aggression as the Soviets demanded, the United States was obliged to agree to language that called for the Belgian troops' immediate withdrawal. This issue was the first of many that caused tension between the United States and Belgium.

One of my first tasks as desk officer was directed at assuaging Belgian sensitivities flowing from this first Security Council resolution. The embassy in Brussels was instructed to remind the Belgians that we had publicly stated our view that they were not an aggressor and that we supported a phased Belgian withdrawal. The embassy was also to remind the Belgians that we had played a key role in keeping out of the resolution far more damaging language proposed by the Soviet Union. At the same time, the instruction expressed confidence that our Belgian ally would continue to adhere to UN resolutions, pointedly observing that Belgium had to demonstrate that it was rapidly withdrawing its forces to Belgium, including from Katanga.[21]

During the ensuing weeks and months, we in the Office of Western European Affairs sought to reassure the Belgians that while we favored moderate and sensible UN actions, we also aimed to prevent actions that would benefit the Soviet Union and radical Congolese political elements and undermine the Western (Belgian) interests in the Congo. We were constantly pressed by our colleagues in the State Department's Africa and UN bureaus to urge the Belgians not to take actions that weakened our ability to keep the UN effort on a moderate course. Thus, while we were expressing our concern to the Belgians about reports of Belgian arms shipments to Katanga,[22] we were also calling on the United Nations to look into reports of Soviet arms shipments into the Congo.[23] Similarly, while pressing the Belgians to support UN resolutions favoring Congolese unity, we were also urging the United Nations to avoid actions that undermined Moïse Tshombe's position as Katanga's leader or Katanga's integrity as the Congo's richest province or that, conversely, acted to facilitate Lumumba's entry into Katanga.[24]

As events unfolded in the summer and fall of 1960—and as the 1960 U.S. presidential campaign came to its climax—the United States continued to tread gingerly among Belgian sensitivities, Lumumba's fanatical anti-Western nationalism, Soviet maneuvers to undermine the United Nations' and the West's positions in the Congo, and the United Nations' own weaknesses and twists and turns as it tried to succeed in its almost hopeless mission of restoring law and order, peace, and stability in an independent Congo without taking sides either in the Congo's internal strife or between the United States and the Soviet Union.

UN troops started to arrive in the Congo on July 15, 1960; by the end of the month some eleven thousand UN troops were there, from African and neutral European nations. However, on July 17, Lumumba demanded that the United Nations remove all Belgian troops within forty-eight hours or he would ask for the intervention of Soviet troops. This provoked ugly incidents between Congolese and UN personnel and led Khrushchev to step up his support for Lumumba—more, perhaps, than he had been inclined to do.[25] In turn, the United States pressed Belgium to begin to withdraw its troops immediately. In the end, the United States and UN Secretary General Dag Hammarskjöld were able to persuade Belgium to have all of its military personnel out of Léopoldville by July 23.

Lumumba's ultimatum to the United Nations and his threat to seek Soviet intervention, coupled with Soviet tactics at the United Nations that appeared designed to undercut a workable UN role in the Congo, fed growing Western suspicions regarding Lumumba's political orientation and ultimate intentions for the Congo. William A. M. Burden, Eisenhower's ambassador in Brussels, in response to the State Department's request for an assessment of the situation, called for Lumumba's replacement by more moderate leadership in Léopoldville (Kinshasa today). At the United Nations, Ambassador Henry Cabot Lodge warned the Soviets not to intervene, and Secretary of State Christian Herter warned that the United States would back the United Nations "with all its moral force and material resources." At the same time, the United States continued to press the Belgians to withdraw their troops "speedily" in order not to give the Soviets further excuse to undermine the UN effort. By the end of August all Belgian troops were out of the Congo except from Katanga—and this focused international attention on that Gordian knot of the Congo problem.

From my vantage point on the Belgian desk of the State Department, I was principally concerned with following the threads of Belgian interests in the Congo affair, the interplay of Belgian and U.S. actions therein, and the impact of these actions on overall U.S.-Belgian relations. My days were taken up with a succession of issues such as the Belgian-supported Katanga secession, the withdrawal of Belgian troops, the reintroduction of Belgian technicians, and the introduction of Belgian mercenaries. On occasion I would accompany the Belgian ambassador, Louis Scheyven, on his rounds of senior State Department officials, trying to solve day-to-day problems and keep U.S.-Belgian relations on an even keel. On other occasions, I accompanied Ambassador Burden on his own rounds of senior levels of the State Department, with similar objectives.

My professional horizons were bounded by the State Department's Bureaus of United Nations and of African Affairs on the one hand, and by my office, the Bureau of European Affairs on the other.[26] My day-to-day combat in the bureaucratic trenches took place for the most part at the office level in each bureau: the Office of UN Political Affairs, headed by William Cargo and his deputy, Joseph Sisco; the Office of Congo Affairs, headed by Sheldon Vance and his deputy, Robert Eisenberg; and my own Office of Western European Affairs, headed by Robert McBride and his deputy, William Blue.[27]

In reality, this major policy problem, the Congo and its fate, was dealt with at levels far above me and, for that matter, far above the office directors. My responsibilities were limited primarily to attending meetings and keeping track of events for my superiors, writing records of conversations with the Belgian ambassador and other visiting Belgian officials in the form of telegraphic reports dispatched normally to New York, Brussels, and Léopoldville.

In dealing with Congo matters at my level, I quickly discovered that many "creative tensions" existed, even within the State Department itself. The bias of our own bureau and office was the preservation and advancement of good U.S. relations with Belgium, an esteemed and valued NATO ally. The UN and Africa bureaus saw Belgium as the cause of much of the problem and as resisting solutions in the long-term interests of the United States and the free world. We "Europeanists" argued that NATO Europe had our highest priority and that insensitive U.S. treatment of Belgium could jeopardize those interests. We also sympathized with the Belgian view that Katanga's stability and wealth should not be jeopardized for the illusory objective of unity of a Congo that was obviously woefully unprepared for it.

The views of each of the three bureaus concerned were put forward to the political leadership with passion, often heatedly, but for the most part in a highly professional, expert manner. Bill Cargo and Joe Sisco in the UN bureau were hard-driving and tough in the bureaucratic fights of the day, and very effective. Everyone concerned was under great pressure. We in the European bureau felt that Cargo and Sisco were fair and straightforward in fulfilling their responsibilities. We did not always feel that way about Vance and Eisenberg, whose bureaucratic practices in the heat of battle were equally hard-driving and tough, but sometimes less open and direct.

It was a classic case of advocacy of differing—often opposing—viewpoints, all aimed at advancing the U.S. national interest as seen through differing parts of the same prism. It was up to the secretary of state, the National Security Council, and finally, the president to set the policy from the different choices offered up by the bureaucracy. For the State Department's UN and Africa bureaus, crucial issues were at stake: the future of the United Nations as an effective force for conflict resolution and peacekeeping on the one hand and, on the other, guiding Africa successfully through the decolonization process to independence and economic well-being while at the same time keeping it well-disposed toward the United States. For the European bureau—my bureau—these issues, while important, were secondary to maintaining a strong, healthy, and effective NATO alliance as the principal element of deterrence and strategic stability in the continuing Cold War with the Soviet Union. Inevitably, the priority of keeping the Soviet Union out of a prize—and gigantic—piece of real estate in the heart of Africa outweighed that of upsetting, irritating—and occasionally offending—Belgium, a good friend and ally, but at best a minor player in the NATO–Warsaw Pact standoff in central Europe.

John Kennedy's accession to the presidency in January 1961 intensified the tension and misunderstanding between the United States and Belgium. Kennedy immediately sought a new initiative on the Congo and overlooked Belgium's expectation to be consulted on any new moves. In his desire to thwart a Soviet success in central Africa, Kennedy pressed the State Department for new proposals. The split between the professional pro-NATO, pro-Belgian Europeanists and their pro Africa, pro-UN colleagues deepened with the arrival of the liberal political appointees of the new administration, including Adlai Stevenson to replace Lodge at the United Nations and G. Mennen "Soapy" Williams, former governor of Michigan, named assistant secretary of state for Africa.

The latter two felt that the Kennedy administration should distance itself from Eisenhower's policies, which had alienated the newly emerging African and Asian nations, now members of the United Nations. Events in the Congo moved so quickly that the new administration's policy deliberations had difficulty keeping up; moreover, these events kept pushing the administration toward accommodating the growing number of newly independent African and Asian nations in an effort to keep that bloc from joining the Soviet Union in turning rapidly against the United Nations and its secretary general, Dag Hammarskjöld.

The event that stunned the world, put the United States, its allies, and the United Nations on the defensive, and enraged the Soviets, Asians, and Africans together was the revelation on February 13, 1961—less than a month after Kennedy's inauguration—of Patrice Lumumba's death in Katanga at the hands of unknown persons. Lumumba's death had actually occurred in late January but had been kept secret by Katangan authorities, who had been holding him prisoner since his capture a month earlier under conditions of confusion and mutiny in Thysville. The Soviet and radical African and Asian reaction was immediate and violent, and directed against the United States, Belgium, the United Nations, and Katangan leader Moïse Tshombe. As Washington sought to recoup the initiative under these circumstances, six more political prisoners were murdered in the Congo, a development that envenomed the situation even further.[28]

Adlai Stevenson, who had hoped to persuade the newly independent African and Asian leaders to agree to moderating amendments to a resolution they were sponsoring in the UN Security Council, found himself obliged to vote for their draft as it was. The resolution called for UN forces to prevent civil war through the establishment of neutral zones and cease-fires. It also called for the immediate withdrawal of all Belgian military and political advisers, the reconvening of Parliament, the reorganization of the Congolese National Army, and an investigation of Lumumba's assassination.

Brussels was shocked to receive a UN cable demanding the withdrawal of Belgian military and political advisers without any provision for their replacement. In Elisabethville, Katanga's capital, Tshombe called the UN resolution a "declaration of war against Katanga and the Congo." In Léopoldville, the Congolese prime minister charged that the resolution violated Congolese sovereignty and warned that the Congo would fight if the United Nations sought to enforce it. When the Soviets continued to attack Hammarskjöld, Stevenson called on the Soviet Union to support the UN resolution and warned it not to try to replace departing Belgians with Soviet personnel.

A new instruction to the U.S. embassy in Brussels, which I drafted and which was authorized by the new secretary of state, Dean Rusk, called for close consultations with the Belgians on the issue of the Belgian military withdrawal in order to avoid damaging U.S.-Belgian relations as well as our interests and goals in the Congo. In return for Belgian cooperation, we would urge the United Nations to develop more productive relations with Belgium, noting that many Belgian civilians in the Congo were playing constructive roles there in developing the economy.[29]

Meanwhile, a new government took office in Belgium in April 1961, three months after the Kennedy administration took over in Washington. Belgium's new foreign minister, Paul-Henri Spaak, in a conversation with our new ambassador in Brussels, Douglas MacArthur II, appeared to be more understanding of the position the United States and the United Nations found themselves in, and to be more willing to cooperate in withdrawing the Belgian military from the Congo. MacArthur urged that the president and secretary of state receive Spaak in June to continue to encourage him in this constructive direction.[30]

In mid-June, I wrote another instruction to the field conveying the Department of State's hope that Spaak could be persuaded to proceed with at least an initial withdrawal of Belgian military personnel in order to maintain the current favorable atmosphere between Brussels and New York.[31] A few days later, another telegram went out from the State Department that instructed MacArthur to make clear to Spaak that the "fact present political picture confused offers no valid excuse for postponing large and dramatic withdrawals Belgian officers."[32]

U.S. relations with Belgium and other NATO allies, Britain in particular, remained tense. As long as the Congo's central government was in Lumumba's hands, or in chaos, the principal U.S. goal of maintaining a unified Congo was moderated by the strong desire—shared by the Belgians and other NATO allies—not to see Katanga's riches brought under radical control. However, once the moderate Cyrille Adoula came to power in Léopoldville, and Tshombe remained recalcitrant, U.S.-Belgian relations came under renewed strain. The Belgian government, as well as powerful Belgian and other European (and American) businesses, did not wish to see their interests, which centered in Katanga, jeopardized by the latter's subordination to a fragile government a thousand miles away in Léopoldville.

In December 1961, with Tshombe still holding out against integration into a unified Congo and threatening the use of force against United Nations and Congolese forces, Washington began building up pressure on Brussels to bring Tshombe around. I prepared an instruction, which was signed by Acting Secretary of State George Ball, calling on Ambassador MacArthur in Brussels to urge Spaak to "give serious consideration to developing convincing program [to] strengthen economic position [of] GOC [Government of the Congo] which includes measures having effect of exercising strong economic pressures against Katanga if Tshombe or his advisers refuse [to] implement basic Kitona agreement [agreement between Tshombe and Adoula under which Katanga would be integrated]."[33]

A report to the president, which I had a hand in preparing, cited our concerns:

> If it becomes clear Tshombe has no intention of negotiating in good faith, we believe it inevitable meeting of SC [UN Security Council] would be called at which Soviets, Africans and Asians would insist on intensified military action against Katanga. Since these demands would be vetoed by UK, French and possibly others, we would most likely find ourselves in an emergency special session of the GA [UN General Assembly] as in September 1960. . . .
>
> An immediate consequence of a clear posture of intransigence by Tshombe would be a sharpened desire of Leopoldville Govt to step up military operations by the Congolese Army. We would make every attempt to delay and divert ANC [National Congolese Army] action recognizing that failure to act would jeopardize stability of present moderate govt. If tangible progress is made on integration of Katanga . . . without cooperation of Tshombe, Adoula would have better possibility [to] keep extremists under control and limit military operations to scope acceptable to us.
>
> If, despite our best efforts, there is renewed heavy fighting in Elisabethville, there would most likely be disintegration of Tshombe Govt. We would then hope the UN would move energetically to maintain peace and stability and would take steps to promote establishment [of] more cooperative but popularly based Katanga Govt. . . .[34]

Meanwhile, we were keeping the pressure on the Belgians. On January 2, 1962, Under Secretary of State George McGhee called in Scheyven, the Belgian ambassador. McGhee confirmed to Scheyven our opposition to the resumption of hostilities but "reiterated that any attempt by Tshombe to resume secessionist status [was] absolutely intolerable to US, to UN, and to many other governments which were aware of all that was at stake in Congo."[35]

In a follow-up message to MacArthur, the department made some additional points to be conveyed to the Belgians. We were particularly concerned that Belgium not oppose the UN's and our threats of economic pressures against Katanga. We feared that if Tshombe learned of Belgium's hesitation, it would weaken the pressure program's impact.[36]

For the remaining weeks of my assignment on the Belgium-Luxembourg desk, events in the Congo moved toward their resolution in ways that were ultimately satisfactory to the United States overall. But this process was not completed until after I had left the desk for my next assignment.

Punctuating the Congo problems within my work horizon were other more routine matters dealing with strictly bilateral issues, such as military assistance levels for Belgium; internal political developments there and in Luxembourg, my other "charge"; routine briefings, oral and written, on these and other matters; preparing for visits of Belgian dignitaries, including members of the Belgian royal family; trying to solve problems of one sort or another for our embassies in Brussels and Luxembourg; and assisting the Belgian and Luxembourg embassies in Washington to find their way around the confusing maze of the Washington bureaucracy.

Both Eisenhower's and Kennedy's ambassadors, William Burden, wealthy New Yorker and patron of the arts, and top career diplomat Douglas MacArthur II, nephew and namesake of the famous wartime general, needed "care and feeding" from the desk officer. Burden, a large, hearty man of action and of conservative ideology, would come to town determined to accomplish his objectives and would set about doing just that. He refused to take no for an answer on any matter and simply concentrated on finding the "right button to push" in Washington to get what he wanted.

On one occasion, the United States and Belgium were preparing to celebrate the arrival in Antwerp of the five hundredth shipment of U.S. military-assistance goods to the Belgian armed forces. This particular shipment consisted of a group of Honest John howitzers. Burden was determined to acquire a model of the Honest John to present as a gift to the Belgian minister of defense to mark the occasion and had asked me to find one. I had learned that the choice for such a gift was limited to either a dime-store plastic model (wholly unacceptable to Burden of course) or one of a half-dozen elaborate (and expensive) models, all of which were claimed and in use. Characteristically, Burden, who had previously served as an assistant secretary of the Air Force and knew his way around the Pentagon, did not accept the situation as I had presented it to him and was determined to raise it with the secretary of the Army. With me at his heels, Burden strode purposefully down the corridors of the Pentagon on the way to his appointment with the Army secretary. By sheer coincidence, we passed one of the Honest John models (expensive version) on display in a sealed plastic case near the secretary's office. By nightfall that item had been boxed up and put on a plane for Brussels—mission accomplished.

On another occasion, Ambassador and Mrs. Burden had been invited to the wedding of King Baudouin to Princess Fabiola of Spain. The ambassador called from Brussels one morning to tell me he had arranged with Harry Winston Jewelers in New York for the loan of a diamond tiara for Mrs. Burden to wear at the wedding. He said he had asked Winston's to send the tiara to me by mail, and he hoped I would be able to arrange for someone to carry it to Brussels in time for the ceremonies. Winston's letter arrived twenty-four hours later, informing me that the tiara would arrive separately by mail and that it was insured for (as

I recall) sixty thousand dollars. Sure enough, the following day, a small, unobtrusive box appeared on my desk. Nervous at the responsibility for assuring the safe onward disposition of this piece of jewelry, I sought an appointment with Wiley T. Buchanan, a wealthy former oilman then serving as chief of protocol, to get his advice. As I explained my problem in hesitant tones, he grabbed the package and tossed it into his briefcase. He said he would be happy to take it himself. When he saw my relief, he said, "Young man, you just have to treat such objects as rocks and ignore their value; otherwise, it will get you down!" Another lesson for a young diplomat with still much to learn!

MacArthur was a different sort: dynamic, smooth, difficult, and self-assured. His wife, "Wahwee," was the daughter of the late vice president Alben Barkley and a terror of Foreign Service wives. "Doug" MacArthur was very much a member of the Foreign Service establishment. Comfortable with his family connections, political adviser to Dwight Eisenhower during World War II, he had served as Eisenhower's ambassador to Japan and then been appointed by Kennedy to Brussels. I arranged for the usual series of briefings for MacArthur and off he went to post.

One day, when Belgian suspicions of U.S. attitudes and actions toward Tshombe were at a peak, MacArthur woke me at 4:00 A.M. (it was 9:00 A.M. in Brussels). He started by saying, "Sorry to wake you, pal!" He then said that the morning headlines in Brussels were charging that U.S. warplanes had bombed targets in Katanga and that he needed to deny the charges immediately and categorically. Could he do so? Acutely conscious, even in my sleepy state, that in many matters of high Congo policy the Belgian desk officer was usually the least informed, I nevertheless assured the ambassador he could deny the story. By fortuitous happenstance, I had been at a meeting the day before on the Congo crisis, which gave me confidence that U.S. planes were not bombing in Katanga. When I arrived at my desk at the opening of business, I found a copy of an "immediate" cable to the secretary of state from MacArthur stating that, on the basis of telephonic consultations earlier that morning with Desk Officer Miller, he had denied the story and thus scotched a mischievous report before it caused any harm.

Louis Scheyven, the Belgian ambassador to the United States, was a sweet and gentle human being who must have found his period of service in Washington unpleasant and disagreeable during the difficult Congo crisis days. Despite the difficult demarches he was often called upon to make to us and the often disagreeable messages he received from a number of our overworked and hard-pressed senior officials, for some of whom diplomatic discourse seemed to be an alien tongue, Scheyven was always civil to me and in fact went out of his way to show kindness to my wife and me despite our junior years. He was an old-school European diplomat caught up in the tensions and crosscurrents of emerging postcolonial forces, which in his case seemed to pit a small but proud old-world NATO country against its leviathan new-world ally.

As 1962 began, I was approaching five years in Washington, and it was time to think about an assignment abroad again. I had been promoted just before joining the Belgian desk and was beginning to hope for another promotion. Our years in Washington had been good ones, but Kaity and I were ready for a new assignment abroad. I consulted my "career counselor," who advised that I should seek a consular assignment in a hardship post in order to vary and broaden my experience. I had developed an interest in North Africa during our stay in Paris as the French Indochina war ceased and the war in Algeria opened. The Bureau of Personnel mentioned several possibilities to me, including Constantine and Algiers in Algeria, Dakar in Senegal, and Kano in northern Nigeria. When Personnel's wheel of fortune stopped, I was assigned as a first secretary, political officer, and deputy chief of the political section at our embassy in Saigon, South Vietnam. I left the Belgium-Luxembourg desk in March 1962 to begin preparing for my departure for Saigon later that summer. My career was about to take a new, different, and major turn.

Within nine months of my leaving the Belgian desk, the Congo crisis for all intents and purposes was over. United Nations forces entered Katanga virtually without incident in January 1963. Even with more than a quarter century's hindsight, in Cold War terms the Congo outcome clearly represented an early major success for the West and for the United Nations, and a major defeat for the Soviet Union. Had the latter succeeded in gaining a foothold in the Congo in the 1960s, the subsequent successes in southern Africa of the 1970s and 1980s—of bringing white-dominated Zimbabwe and Namibia to independence, of removing Cuban and other external military forces from Angola and Mozambique, and of encouraging South Africa to replace its racist apartheid regime with a representative, democratic government—would undoubtedly not have been possible without far more bloodshed than actually occurred. Even the parlous state of the Congo today, the product of a leader—Mobutu Sese Seko—who stayed in power with U.S. backing far longer than he should have, transforming and corrupting that power from promoting national unity and economic development to that of enriching himself, corrupting the political system, and draining the economy, does not detract from that immediate judgment.

Moreover, without strong U.S. support for a unified Congo early in the

Cold War—and early in the decolonization process—the Congo itself would have almost certainly broken apart, with powerful Western (European and American) business interests centered in the resource-rich Katanga province. In this event, Katanga would have probably become another regime in southern Africa dominated by a white minority determined to hold onto its interests at all costs. Almost certainly, too, the large, remaining portion of the Congo would not have been a viable state and would have been much more vulnerable to Soviet subversion and exploitation than a unified Congo. The resulting expanded polarization of southern Africa between black-dominated and white-dominated regimes and the inevitable Cold War confrontation in the region between the West and the Soviet Union that would have occurred would undoubtedly have been even worse—more prolonged and bloodier—than they actually were.

PART II

Vietnam

CHINA
Gejiu
Wenlan
Kaihua
Xinjing
Gui Xian
Simao
Nanning
CHINA
Yulin
Lao Cai
Black River
Red River
Yen Bai
Lang Son
Phong Saly
NORTH VIETNAM
Viet Tri
Dien Bien Phu
Hanoi
Hon Gai
Zhanjiang
Luong Nam Tha
Muong Sai
Hoa Binh
Hai Phong
Samneua
Nam Dinh
LAOS
Nam Binh
Luang Prabang
Thanh Hoa
Xiangkhoang
HAINAN ISLAND
Sayaboury
Gulf of Tonkin
Mekong River
Vinh
Vientiane
Nong Khai
Dong Hoi
Udon Thani
Nakhon Phanom
Vinh Linh
DEMILITARIZED ZONE
Phitsanulok
Muong Xepon
Cam Lo
Quang Tri City
Savannakhet
Khe Sanh
Phu Bai
Khon Kaen
Hue
Da Nang
An Hoa
THAILAND
Saravane
Tam Ky
Chu Lai
Ubon Ratchathani
Si Sa Ket
Attopeu
Surin
Pakse
My Lai
Warin Chamrap
Nakhon Ratchasima
Dak To
Sara Buri
Kontum
Bangkok
Aranyaprathet
Pleiku
Qui Nhon
An Khe
Sisophon
Siem Reap
Stoeng Treng
Lomphat
SOUTH VIETNAM
Tuy Hoa
CAMBODIA
Battambang
Kompang Thom
Ban Me Thuot
Pursat
Nha Trang
Gia Nghia
Kompong Cham
Cam Ranh
Phnom Penh
Phuoc Binh
Da Lat
Gulf of Thailand
Kompong Speu
Phan Rhang
Bao Loc
Tay Ninh
Saigon
Phan Thiet
Kampot
Kompong Sam
Long Binh
My Tho
Ha Tien
Vung Tau
Rach Gia
Can Tho
Bac Lieu
South China Sea
CON SON

VIETNAM

THREE

The Cold War Turned Hot

BY 1962, when I was assigned to the American embassy in Saigon, the United States was already deeply involved in the former French colony of Vietnam. The roots of that involvement dated back to the Truman and Eisenhower administrations.[1] France's postwar position contrasted sharply with that of Belgium, both in Europe and in their respective far-flung colonial empires. The Congo was strategically important, for its raw materials and for America's Cold War goals of bringing the African nations to independence outside the Soviet orbit. However, the Congo was on the Cold War's periphery, and the United Nations was the chosen instrument through which the United States pursued its interests there without directly confronting the Soviet Union. Indochina, in contrast, was perceived to be on the Cold War's front line in Asia, where communism and the "free world"[2] were seen to be joined in actual conflict. Indochina, like Korea, was a battlefield where the United States saw the Sino-Soviet threat as real and immediate—and where force had to be met with force. The conventional Cold War wisdom, following China's fall to communism in 1949, was that, if the communist tide could not be stopped in Vietnam, the rest of Southeast Asia could fall "like a row of dominoes."[3]

France, in contrast to Belgium, was key to America's plans for Western Europe—reconstruction of its devastated economies and integration of a rebuilt, restored democratic Germany into a Western defense structure. Not only did France occupy geographically important territory between the English Channel and Germany, at whose hands France had suffered aggression three times in the preceding century, but Europe's reconstruction and Germany's integration would have been infinitely more difficult, if not impossible, without France's cooperation. Moreover, in the immediate postwar years, France's Communist Party had made deep inroads into France's body politic.

In May 1950, therefore, after China had finally fallen to Mao Zedong's forces and Chiang Kai-shek's forces had fled to Taiwan, Truman approved Acheson's recommendation that the United States provide economic support and military supplies for France's use in Indochina. Despite his own and Acheson's deep reservations, Truman was willing to help France restore its position in Indochina by preventing Ho Chi Minh's communist-backed forces from taking control in Vietnam, Laos, and Cambodia.

One month later, North Korea invaded South Korea, and by Thanksgiving, China had intervened there in a major way. The widening war against Ho Chi Minh's communist forces in Indochina, North Korea's invasion of South Korea, and China's massive intervention in the Korean conflict convinced Washington policymakers that Sino-Soviet aggression was indeed a direct threat to America's security. Truman sought augmented military-aid funds for the Philippines and Indochina.

By 1951, we were providing a half-billion dollars in support of the French effort in Indochina, although the Truman administration was unanimously opposed to the direct involvement of U.S. combat forces there.[4] In effect, the fall of China to communism in 1949 and North Korea's unprovoked attack on South Korea the following year made virtually inevitable America's response to what it perceived to be the communist threat to free-world interests in Southeast Asia. The Truman administration had made some early efforts to reconcile differences with Communist China, as we all called it in those days. However, chances of such a reconciliation dwindled to zero after China's entry into the Korean War, triggered by Truman's and Acheson's ill-advised acquiescence in General Douglas MacArthur's drive to the Yalu River in an effort to reunify Korea by force. The administration apparently gave little thought to exploiting signs of growing Sino-Soviet differences. On the contrary, U.S. decisions to try to stop communism in Vietnam had the opposite effect. The Eisenhower administration continued to pour millions of dollars into support for France's increasingly untenable position in Indochina, arguing that Southeast Asia was "of the most transcendent importance" to the United States.[5]

In 1954, France extricated itself from Indochina via the Geneva Accords, and the United States, unhappy that France had abandoned the northern half of Vietnam to communism, took up in South Vietnam where the French had left off. The Eisenhower administration threw its full support behind South Vietnam's new nationalist leader, Ngo Dinh Diem. Indeed, it was instrumental in installing Diem as South Vietnam's first independent leader. Eisenhower and Dulles also grudgingly agreed to do nothing to upset the terms of the Geneva Accords, which had provisionally partitioned the country until national elections could be held in 1956.

At the same time, the United States had persuaded Britain, France, Australia, New Zealand, and Pakistan to join with Thailand and the Philippines in forming the Southeast Asia Treaty Organization (SEATO) in the hope of preventing further communist expansion in Southeast Asia. Although South

Vietnam, Laos, and Cambodia were precluded by the 1954 Geneva Accords from joining a defensive alliance, the 1955 Manila Treaty that created SEATO formally extended its protection to those states. This treaty commitment, which was overwhelmingly approved by the U.S. Senate with a minimum of debate, served as a major rationale for the Kennedy-Johnson Vietnam policy over the ensuing twenty years.[6] Ironically for both the Eisenhower and Kennedy administrations, U.S. Vietnam policy remained trapped between Scylla and Charybdis: The 1954 Geneva Accords severely limited the military assistance that external powers could legally provide South Vietnam; yet the 1955 Manila Treaty's commitment justified growing quantities of such assistance to that beleaguered country. Only a decade later, when Lyndon Johnson decided to send combat troops in increasing numbers, did the United States feel free to ignore the restrictions of the Geneva Accords that Hanoi had in any case so long ignored.

Meanwhile, unstinting U.S. support had allowed Diem to consolidate his position internally. In 1956, Eisenhower and Dulles accepted Diem's decision not to proceed with the nationwide elections called for by the Geneva Accords on the grounds that Communist North Vietnam would allow genuinely free elections neither in the north nor in areas in the south under its control. This was another early decision that gave the United States growing responsibility for the fate of South Vietnam—and that sowed the seeds of later domestic controversy in the United States over the wisdom and legality of U.S. policy supporting Diem and opposing North Vietnam.

Thwarted in its objective of using the electoral process blessed by the Geneva Accords to dominate South Vietnam, Hanoi renewed its insurgency against the South with the full backing of the Soviet Union and China, themselves in bitter competition with each other. When John Kennedy came into office in January 1961, Eisenhower warned him that Laos (apparently without mentioning Vietnam specifically) would be his biggest headache. Kennedy resisted recommendations that U.S. ground force units be sent to South Vietnam, but he directed a major increase in the U.S. advisory effort. The Kennedy administration's determination "to win"[7] in Vietnam was widely shared in the Congress and in leading newspapers, including the *New York Times* and the *Washington Post.*

In July 1962, in preparation for my new post as political officer in Saigon, I attended the first session of the Kennedy administration's new "counterinsurgency course." On graduation, the class was bused to the White House rose garden to hear from President Kennedy himself the importance his administration—and he personally—gave to our assignments. The president spoke to us briefly, then moved through the group greeting each of us personally and shaking our hands. A year and a half before, the nation had been stirred by his inaugural address, and now we were going to be a part of his call to "bear any burden, pay any price" for freedom. The ease with which he met each of us, recalling seemingly without effort those whom he had met before, sealed our contract with him. His brother, Attorney General Robert Kennedy, lean and intense, observing the spectacle from above on the White House steps leading to the rose garden, added his stamp of approval to the contract. We were the Kennedy administration's "shock troops," being sent to do unconventional battle in far-off Vietnam and other far-flung troubled countries beset by externally supported insurgencies.

It was a sparkling day. The president was serious, yet relaxed, warm and outgoing. For me, a career Foreign Service officer with then nearly ten years' experience in European affairs, it was an inspiring send-off to Vietnam. Meeting the president in the White House Rose Garden climaxed four months of orientation on the State Department's Vietnam desk and in more formal training at the department's Foreign Service Institute in Southeast Asian studies and later in the counterinsurgency course.

I went to Vietnam with no reservations. In the four months I spent immersing myself in the area and in the bureaucratic lingo, the atmosphere of confidence and determination that the Kennedy administration inspired caught my imagination as it did for many others. I understood that the struggle in Indochina was "unconventional": It was not for territory but for the hearts and minds of the Vietnamese people. Crucial to victory were political and economic reforms, not military might. I learned these "truths" from people like Averell Harriman, Bobby Kennedy, Roger Hilsman, Lucian Pye, and many senior military and civilian colleagues. Conveying the mind-set of the era was a Peanuts cartoon someone later stuck on a wall in our Saigon embassy showing Charlie Brown marching resolutely onto the baseball field with his bat over his shoulder and his glove slung over his bat. The caption read, "How can we lose when we're so sincere?"

Kaity and I and our two children, now ages eight and six, adapted quickly to our life in Vietnam. We occupied a modest villa in an embassy compound of five villas on Tu Xuong, a quiet, unprepossessing side street in a Westerners' residential quarter. We developed a circle of Vietnamese friends and acquaintances, both through my own contacts and through a group of wives of officials and professional men to whom Kaity and other American wives gave English lessons.

Occasional terrorist attacks in the city did not make us unduly fearful or apprehensive. We took moderate precautions within Saigon and obeyed embassy prohibitions against driving outside the city other than to nearby Bien Hoa. Our personal car was a secondhand, black Volkswagen Beetle convertible, remarkable only for its U.S. embassy diplomatic license plates. We often took local taxis, the ubiquitous blue-and-cream-colored Quatre-Chevaux Renaults, and pedicabs, or *cyclopousses,* the ever-present, three-wheeled conveyances with a canopied carriage seat in front and a pedaling driver behind.

From the start we were taken by our surroundings—the graceful, towering palm trees, the lush foliage, the heavy, simmering heat, the city's pleasant, French-provincial, tree-lined streets, the delicately built Vietnamese people, the sounds, the smells, everything. I was delighted to be there and to be a part of this great effort. It was exhilarating.

I immediately got caught up in my work, even as we settled in. The issues were constant: Was the war going well or badly? And, were President Diem and Ngo Dinh Nhu, his brother and trusted adviser, serious about political and economic reforms or only going through the motions to please us and get our ever-increasing aid? In addition to cultivating official and nonofficial contacts in Saigon, the embassy's political section had a group of young officers trained in the Vietnamese language who spent much of their time in the provinces gathering information from many sources and reporting their findings. Other U.S. officials, AID officers, CIA officers, and USIA personnel traveled or worked in the countryside and provided us with information, opinions, and analysis. American military personnel throughout the country advised Vietnamese forces and developed their own views of the war's progress. Other sources included the foreign press, foreign diplomats, and the Vietnamese themselves. Information and analysis were abundant, as were judgments. Only the truth was elusive.

Among those assigned to the embassy in Saigon during this period were a number of young, unusually talented and ambitious Foreign Service officers whose Vietnam experience defined their entire subsequent careers. In no small measure this handful of young men have had a disproportionately large impact on the shaping of American foreign policy from the 1970s to the 1990s. Anthony Lake, Richard Holbrooke, John Negroponte, Peter Tarnoff, and

Frank Wisner II, all junior officers in South Vietnam on their first assignments in the Foreign Service, were not content with submitting their views only through the normal bureaucratic channels, where they could be deflected, buried in some midlevel inbox, or watered down on the way to the people who counted. Frustrated with what they saw as ineffective, overbureaucratized U.S. efforts and lackluster South Vietnamese responses to those efforts, they sought to shake up U.S. policymakers and to make U.S. policies and programs in South Vietnam winning ones. To this end, they cultivated relationships with senior U.S. officials in Saigon and with high-level officials who regularly visited from Washington.

Far from being rebuffed as young men with no experience, these junior officers found a ready, even eager, audience at the top levels of the U.S. government. There, virtually unanimous skepticism—and enormous frustration—regarding official reports and assessments of progress in the war merged with an eagerness to learn the truth. All sought a winning formula to prevent a communist takeover of South Vietnam. The young officers also quietly cultivated members of the American press, many of them of the same generation, who were strongly influencing American public opinion—mostly negatively—about the effectiveness of U.S. policy in Vietnam.

The senior officials whose ear these young officers captured on Vietnam themselves continued to rise in power and influence and called on these younger men to fill government positions of increasing responsibility. Although, like the rest of us, these rising stars had little impact on U.S. policy or actions in Vietnam, they all advanced rapidly in their careers, either in the Foreign Service or, eventually, outside the service.[8]

I myself was a moderate optimist on Vietnam. I was skeptical of the consistently positive evaluations of military progress by military officers under great pressure to show—whose promotions depended on—progress. I was equally skeptical of those, mostly civilians, who believed we were supporting a corrupt, inept regime incapable of capturing the hearts and minds of the people. I considered our growing effort justified by Hanoi's blatant violations of the Geneva Accords with its infiltration of troops and arms into South Vietnam.

Like all of my colleagues in the embassy's political section—and elsewhere in the mission—I tried to develop my own sense of the Vietnamese people and their desires for their country's future. The expanding circle of Vietnamese friends and contacts—young and old, official and unofficial, men and women, military and civilian—that my wife and I cultivated all came from a limited segment of Vietnamese society: educated, urbanized, middle class. More important, they were approved of, or at least tolerated by, the Diem regime and its successors.

Little by little, from numerous conversations, certain things became clear to us about the Vietnamese. Many of our friends and contacts were refugees from North Vietnam who had fled when the Communist Viet Minh took over the northern half of the country, as provided for by the Geneva Accords of 1954. Many of them were Catholic, but Catholic or Buddhist, most were bitterly anticommunist. Vietnamese from the north, those from the south, and those from central Vietnam were also deeply divided by regional antipathies and cultural differences. These antipathies and differences lay just beneath the surface in the body politic and affected people's ability to cooperate on any common national goals—including uniting against the communists.

Years of Vietnamese resistance against the French colonizers had led to bitter and ruthless factional strife as well, not just between communists and anticommunists but also between and among a wide spectrum of anticommunist and noncommunist political parties and factions. Differences among these groups and their leaders were as deep and bitter as those between communists and anticommunists. These disputes weakened their ability—and even their motivation—to unite against the Viet Cong and their North Vietnamese managers to a degree that Americans could not believe or even begin to comprehend. As the U.S. presence grew and assumed increasing responsibility for the conduct of the war and for South Vietnam's future, some South Vietnamese sought favor with the Americans to promote their own political fortunes and to undermine and destroy the prospects for their political rivals and enemies.

Even with the benefit of hindsight, I remain convinced that the bulk of the South Vietnamese people did not wish their country to be taken over by communism; but neither did they willingly accept domination by a foreign power, not by the French nor, later, by the United States. Washington reacted with great impatience and irritation to the disunity of the South Vietnamese, unable to understand why, with the great generosity and determination of the United States behind them, the Vietnamese could not put aside their differences and unite against the communist menace. Yet all of Washington's actions—perhaps most strikingly its encouraging the coup d'état against Ngo Dinh Diem—seemed designed to undermine the very unity and cohesion that Washington sought to promote.

The years I spent in Vietnam, 1962–1965, were fateful ones for the United States and for Vietnam. Decisions made in those years assured the ultimate, failed outcome: in 1963 the decision to withdraw support from Diem that led to his overthrow and assassination; the decision to begin bombing selected military targets in North Vietnam after the still-controversial Tonkin Gulf incident in August 1964 and the ensuing congressional Tonkin Gulf Resolution; and the decision in 1965 to begin sending American combat troops into South Vietnam. During those same years, our policy finally extricated itself from the constraints of the 1954 Geneva Accords to better confront Hanoi's blatant violations of those accords. Hanoi's massive infiltration of troops and equipment into the South, we argued, justified our own growing overt combat role. By the time we openly threw over those constraints, however, the American people had already tired of mounting casualties and of supporting a Vietnamese leader unable or unwilling to mobilize his own people against the communist invader. Americans had grown skeptical, too, of the official U.S. claims that this struggle was vital to America's security.

By 1962, Diem faced three problems. In Saigon, he faced pressures from the intellectual and Western-educated Vietnamese elite to liberalize his regime—to be responsive to a variety of shifting and contradictory oppositionist pressures. It was to these elements of Vietnamese society that members of the U.S. mission, and the U.S. press corps, had the easiest access and by whose views we tended to assess events. It was thus this elite who convinced U.S. officials and journalists of the Diem regime's increasing unpopularity, which they believed was only helping the communist cause by alienating its own people. Yet Diem knew that if he gave in to those pressures—domestic and American—he was finished, and so was his country. This would not be so much because justice had won out over an evil regime, as many in the United States saw it. Rather it would be because a developing society, plagued for at least a generation by the struggle between a dying colonialism and a growing nationalism exploited by a disciplined, well-led communist movement, would shatter under a less than firm hand.

As his second problem Diem faced a determined, ruthless, and bitter enemy waging an organized campaign in the countryside to terrorize the people and destroy the government presence there by assassination and attack. The Viet Cong wished to show that the Diem regime was unable to protect the people, that the regime was indifferent to their needs, and that it was the Viet Cong, not the Saigon government, that was the wave of the future.

The wholly different views and largely different aims of Diem's chief ally, the United States, constituted his third problem. The United States saw the struggle in Diem's land as a war to win in a foreign country that the United States would leave after its mission was accomplished—as Lyndon Johnson later put it, another coonskin for frontier America to nail on the wall. The United States had no intrinsic interests in Vietnam; its interest was to see that a hostile power did not succeed in dominating Vietnam and thereby set in motion a series of "falling dominoes" throughout the region.

Diem, his brother Ngo Dinh Nhu, and their compatriots were fighting a different war. For them the war was a historic fratricidal struggle from which the Vietnamese people had no escape, a condition of life to which they must adapt to survive. Diem desperately needed American material help to stay in power. As its price, he had to accept American advice—and advisers. The latter he mistrusted and belittled, but he had to get along with them, as with an overbearing mother-in-law who provides the house to live in and the furniture and then offers endless advice about the cooking and cleaning.

When I arrived in Vietnam, some ten thousand U.S. military advisers were already there. Even then they were skirting very close to a combat role—frequently "advising under combat conditions" but staying out of combat themselves except in the clear case of self-defense. The thin line between combat and noncombat status was stretched even thinner in air operations. American personnel flew in observer aircraft and in strike aircraft as well, but no American was to fly in the latter during combat without being accompanied by Vietnamese pilots who were supposed to pull the trigger. U.S. military authorities labeled these air operations "Farmgate."

Soon after my arrival, one advisory role I participated in directly was what was then a small, tentative, experimental program of chemically defoliating tropical vegetation and crops, dubbed "Ranch Hand."[9] Only a few experimental defoliation missions had until then been flown in the delta southwest of Saigon along canals and roadways and around base areas to clear fields of fire and to reduce the risk of Viet Cong ambush. On one occasion, I accompanied General Paul Harkins, the first commander of the U.S. Military Assistance Command, Vietnam (MACV), on an inspection flight over sprayed areas in the delta.

Later on, I flew on a number of Ranch Hand C-123 missions north of Saigon in Tay Ninh and Phuoc Long provinces whose purpose was to select isolated Viet Cong crop areas for destruction by defoliant spraying. The Phuoc Long test operation, along with one or two others, laid the basis for decisions in Washington to continue the program on a limited and carefully controlled basis. After evaluation of these operations in Washington, President Kennedy agreed to delegate to the ambassador in Saigon the authority to approve carefully defined defoliation operations but insisted that crop destruction proposals had to receive senior approval in Washington.[10]

The C-123 Ranch Hand flights were not without their drama or their risks. We would take off from Saigon's Tan Son Nhut airport in the early morning with Vietnamese military and agricultural experts, MACV representatives, and myself, the lone diplomat representing the political judgment of the embassy and the State Department. Before taking off in the relative cool of what invariably became a hot, steamy tropical morning as the sun climbed higher, each passenger was handed a parachute (usually accompanied by some black humor—"if it doesn't work, turn it in for a new one!"—from the crew member) and told to strap himself into his bucket seat. The C-123 was a cargo plane—bucket seats for the few passengers, no interior finish or furnishing. As we reached our cruising altitude, the crew would open the rear cargo ramp to improve the air circulation inside the aircraft. When we reached the province in which our prospective targets were located, we would usually land on a dirt airstrip to pick up local officials, Vietnamese and American, who were more familiar with the local terrain and security conditions.

Over the proposed target area, we descended to a relatively low altitude for better viewing of the rice or vegetable plots that were our tentative targets, in order to make judgments as to their suitability for chemical defoliation. This is when we were most vulnerable to Viet Cong sniping or antiaircraft barrages—happily, something that never occurred on the flights I went on.

Under guidance from the State Department, the U.S. mission followed elaborate criteria to prevent spraying operations from hitting populated areas or crops near populated areas. This meant flying conditions had to be nearly ideal—with a minimum of wind and precipitation. It meant, too, devising a scheme for compensating villagers if their crops were destroyed in error. Categorical assurances were repeatedly given by the chemical experts of the U.S. Army and the Advanced Research Projects Agency (ARPA) that the defoliants, "agents orange and purple," were harmless to humans and animals.

We kept detailed records of every operation, assessing the process of selecting targets, the operation itself, and the results. The State Department had serious concerns that destroying food with chemicals would lead the communist side to charge the United States with engaging in chemical warfare in Vietnam. The department insisted that an embassy political officer participate in the selection of possible crop targets to assess the potential political risks. The volumes on Vietnam in *Foreign Relations of the United States 1961–1963* (see notes 9 and 10) reflect the controversy that swirled around this issue in Washington as the policymakers grappled with the potential benefits and liabilities of such a program.

Ranch Hand ultimately grew from its modest beginnings to a program of gigantic proportions. It was perhaps the most egregious—and tragic—example of how America's frustration with its inability to achieve its purposes in Vietnam led it to lose all perspective—moral and otherwise—regarding the methods it employed. Americans and Vietnamese alike continue to bear Ranch Hand's damaging consequences.

The Washington debate was complicated further by the American desire to describe Ranch Hand as a South Vietnamese program for which Saigon had requested our technical assistance. This ran smack into the Vietnamese desire to get on with the program without paying too much attention to U.S. restrictions. It became just one more source of tension between the Vietnamese and ourselves.

The year 1963 opened with several body blows to U.S. policy and actions in South Vietnam. On January 2, South Vietnamese forces engaged a Viet Cong battalion at Ap Bac, a village in the Mekong Delta. Despite a four-to-one numerical advantage, South Vietnamese units suffered heavy casualties and three Americans were killed. The ensuing widespread coverage of the battle in the U.S. press and the open, bitter criticism by U.S. advisers of the weak South Vietnamese performance fed the growing doubts and disagreements in Washington about the U.S. effort in Vietnam. The incident added to the growing tension between the Americans and their South Vietnamese allies.[11]

In February 1963, in the aftermath of the controversy over the Ap Bac battle, Senator "Mike" Mansfield released a report of his December 1962 visit to Vietnam. An early admirer and supporter of Diem, Mansfield was by then highly critical of Diem's government and of the U.S. effort there. His report, coming on the heels of the Ap Bac disaster, stoked the fires of controversy even more and heightened tensions in both Washington and Saigon.[12]

Against this backdrop in March 1963, Washington asked the embassy in Saigon to reassess the use of U.S. air power in support of South Vietnamese forces. The State Department's instruction, issued only three months after the president had agreed to a significant augmentation of Farmgate aircraft to perform these support missions, noted that "present interdiction missions appear to go beyond 'air-ground support techniques'" authorized by the president in November 1961. The department's instruction weighed the pros and cons of the growing U.S. involvement in these air missions, noting that in a political war, the widespread killing of civilians by U.S. air strikes would be self-defeating; that the use of U.S. aircraft and personnel in combat missions was in violation of the Geneva Accords; and that such use in interdiction strikes "badly stretches, if it does not actually break, the mandate under which American air power was first engaged in the Vietnam conflict."[13]

A month later, Saigon submitted its review, which I had prepared on the basis of information gathered throughout the mission and which General Harkins had cleared and Ambassador Frederick E. "Fritz" Nolting had approved. This report,[14] like the embassy's assessments of the pilot defoliation and crop destruction test operations, illustrated how incremental assessments were invariably stated in positive terms by the mission in the field. Such reports reflected the honest judgments of the professionals, myself included, based on often spotty and inconclusive information and evidence then available—and undoubtedly often weighted with a "get with the program" bias from those whose operations were being assessed. At the same time, underlying all such assessments was the unspoken understanding that to come up with a negative assessment would have called into question basic U.S. policy in Vietnam, which the ambassador and the U.S. commander were under heavy pressure to bring off successfully. Ironically, such reports, which made eminent sense to those charged to "win" in the field, compounded frustration and irritation and fed the policy divisions between hawks and doves within the administration, both political and career.

A case in point: Michael Forrestal, a member of President Kennedy's National Security Council staff, in forwarding the embassy's study of the use of U.S. air power in Vietnam to the president added a memorandum from Roger Hilsman, assistant secretary of state for Far Eastern affairs. According to Hilsman, a military officer recently returned from Vietnam had cast doubt on the study's conclusion that the use of air power in Vietnam was under tight control. Forrestal's brief memorandum advised the president: "I don't think that the problem raised by Roger's memorandum can be effectively handled from Washington. What we need is fresh leadership in the field." Forrestal's memorandum went on to argue for the replacement of Fritz Nolting as the U.S. ambassador in Saigon.[15]

Diem had skillfully and shrewdly used growing U.S. material and political support as a substitute for his own sagging domestic political support. With equal skill, he used his brother Nhu, his principal ally in keeping domestic political pressures in check, to reassure the United States that his government was capable of organizing itself to meet the challenge from the Viet Cong and their leaders in Hanoi. At the same time, when he felt it necessary in response to U.S. pressures, he would assure us that he intended to liberalize his regime and broaden its political base as much as the conditions of his beleaguered country would permit.

This uneasy but more or less workable partnership was upset by totally unforeseen developments triggered from a wholly unexpected quarter—the third and most damaging body blow to U.S. policy in Vietnam that year. In May 1963, traditional celebrations of Buddha's birthday in Hue, the old imperial capital in central Vietnam, touched off an ugly incident between the crowds and Diem's security forces. Several people were killed and others injured, setting in motion events that were to lead six months later to the downfall and death of Diem and his brother Nhu.

Diem and Nhu badly misjudged and mishandled the Hue incident. They had underestimated the shrewd determination of the Buddhist leadership and the strength of long-festering Buddhist feeling against a Catholic-dominated regime in Saigon, in particular that the Buddhist leadership associated Catholicism with Western colonialism. Diem and Nhu mistakenly assumed that their regime could use U.S. support as leverage against the Buddhists to revive the country's concentration—and that of the United States—on the principal struggle, the war against the Viet Cong.

The United States, too, misjudged and mishandled the affair. Ultimately, in encouraging Diem's generals to overthrow him, the United States accepted responsibility for a war that, without Diem, became an increasingly losing struggle. Throughout this period the U.S. embassy was manned by career Foreign Service officers who had had no previous experience in Asia. Fritz Nolting, the ambassador when I arrived, had had no Asian experience; neither had William Trueheart, the deputy chief of mission, nor Melvin Manfull, the political counselor, nor I, Manfull's deputy. All of us had served together in Paris with the U.S. delegation to NATO, and it was undoubtedly no coincidence that we ended up together in Vietnam. Nolting and Trueheart, longtime personal friends, were presumably instrumental in seeing that Manfull and I were assigned to lead the political section in Saigon under their direction.

Opinions and biases differed within the embassy proper, and even more so within the mission as a whole (including MACV, the intelligence community, the AID mission, and the U.S. Information Service [USIS]). But all generally agreed that the Diem regime's heavy-handed response to the events in Hue gave impetus to what became the Buddhist revolt and helped it spread and gain the sympathy of leadership groups throughout central Vietnam and

Saigon, even within South Vietnam's military establishment. (Interestingly, the densely populated area of the Mekong Delta south of Saigon was never seriously affected.) We all agreed, I think, that the Buddhist ringleaders were so encouraged by their success in exploiting the deep restiveness of the country, and by the regime's inept playing into their hands, that their protest struggle gradually transformed itself into a crusade to bring down the regime. Despite Diem's serious shortcomings, we in the mission were unanimously perplexed that the Buddhist leadership could so irresponsibly and foolishly risk handing the country over to the Viet Cong by creating widespread political instability. This was yet another example of how little we understood the mood of the South Vietnamese people.

In June 1963, the dramatic, grisly picture of a seated Buddhist bonze (monk) in saffron-colored robes engulfed in flames in an act of self-immolation in the middle of a main Saigon thoroughfare flashed across television screens in America and around the world. The shock and revulsion were instantaneous. That one horrifying picture doomed Diem's prospects for retaining control—and American support. He was never able to regain the momentum and restore order. Meanwhile, American press and television coverage of the spreading unrest fueled the controversy surrounding our growing commitment. As Diem fought for control of events in South Vietnam, the Kennedy administration fought for understanding and support for its Vietnam policy at home.

In July, President Kennedy replaced his ambassador in Saigon as a sign of Washington's displeasure at Diem's clumsy handling of the Buddhist affair and as a sign to the American people and Congress—and to the communist world—of a growing U.S. determination and involvement. In 1961, Kennedy had chosen Fritz Nolting as his ambassador in Saigon after the new administration's basic policy decisions had been taken. Nolting's instructions had been to give full support to the Diem regime to forestall a communist takeover of South Vietnam. Kennedy's advisers deemed it possible to succeed in this goal; so did Nolting. Nevertheless, there were those in the Kennedy administration who had always been uncomfortable with the administration's growing support for the authoritarian Diem and who had long doubted that Diem could be induced to broaden his government's political base enough to erode communist pressures and blandishments. Doubters included W. Averell Harriman, under secretary of state for political affairs; Roger Hilsman, assistant secretary of state for Far Eastern affairs; Chester Bowles, ambassador at large; Arthur

Schlesinger, presidential special assistant; and Mike Forrestal, a member of the National Security Council staff.

For months this group had militated to get rid of Nolting. For them, Nolting symbolized what was wrong with Kennedy's policy of maintaining support for Diem as the principal means to defeat the communist insurgency in South Vietnam. Every time they asked Nolting and his staff —or Harkins and his command—for an assessment or an appraisal of a program or of the progress of the war, the assessment came back positive rather than negative—the glass was always half full, never half empty. Nolting's responsibility—and that of Harkins—was to make the policy work. The perceived alternatives were either to scrap the policy and withdraw, leaving the field to the communists—unthinkable—or to scrap Diem and his regime and get on with the war. In the end, the administration scrapped Diem, but this option proved unworkable.

Forrestal and Hilsman had been gunning for Nolting since the battle at Ap Bac in January 1963. Hilsman, then director of the State Department's Bureau of Intelligence and Research, had visited South Vietnam soon after the battle. On his return, on January 25, he sent the president a detailed assessment of the situation and of the effectiveness of the U.S. mission and its leadership. In an "eyes only" annex, he argued for Nolting's replacement by a "single, strong executive"—either a military figure or a civilian public figure who could dominate all elements of the mission.[16]

As the debate between Washington and Saigon continued in the wake of Ap Bac, Nolting made clear his views in a February 1963 exchange of letters with Harriman, then assistant secretary of state for Far Eastern affairs. Harriman conveyed to Nolting Forrestal's concerns that the embassy was insufficiently in contact with opposition political figures in Saigon. In reply, Nolting forcefully stated his views:

> [A]fter the unequivocal public pronouncements of Vice President Johnson two years ago, and more recently the Attorney General and other high US officials, which I myself thought right and proper, I would not find it possible to be the agent in a change of US policy away from forthright support of the legitimate government which happens also, in my opinion, to be the best available at the present time.[17]

When the Hue incident occurred, Nolting unwisely decided to continue with his home-leave plans, presumably with Washington's agreement—a normal step after two years in a difficult assignment.[18] He judged that the Hue incident, like others before it, was an isolated one, but the situation continued to worsen in his absence. While cruising in the Mediterranean, he learned from a ship's radio that he had been replaced by Henry Cabot Lodge. In midsummer, Nolting returned briefly to say good-bye, a deeply embittered man—which he remained until his death many years later.

Aside from his chagrin at learning about his replacement from a ship's radio, Nolting believed that the embassy in his absence had overdramatized the internal political turmoil in its reporting to Washington. Such reporting further undermined Washington's confidence in what it already saw as Diem's shaky ability to protect the growing U.S. investment in South Vietnam—confidence that Nolting had painstakingly cultivated over two years, building on the efforts of his predecessors. Nolting believed that slipshod and irresponsible embassy reporting was undoing all of his work. Most of all he blamed the man he had left in charge in his absence, Bill Trueheart. Sadly, the long-standing personal friendship between these two fine men, both with deep personal integrity and highly developed professional skills and reputations, was an early casualty of the Vietnam war: Their friendship was never restored.

By this time—midsummer—I had turned over my defoliation "portfolio" to Robert Burke, who became responsible for liaison with MACV. As deputy chief of the political section, I focused more and more on coordinating the mission's reporting on the internal political situation. During Nolting's final brief period in Vietnam, I drafted a report to Washington on the preparations for the national assembly elections coming that September. The report was based on numerous conversations my colleagues and I had had with candidates, election officials, and national assembly staff members. A pattern had emerged from these conversations indicating clearly that the elections were to be as carefully controlled as they had been in the past. Diem undoubtedly was convinced that he could ill afford the luxury of an open election in the face of pressures from the communist insurgents in the countryside, the noncommunist elites in urban centers, the American government, the American press, and finally, the new element of militant Buddhists.

Before releasing the report for transmission to Washington, Nolting questioned me closely on its accuracy and balance. It differed strikingly from Diem's previous assurances to Nolting. Reluctantly, he agreed to send it.[19]

Henry Cabot Lodge, Boston Brahmin, archetypal Republican, former U.S. senator, former ambassador to the United Nations, former vice presidential candidate, and still a figure of national prominence, arrived to take up his duties as U.S. ambassador to South Vietnam on August 22, 1963. Lodge was ordered to speed up his arrival following Diem's declaration of martial law and his brother's use of South Vietnamese special army units to attack Buddhist pagodas in Saigon and elsewhere as centers of subversion against the state. Thich Tri Quang, the key Buddhist ringleader, sought and was given asylum in the U.S. embassy.[20] Vu Van Mau, Diem's foreign minister and a devout Buddhist, resigned and shaved his head in protest over the government's actions.

Lodge's orders were to determine whether U.S. objectives in Vietnam could any longer be achieved with Diem at the helm; whether, to salvage U.S. objectives, Diem could be persuaded to divest his regime of his brother's malign influence; or, if neither were likely, whether it would be possible to continue to pursue U.S. objectives if Diem were removed by a coup d'état and, if so, whether senior military officers in South Vietnam's armed forces would be disposed to engineer a coup if assured that the United States would not stand in their way. Lodge received the first of numerous instructions in this vein two days after he arrived in Saigon. Controversy still swirls today around the process by which that first instruction was (or was not) coordinated at the highest levels of the U.S. government.[21]

Over the next few days, those highest levels of the U.S. government were consumed by the issue of what to do about Diem. The president met regularly with his advisers to review Lodge's latest reports on the unfolding situation in Saigon, in particular the generals' vacillation as to whether to move against Diem and, if so, when. Kennedy himself did not appear eager to proceed with a coup if its success were problematical. When the president queried Lodge for his best assessment of the likelihood of success, Lodge replied, "We are launched on a course from which there is no respectable turning back."[22] Vacillation in Washington and among the Vietnamese generals in Saigon continued until the coup actually took place.

Most of us in the embassy were not privy to the volleys of highly sensitive messages flashing back and forth between the two capitals. Rather, we were engrossed in answering Washington's repeated requests for assessments of the situation to fine-tune its judgments about possible courses of action to take. In early September, Marine Major General Victor Krulak of the Pentagon's Office of the Joint Chiefs of Staff and Joseph Mendenhall of the State Department (and formerly political counselor at the embassy in Saigon) were dispatched to make (yet another) independent assessment of both the military situation and political attitudes in the wake of the raid on the pagodas. Krulak visited MACV and the military structure in the delta south of Saigon (III and IV Corps), while Mendenhall visited the embassy and, accompanied by me, Hue and Da Nang. Mendenhall met principally with civilians—Vietnamese and American.

Back in Washington they reported to the president and his senior advisors. Krulak gave an optimistic assessment of the war's progress and of the absence of any serious impact on it from the Buddhist crisis. In contrast, Mendenhall gave a pessimistic assessment of political attitudes. He argued that if the Buddhist crisis continued, it would lead to the collapse of the war effort and that the United States could not win with Diem. These two totally conflicting assessments prompted President Kennedy's well-publicized remark that they must have visited two different countries.[23]

In conjunction with the Krulak-Mendenhall visit, the U.S. mission was instructed to assess support for the Diem regime among the various leadership groups in the country—notably professionals, academics, business leaders, the military, students, and religious groups.[24] We reported as we learned. When the Hue incident occurred, the embassy's file on Buddhism in Vietnam had consisted of two or three musty sheets of paper—sheets that I am sure did not contain the names of the new ringleaders, and ultimate rivals, Thich Tri Quang and Thich Tam Chau. Embassy officers were unaccustomed to this kind of reporting in Vietnam, having focused primarily on activities of the regime, the security situation, the developing Viet Cong threat, the escalating infiltration of troops and supplies from North Vietnam, and the lackluster activities of military leaders and a few perennial opposition figures. Diem would have deeply resented our going further than this in our inquiries, and we had no desire to complicate our relationship with him by encouraging opposition leaders through extended contacts with them. In fact, Diem made sure that any potential opposition was effectively neutralized through exile, imprisonment, or intimidation. Our support for him thus made contacts with opposition figures largely irrelevant.

Diem's political strategy and our acquiescence in it ensured that effective alternative, noncommunist leadership in the country could come only from within his own military establishment. That indeed was the ultimate source of his death blow. As early as 1960, the military, with political backing, had led an unsuccessful coup attempt against Diem; and a few months before I arrived in Saigon, a lone pilot had bombed Diem's palace in a bungled attempt to take Diem's life. Diem's firm rule, in effect, rendered virtually all political opposition impotent; he relied instead on the United States as a substitute for internal political support. The United States, correctly judging that there was no alternative to Diem under the circumstances, was obliged to support him all the more strongly (that is, until the Buddhist revolt began to get out of hand).

Embassy staff were by no means unanimous in their views, but disaffection was clearly on the rise among the population as brutal police methods against demonstrators began touching an increasing number of urban, educated families, including those associated with the government. Nevertheless, we tended to maintain a distinction between Diem himself and his brother and sister-in-law, the infamous Nhus. We believed the regime could be salvaged if Diem could somehow distance himself from his ruthless brother and his brother's fanatical, outspoken, anti-American wife. We inadequately understood that Diem could not bring himself to get rid of the only ones around him he could really trust. For him to have done so would have been to accept defeat.[25]

Some days before the coup, when the handwriting was clearly on the wall—perhaps even as we were holding the pen—I was entrusted with a delicate mission. Washington had asked some time before that we call discreetly on Diem's figurehead vice president, Nguyen Ngoc Tho, to convey the message, ever so indirectly, that if the Vietnamese people should in fact withdraw their mandate from President Diem, the United States government hoped Tho would agree that a constitutional succession—namely by Tho himself—would be highly desirable. Trueheart, who by then was chargé d'affaires ad interim after Nolting's definitive departure and before Lodge's arrival, had advised putting off any such conversation with Tho unless and until it was clear that Diem was unmovable on his handling of the Buddhist crisis.[26] My conversation with Tho was brief and amiable. When the coup came, however, Tho succeeded Diem for only the briefest of periods, soon giving way to the generals who led the coup and who chose one of their own, General Duong Van Minh ("Big Minh"), as chief of state.

The coup generals remained in power for less than three months before they in turn were overthrown by thirty-eight-year-old General Nguyen Khanh, thus beginning a succession of revolving-door governments and regimes that lasted until Nguyen Van Thieu wrested power from Nguyen Cao Ky and remained in power, with Ky as his vice president, until North Vietnamese tanks pushed through the wrought-iron gates of the presidential palace on April 30, 1975.

In the final weeks before the coup, beginning especially after Nhu's raid on the pagodas, tension grew between the South Vietnamese and the official American community. Vietnamese government officials, up to and including Diem himself, believed that the U.S. government was undermining the regime, if not actively fomenting a coup d'état. Inspired articles and editorials began appearing in the local Vietnamese press openly accusing the United States of interfering in South Vietnam's internal affairs. Madame Nhu made highly intemperate, accusatory statements about the United States and spoke contemptuously about Buddhist bonzes "barbecuing" themselves. The American press corps eagerly reported her statements in the *New York Times*, the *Washington Post*, and other key media, thereby escalating home-front opposition, not least in an increasingly restive Congress, against the Diem regime and against U.S. policy.

In Saigon, Vietnamese officials and even nonofficial friends were reluctant to be seen socially with official Americans for fear of being harassed by Nhu's police. Americans had the impression that their household servants were pressured by the police to report on who was visiting them. We began to suspect, for example, that our houseboy was collecting seating place cards from our dinner table and handing them over to the police.

When martial law was declared and a curfew decreed after the August raid on the pagodas, Americans were advised to observe the curfew and to carry their diplomatic documents with them at all times. The night of the pagoda raid, I worked late at the embassy and, unhappily, ran out of gas on my way home in my little Volkswagen Beetle. As I stood beside the vehicle wondering what to do, a patrol of tanks rumbled by, fortunately paying no attention to me. Shortly thereafter, a colleague came by, saw my predicament, picked me up, and drove me home.

The coup came on November 1. On that day, I was getting ready to return to work after lunch at home when I heard the sound of gunfire. I immediately drove to the embassy, ten minutes away, noting along the way that concertina barbed wire had been strung across the streets leading to the palace and that several armored vehicles had been placed in defensive positions in the area. This in itself was not so unusual, as such precautions had become a fairly frequent occurrence over the previous few months.

On arriving at the embassy, I learned that a coup was indeed in progress. I spent the rest of that day and night at the embassy trying, along with others, to monitor reports of what was happening. Sporadic gunfire continued throughout the afternoon and evening. After nightfall many of us went up on the embassy roof to watch the fighting. In the early morning hours came a final tank-led assault on the palace, and by daylight it was all over. Diem and his brother had gone into hiding. When they eventually surrendered, they were executed by their captors. Their deaths shocked Washington, especially President Kennedy. But the coup had succeeded, and the generals were in charge. I felt a sense of elation, a sense of a new beginning. These emotions proved to be short-lived. Exhausted and tense from the all-night vigil, I went home. During the night I had tried several times to call home to check on my family and constantly got a busy signal. As I drove home anxiously, I saw very few signs of battle damage along the route; indeed, the streets thronged with people in a holiday mood. Home at last, I was relieved to find all well and Kaity unaware that the phone had been placed improperly on the hook from an earlier call.

The family had had a less than tranquil twenty-four hours, nonetheless. The sporadic gunfire induced Kaity to keep moving children and servants downstairs, where there were no windowpanes to shatter, then back upstairs into the air-conditioning when the firing stopped. Once during the afternoon a loud explosion nearby had frightened them all. A stray rocket from an aircraft had exploded in the yard next door. Aside from the minor damage it caused, the explosion had freed a pet boa constrictor from its cage!

Two months before the coup, the U.S. government had begun to get intelligence reports "of varying credibility" that Ngo Dinh Nhu was clandestinely in touch with Hanoi authorities—with French encouragement—to explore Hanoi's willingness to negotiate on South Vietnam's future.[27] In an "eyes only" message to Secretary of State Dean Rusk on September 13, 1963, Lodge said he hoped "some study will be given to what our response should be if Nhu, in the course of a negotiation with North Vietnam, should ask the US to leave South Vietnam or to make a major reduction in forces."[28] By the time the coup occurred on November 1, the possibility that Nhu was putting out feelers to Hanoi behind our backs had become an important secondary factor in our decision not to stand in the generals' way. On November 1, as the coup was under way, the State Department, with McGeorge Bundy's concurrence and Dean Rusk's approval, sent the following message to Lodge:

> If coup succeeds, acceptance and understanding of its purpose here will be greatly increased if Generals and their civilian associates continue to develop strongly and publicly the conclusion reported in one of their broadcasts that Nhu was dickering with Communists to betray anti-Communist cause. High value of this argument should be emphasized to them at earliest opportunity.[29]

Two weeks after the coup, I reported that I had been told by a South Vietnamese official that "friends of his had seen papers indicating the late Brother Nhu had reached an advanced point in negotiations with the DRV and that terms had been set under which Ho Chi Minh would be President of reunified Viet-Nam, and Nhu Vice President." This report excited some interest in the

State Department, and a colleague of mine wrote me informally seeking more details.[30] In hindsight, it seems hard to believe that we resisted a South Vietnamese initiative to find a South Vietnamese solution directly with North Vietnam—one that might have spared us the heavy responsibility for South Vietnam's fate.

Twenty-two days after Diem's downfall and assassination, John F. Kennedy was in turn assassinated. I was in the shower before breakfast when I heard the first news bulletin that he had been shot in Dallas, Texas. I was sure that the noise of the shower had played tricks with my hearing. This impression was reinforced by the Armed Forces radio station's immediate return to its normal popular-music programming. The shocking news was confirmed, however, as soon as I arrived at the embassy. On top of our personal emotions at this tragic event, the outpouring of grief among the Vietnamese was overwhelming. In the continuing popular euphoria at Diem's overthrow, the Vietnamese had given Kennedy full credit. Streams of Vietnamese, especially students, came to the embassy in tears to present their condolences. Deputy Chief of Mission Bill Trueheart, near tears himself, went to the embassy entrance to receive and thank them. Vietnamese friends, again particularly young people, came to our home, as they did to those of many of our colleagues, to offer their condolences and share their tears.

The year 1964 was a turbulent one in South Vietnam—and one of growing restiveness in the United States. Kennedy's brief presidency had set the stage for the future disastrous course of events in Vietnam. In 1961, he had sent his first ambassador, Fritz Nolting, a career professional, to Saigon under instructions to "win with Diem." Soon key advisers around Kennedy had begun to press for Nolting's replacement on grounds that he was not pushing Diem hard enough to broaden his political base through more democratic elections and thereby undermine the political attraction of the Viet Cong. They also faulted Nolting for allowing U.S. military advisory activities to spill over into actual combat operations, thereby risking U.S. casualties and growing opposition to the war at home.

Kennedy's choice of Henry Cabot Lodge as his second ambassador to South Vietnam was made primarily, if not entirely, for domestic political reasons, namely, to solidify Republican support for his Vietnam policy and actions. In contrast to Nolting's instructions, those given to Lodge ordered him to assess the viability of "winning with Diem" in light of the growing Buddhist-led unrest, and to encourage Diem's generals to remove him from office if it became clear that he no longer served the U.S. objective of keeping South Vietnam out of the communist orbit. No analysis seems to have been made, either in Washington or Saigon, nor any strategy formulated, for achieving this objective if Diem were to leave the scene. In Saigon, neither Nolting nor Lodge had any background in Southeast Asia. Nolting, a career professional, believed in the policy he was sent to carry out, underestimating the threat to that policy that Diem's inept handling of the Buddhist crisis represented. Lodge, a prominent Republican political figure who had spent eight years fighting the Cold War as Eisenhower's ambassador at the United Nations, exercised no independent judgment regarding the consequences for the United States of Diem's removal. Nor had he formulated any contingency plans for the unexpected turn of events that followed. And in Washington, no serious consideration was given to alternative courses of action. In a word, if we could not win with Diem, we would win without him.

The difficulties of following this course became clear as 1964 progressed. Lyndon Johnson, who as vice president had had serious reservations about removing Diem from office, tried to pick up the pieces from his fallen predecessor but with his options seriously narrowed. Not surprisingly, long before the year had run its course, Johnson's advisers were advocating replacing Lodge with a more forceful, overall manager of the war effort who could keep the components of the sprawling U.S. mission in Saigon talking to each other and working for the same goals. Above all, they wanted someone who could effectively and simultaneously pursue U.S. political and military goals. This, alas, proved to be no easier in 1964 under Johnson than it had been in 1963 and before under Kennedy.

My own sense of new beginnings quickly waned as 1964 began. Less than three months after overthrowing Ngo Dinh Diem, as noted earlier, the coup generals were themselves toppled in a bloodless coup by one of their younger colleagues, General Nguyen Khanh, who sequestered them in the town of Dalat, north of Saigon in the central highlands. The United States, which was pouring ever more resources into South Vietnam, was powerless to stop Khanh. Indeed, so unfamiliar were we with the political dynamics of the body politic (and military) in the wake of Diem's demise that we were uncertain whether Khanh's coup was a good thing or a bad thing for U.S. goals and objectives. Khanh persuaded Lodge that the "Dalat generals" who ousted Diem favored a neutralist solution for South Vietnam, a solution also promoted by France under General Charles de Gaulle.[31] Lodge was thus persuaded that the young, vigorous, and decisive Khanh was good for U.S. objectives. Washington had no choice but to go along with Lodge's judgment.

Shortly after Khanh came to power, I was visited at the embassy by Nguyen Xuan Oanh, to whom I had been introduced in Washington by a mutual friend. Oanh, known to his friends as "Jack Owen," was the first Vietnamese I met. He had a Ph.D. in economics from Harvard University and had worked for many years for the International Monetary Fund in Washington. On arriving in my office, he announced that Khanh was about to name him deputy prime minister and asked to be introduced to the ambassador. I obliged him by getting him an appointment. No one in the embassy, including the ambassador, had any idea that Oanh was about to spring upon the local political scene, but spring he did—he even became acting prime minister very briefly after Khanh was driven from office. (In the end, "Jack Owen" had more durability than most South Vietnamese politicians of the day. After Saigon collapsed, Oanh ended up in Hanoi as a member of Hanoi's Parliament. Today, he lives in Ho Chi Minh City as a businessman—without great influence but with many eager American business contacts.)

Khanh's stewardship of South Vietnam's fate—and of U.S. policy aims—was short-lived and disastrous. The South Vietnamese government's attention was increasingly diverted from the deteriorating security situation in the countryside to the growing political instability in Saigon and other major cities and towns. In response, the United States, in its frustration, focused more and more on plans for taking the war to its source—North Vietnam itself, the Ho Chi Minh Trail in Laos, and Viet Cong sanctuaries in Cambodia. The United States also increasingly took the reins of command away from the faltering South Vietnamese governmental and military authorities, deluging them with political, economic, and military advice. Our advice and our progressive intrusiveness into South Vietnam's internal affairs merely served to increase resentment toward the United States and its already huge and growing presence in South Vietnam. Such actions also made us the target of blame for the deteriorating situation.

As the American participation grew, Washington changed ambassadors yet again. Lodge had been appointed by John Kennedy. Lodge and Kennedy both came from prominent Massachusetts political families, albeit one Republican, the other Democratic. Kennedy had been looking for a Lodge to represent him in Saigon to strengthen bipartisan support for a controversial foreign policy commitment. But Texan Lyndon Johnson, uncomfortable with many of Kennedy's eastern establishment appointments, accepted Lodge's resignation with alacrity when Lodge asked to be relieved of his post to enter the 1964 Republican presidential sweepstakes against Senator Barry Goldwater.

After the White House announced Lodge's resignation and General Maxwell Taylor's appointment to succeed him, Lodge convoked his staff to explain his decision. When Kennedy had appointed him ambassador to South Vietnam, he said, he had had no thought of entering politics again and had accepted his new assignment as a chance to serve his country in a crucial area. All that had changed when President Kennedy was killed, although he had not realized it at the time. Then came Lodge's unexpected political "radioactivity," as he liked to call it—his victory in the New Hampshire primary—and other indications that he had some political strength in his own right. Following the Oregon and California primaries, and particularly the latter, which had put Goldwater far in the lead for the Republican presidential nomination, Lodge said he began receiving letters from friends and acquaintances whose views he respected suggesting he was neglecting his duty by remaining in Vietnam instead of returning to fight the Goldwater nomination. Lodge claimed this reasoning had startled him: He thought he was serving his country "on the front lines" and that this was the most useful contribution he could make. Then by chance he met an American military officer who asked him if he was going home to head off Goldwater. He felt accused of shirking his duty when he replied "no." As Lodge put it, "If an American officer, risking his life in Vietnam, felt that Henry Cabot Lodge was shirking his duty by remaining there . . ." So he had decided to return home, he said, to try to help William Scranton win the Republican nomination.[32]

Lodge left and Taylor arrived in early July 1964. Taylor was accompanied by career diplomat U. Alexis Johnson, given the rank of deputy ambassador. Taylor and Johnson were no more successful than Lodge had been in ensuring that the U.S. effort keep South Vietnam out of the communist orbit. Lodge had arrived in Saigon in the midst of Diem's and Nhu's crackdown on the Buddhists and had concentrated on seeing Diem removed as an obstacle to the pursuit of U.S. goals. On their arrival, Taylor and Johnson were obliged to deal with the running sore of political instability that Diem's removal had opened. Moreover, Taylor and Johnson were faced with a deteriorating military situation, which moved the United States inexorably in the direction of carrying the war to North Vietnam. Washington had hoped that Taylor's military background and prestige would improve on Lodge's management of the huge U.S. advisory effort, in particular on MACV's critical part therein, and even more important, that it would pull the bickering South Vietnamese generals running the country and the war effort together. Alas, Taylor, reserved and aloof where Lodge had been reserved and arrogant, tended to treat the Vietnamese generals as a group of insubordinate shavetail lieutenants who would not follow orders from a superior officer.

Moreover, as the situation deteriorated, Taylor, like Lodge before him, apparently made no effort to suggest to Washington any options other than simply continuing down the same track of deeper and deeper involvement. Taylor even favored carrying the war to North Vietnam, although he did object to Washington's decision to send combat ground units to South Vietnam with no real prior consultation with the South Vietnamese government.[33] In the end, Taylor stayed no longer than Lodge had—one year—not long enough to have any lasting impact on the situation on the ground. And, symbolizing its inability or unwillingness to break new ground on Vietnam, Washington sent Henry Cabot Lodge back for a second one-year tour as ambassador in Saigon, another short tour that did nothing to change an increasingly somber picture of frustration and failure.

In mid-1964, in rapid succession, Viet Cong terrorist attacks increased on U.S. installations; Khanh promulgated a new "charter," which he was quickly forced to withdraw in the face of strong Buddhist opposition and demonstrations and which fatally weakened his ability to govern; and the Tonkin Gulf incident or incidents occurred—North Vietnamese torpedo boat attacks on U.S. Navy vessels in international waters of the Tonkin Gulf off North Vietnam—that led to U.S. reprisal air strikes against military targets in North Vietnam. All three developments precipitated a new phase of the war by bringing the United States ineluctably closer to a direct combat role. Also, Lyndon Johnson's use of the Tonkin Gulf incidents to obtain a near-unanimous congressional endorsement of the Tonkin Gulf Resolution provided him with the authority to use whatever force he deemed necessary to achieve U.S. objectives in Vietnam. In the event, the use of force did not occur until well after the 1964 presidential election, in which Johnson roundly defeated Barry Goldwater, in part because Goldwater advocated the systematic bombing of North Vietnam.

My own responsibilities centered more and more on assessing the war's progress (or lack thereof) and analyzing internal political developments. Washington agencies were constantly dissatisfied with the mission's reporting out of South Vietnam and forever sending out officials to make "independent" assessments. Depending on the professional bias of the officials, these assessments were either pessimistic or optimistic and thus added to the confusion and frustration at top levels of our government.

In yet another effort to get at the truth, Ambassador Taylor asked that I coordinate a weekly missionwide report to Washington assessing U.S. and South Vietnamese programs aimed at protecting the population, rural and urban, from Viet Cong intimidation and attack. Much has been written about the reporting from Vietnam—both official and press reporting. The U.S. mission and the press accused each other of distorted reporting—of describing the glass as half full when it was really half empty, and vice versa. The mission was accused of managing the news, the press of becoming a player on the stage and influencing events instead of objectively reporting them. Hawks and doves abounded in both camps, to say nothing of dovish hawks and hawkish doves.

All these accusations contained some truth. We were under great pressure to show that administration policy was succeeding. Much press reporting, on the other hand, started from a bias hostile to the administration's policy goals. Embassy reporting was largely programmatic; it focused on programs we were deeply involved in, such as civic action, hamlet security evaluation, Chieu Hoi (program for Viet Cong returnees), and leaflet and other propaganda programs. Weekly reporting on a series of programs expected to succeed, and therefore seen by those responsible for them as succeeding, was not a satisfactory basis for meaningful assessment. Many of these programs had been presented to, or conceived by, Washington as part of a winning combination. We were therefore careful not to judge small setbacks or program weaknesses too harshly. With everything at stake on these programs, who was to judge whether a negative development was significant or not? A judgment that all mission elements could agree on for purposes of coordinated weekly reporting to Washington was often a "lowest common denominator" judgment, whether negative or positive.

The press had different, even opposite, kinds of institutional restraints on them. Many of them could not afford to make positive assessments of developments for fear they would be seen by their colleagues and their editors as patsies for the U.S. or South Vietnamese government. Young reporters like David Halberstam of the *New York Times,* Malcolm Browne of the Associated Press, and Neil Sheehan of United Press International were out to make names for themselves. Increasingly bitter, they saw the United States as throwing good money after bad in a failing policy in South Vietnam, thus exacerbating the tension between them and a U.S. mission whose task their aggressive and bare-knuckled reporting rendered infinitely more difficult.[34]

In any case, the mission's routine reporting had little influence on Washington's policy judgments and decisions. It dealt with program "nuts and bolts" and specific weekly developments geared to the working-level experts in the Washington agencies, who were constantly being called on for assessments, briefings, talking points for meetings, and the like. It was part of the struggle's bureaucratic trappings, not of the struggle itself.

My colleagues and I in the political section were also kept busy reporting on the many confusing political developments surrounding the constant governmental turnovers in Saigon. Our most interesting work professionally was trying to anticipate who was likely to end up next at the top of the heap and why. On one occasion in particular when we were wrong in our predictions, we received the clear impression from our embassy leaders (who were under even greater pressure to "keep on winning") that it would somehow be our fault if the actual Vietnamese choice led to defeat.

The incident arose when we tried to find out who would emerge as South Vietnam's latest leader after Khanh's withdrawal of his short-lived charter and concessions to Buddhist pressures. In the aftermath of this turmoil, which incidentally included yet another unsuccessful coup attempt against him by another group of generals looking for the main chance, Khanh had formed a High National Council to formulate a new basis for governing South Vietnam—and we hoped for getting on with the war. The High National Council was composed of twenty or so prominent Vietnamese civilian figures, some political, some nonpolitical. Most of them had been in opposition to Diem; some Diem had jailed. Some my colleagues and I had known; some we had not known or had gotten acquainted with only after Diem's fall.

When the council was formed, my colleagues and I divided up the membership for purposes of getting to know them and thereby keeping informed about the council's deliberations. Ambassadors Taylor and Johnson were of course also in direct contact with council members.

My assigned contacts were Le Van Thu, a lawyer little known to the embassy, and Tran Van Van (known irreverently to the political section as TV^2), a prominent political figure whom I had known earlier as an "out" politician during the Diem era. (Van was later tragically assassinated in a booby-trapped vehicle.) However, try as we (and the ambassadors) might and despite our reasonably good contacts among the High Council's members, we could not learn whom the council was going to choose as chief of state, simply because there was absolute discipline among the council members. They did not want the Americans to influence, or interfere with, their choice, and they successfully kept their own counsel.

When the victor was announced—a widely known, widely respected, and wholly ineffectual ailing old man, Phan Khac Suu—Taylor was furious, both at the choice and at being surprised. Suu was hardly a strong vehicle for U.S. policy and for our growing commitment. But Suu was only another passing palpitation in Saigon's body politic. He and his government lasted only a matter of months before being replaced by Air Force head General Nguyen Cao Ky.

The High National Council selected another venerable gentleman as prime minister, Tran Van Huong. Huong, a gentle southern schoolteacher by profession, had been mayor of Saigon. Like Suu, Huong was in his late sixties and presented a grandfatherly image. I had met him not long before the High Council's action at a reception given by the embassy security officer for his contacts in the Saigon city government. When Huong was named prime minister, I was asked to call on him to assess his qualities and his attitude toward the common struggle and toward cooperation with the United States. He struck me very favorably, although he was not the most dynamic of men by our cultural standards. We had an amiable conversation, in which he seemed well disposed toward the United States, believing that with America's help South Vietnam should continue to defend itself against North Vietnamese and Viet Cong forces.

When Secretary of Defense Robert McNamara paid a visit to South Vietnam in 1964, I accompanied his party on a daylong trip to the central highlands north of Saigon. Robert McNamara was a difficult man to keep up with on a fast walk over rough terrain. We paid a memorable visit to a protected hamlet of mountain people—Montagnards. A local official was explaining the election process to a group of fifty or so Montagnards—uneducated, primitive, dressed in dirty ragged clothes and traditional headdresses—who squatted together uncomprehendingly within a barbed-wire enclosure facing the official, who stood beside a blackboard. On the blackboard a copy of the ballot had been drawn, and chalked in on the ballot appeared only one name.

In late November 1964, I accompanied Taylor back to Washington for consultations. His discussions related principally to plans for bombing North Vietnamese military targets, for introducing U.S. combat troops into South Vietnam, and for evacuating families of American officials from South Vietnam "to clear the decks for action." Taylor's mission had been made all the more urgent by a bold Viet Cong mortar attack on October 31 against the Bien Hoa air base a few kilometers from Saigon where the U.S. Air Force kept a number of B-57 strike aircraft. Four Americans were killed and thirty wounded, and twenty-seven aircraft were destroyed or damaged.[35]

We returned to Saigon after a week. Taylor was armed with new instructions from the president to strengthen the faltering South Vietnamese government and the faltering war effort against the Viet Cong. He was also instructed to tell the Vietnamese leaders that the United States was prepared to strike harder at the infiltration routes in Laos and at sea and to consider more direct measures against North Vietnam, if and when the South Vietnamese government could overcome its divisions and its disorganization.

Taylor had not been back two weeks before the South Vietnamese generals had formed a new Military Council and dissolved the High National Council. These actions ushered in a new period of prolonged uncertainty and political instability. They also led to a confrontation between Taylor and the younger Vietnamese military officers that nearly led to Taylor's being declared persona non grata by the very allies we were seeking to assist. Out of this political maneuvering by the Vietnamese military were to emerge the two figures that ended up directing the fate of South Vietnam until it disappeared in 1975: Generals Nguyen Cao Ky and Nguyen Van Thieu.

On Christmas eve 1964, as we lifted our glasses of champagne at the embassy for a holiday toast, we heard a huge explosion—a bomb had gone off at the Brinks U.S. military bachelor officers' quarters, killing two and injuring fifty. Despite the top-level deliberations in Washington, little had changed on the ground in South Vietnam. Both the political situation in Saigon and the war in the countryside continued to deteriorate. The prospects for 1965 did not seem bright.

And indeed they were not. In February 1965, families of U.S. mission employees—including my own—were evacuated from Vietnam as Lyndon Johnson, fortified with the Tonkin Gulf Resolution, ordered the first systematic air attacks against military targets in North Vietnam and introduced the first U.S. combat troops in South Vietnam—two battalions of marines and a Hawk missile unit—to Da Nang. By then Suu and Huong had been swept out of office—bloodlessly—by Nguyen Cao Ky more or less with official U.S. satisfaction, if not outright approval.

At the end of March 1965, the embassy was subjected to a massive terrorist attack with an estimated 250 pounds of plastic explosive. A car containing the explosive appeared to have broken down on the side street next to the embassy (which was flush with the sidewalk and, with only routine police protection, wholly vulnerable to such an incident). When a motorcyclist seemed to become involved, the police guards became suspicious and fired warning shots. The terrorists, having completed their work, sped away on the motorcycle, and the massive explosion occurred.

In my fourth-floor, inside office I had heard the shots but had dismissed them as a hammer pounding somewhere in the building. With my mind on something I needed to discuss with Political Counselor Mel Manfull, I rose from my desk and entered the hallway connecting the offices of the political section. Just as I passed a doorway to an office facing the street side, the explosion occurred. The impact knocked me down, the lights went out, and dust and debris were everywhere. I remember picking myself up and realizing that I felt all right, that I could see and hear, and that such incidents could, indeed, happen to me. While those thoughts ran through my mind, I became aware that blood was running down the left side of my face and head. I reached up and felt a piece of glass sticking out of my temple. Reflexively, I gingerly pulled it out and continued my way up the hall through the murk. I was conscious of bodies lying on the floor in offices facing the street and of one of my colleagues whistling as he moved. I then retraced my steps back down the hall, passed my own office, and entered the inside office where two secretaries worked and where there were other inside offices not affected by the blast. When the secretaries saw me, I thought they were going to be sick—I was bleeding profusely about the face and head. They sat me down in a chair and with some tissue my secretary started sopping up the blood running down the left side of my head. When the bleeding did not stop after a few minutes, I walked down the five flights of stairs to the street, where I presumed there would be help.

As I came out into the street, I—and many others—faced a crowd of journalists and photographers—mostly American, it seemed to me. I remember silently cursing them as I stood leaning against the wall because they were exploiting the event instead of lending a helping hand. The scene outside the embassy was one of blood and confusion. Seriously wounded people, Vietnamese and American, lay on the ground, while others like myself leaned against the building. Ambulances and other readily available vehicles began to take away the wounded.

After a short wait—always in front of the mass of journalists and photographers—I was led to a nondescript panel truck. A wounded person on a stretcher was put in the truck on the floor, and several of us "walking wounded" were seated on benches on both sides in the back. As we were driven to the U.S. Navy dispensary some miles away, I found myself in my state of shock staring at a gaping wound in the arm of one of my colleagues. Another colleague was seated in front next to the driver, holding the door closed—for some reason it would not stay shut.

After a wait at the dispensary while the more seriously wounded were taken care of, my own wounds were dressed. They were all superficial, all on the left side of the head, facing the blast, and all taken care of with about eighteen stitches. I was kept in the dispensary overnight for observation and then released. I had apparently received a blow on the head because for several days I sported a swollen purple bruise the size of half a grapefruit on the left side of my head. But I was lucky. Two Vietnamese consular clerks and one American secretary were killed, and a number of employees had been seriously wounded—some blinded or partially blinded by flying glass.

While waiting at the dispensary to be sewn up, I composed a cable to Kaity assuring her that I was safe and—mostly—sound. I learned later that the cable was never sent. The embassy had been assured that MACV, with great military efficiency, would send out all such messages. Unfortunately, MACV sent messages only to the United States, ignoring families residing elsewhere. Kaity and the children were with her mother in Greece, where early press reports indicated that I had been seriously wounded. My mother-in-law frantically tried to keep the newspapers away from Kaity until definitive word of my condition was received. I of course assumed my message had gone, since I was never informed to the contrary.

In Seattle, my father, who lived without a telephone, could not be reached by the State Department. His first word of the explosion came from a *Seattle Times* reporter, who knocked on his door in search of my photograph. The reporter had no idea of my condition, so Dad sat glued to the television, where he was reassured by glimpses of me standing outside the embassy.

Within six weeks I was on my way back to Washington (via a long home leave) to become director of the Vietnam Working Group in the State Department. In that job I became acquainted with a different Vietnam war—the bureaucratic war, the war of the media, the war of protest demonstrations, frustration, fatigue, and doubt.

FOUR

The Home-Front War

I HAD gone to Vietnam without reservation. I had had few questions about what we were doing in Vietnam or about the eventual outcome there. I came home a skeptic on both counts. When I went to Vietnam in 1962, there were some ten thousand U.S. military personnel there, advising a South Vietnamese military force that was doing the fighting. The Diem government seemed to be well established and capable of using U.S. aid effectively. To be sure, U.S. policy in Vietnam was already controversial at home and abroad; but the prospects for succeeding seemed good, and success would have silenced the doubters and the critics.

By the time I joined the Vietnam desk in mid-1965, we were living with the consequences of our decision to encourage Diem's overthrow. We were building up our combat forces in South Vietnam as Hanoi exploited the growing political instability there, our casualties were growing, and the protests at home against the war were beginning in earnest. We were overwhelming successive weak South Vietnamese regimes with aid and advice they could not absorb. In our frustration we pushed them aside more and more and were taking full control of the war, thereby undermining what motivation they had for fighting their "brother enemy," the Viet Cong and the North Vietnamese.

Nevertheless, I was delighted with my new assignment. It was arguably the best job in the State Department for my rank at the time: Vietnam was the "hottest" foreign policy problem of the day, it was the focus of everyone's attention—that of the president, the secretary of state, the Congress, the media, and the public at large. While in Vietnam, I had received two promotions: When I went there in 1962, I was a junior officer, a second secretary; three years later, in 1965, I came home a senior officer, a counselor.

William Bundy was the assistant secretary of state for Far Eastern affairs. Leonard Unger, a career officer who had been ambassador to Laos and who recruited me for the Vietnam desk, was Bundy's deputy for Southeast Asia. Bundy, whom I had met in Geneva some years before, was brilliant, self-possessed, and aloof, his attention focused upward and not on his staff. Unger in many ways was Bundy's antithesis: also highly intelligent, but approachable, disciplined, and thoroughly professional. I found working with Unger agreeable and productive. With Bundy, it was more difficult.

When I joined the Vietnam desk in the summer of 1965, Lyndon Johnson still basked in his one-sided victory over Republican candidate Barry Goldwater at the polls the previous November. Once reelected, Johnson had begun sending U.S. combat forces to South Vietnam in response to the deteriorating military situation there. He also had begun regular bombing attacks against targets in North Vietnam in retaliation for the accelerating pace of terrorist attacks against U.S. facilities in South Vietnam. Johnson was determined to win—to nail that coonskin to the wall. Neither he nor any of his top advisers—Secretary of State Dean Rusk, Secretary of Defense Robert McNamara, presidential adviser McGeorge Bundy, Ambassadors Maxwell Taylor and Henry Cabot Lodge, and General William Westmoreland—seriously considered cutting losses and changing course. Even though their prognostications were largely gloomy, they all believed that the stakes in the context of the global confrontation with the Sino-Soviet bloc were too important to allow us to abandon the effort in Vietnam—failure there risked failure for the rest of Southeast Asia; it would undermine U.S. credibility with its allies around the world and damage Lyndon Johnson's own reputation at home.

Meanwhile, in South Vietnam, political turmoil continued in the aftermath of the Diem coup. General Nguyen Khanh had been pushed aside by two other generals, Nguyen Cao Ky, head of the Air Force, and Nguyen Van Thieu, a senior Army general. Ky and Thieu engaged in their own power struggle against each other, with Thieu eventually coming out on top and Ky relegated to the second spot. With the advent of Thieu and Ky, political stability finally returned to Saigon—but too late, as it turned out, to save South Vietnam from ultimate defeat or to turn American public opinion around in its favor.

Elsewhere in the region, in the Philippines and Malaysia, communist insurgencies had effectively been defeated by 1965. That same year, the greatest prize of all in the region, Indonesia, put down by a hair's breadth a coup d'état that might well have moved that huge country into the communist orbit. Despite these favorable developments, the U.S. government continued to adhere to the "domino theory" rationale, believing that a communist victory against South Vietnam could turn the tables and lead to communist victories throughout the region. The judgment at the time continued to be that a communist victory in Vietnam would demoralize the nearby newly independent governments, thereby tipping the balance away from the nationalists in power in favor of communist insurgent elements. Indeed, instead of interpreting the anticommunist coup in Indonesia as an opportunity to reassess the validity of the domino theory, that coup was seen as justifying an even greater American effort in Vietnam in order to consolidate the gains made elsewhere in the region.

Thus, in addition to constantly increasing our military operations in South Vietnam, we quashed any instinct of the South Vietnamese to seek a political solution with their Vietnamese brothers to the north and rebuffed any and all efforts by outsiders to promote such a solution. Our policy in effect sought with each escalatory step to convince the other side to settle on terms acceptable to us. Despite the favorable auguries in the rest of the region, we could not bring ourselves to change direction in South Vietnam for fear that its loss, by itself, would undermine U.S. credibility and reliability in the eyes of its allies around the globe, raise doubts about our treaty commitments to those allies, and betray the sacrifices in blood and treasure we had already made in Vietnam. For the United States to have done otherwise in the mid-1960s would have called for unusual political acumen and leadership in either major party to buck mainstream domestic political trends and beliefs.

In effect, with its inflexible policies, the United States had placed itself in a no-exit situation in Vietnam. We were spending more and more money underwriting more and more civilian programs, sending more troops, sustaining more casualties, and witnessing an ever-growing protest movement against the war at home. There was apparently no way out. The situation on the ground in South Vietnam, although stabilized politically under Thieu and Ky, offered no prospect for a solution or even a breakthrough politically or militarily. We kept saying that all we sought was South Vietnam's right to determine its own future—which was the last thing Hanoi wanted—yet nothing we did persuaded Hanoi to change its course or reduce its pressure. As public opposition at home grew, the administration began exploring possibilities for negotiations with Hanoi but could not bring itself to soften its own position—or to prepare the South Vietnamese government for compromise, for example, to broaden its domestic political base in order to accommodate other political points of view, at least to some extent. We ourselves had for so long opposed compromise with Hanoi and discouraged any hint of compromise on the part of the South Vietnamese that we were on dead center with no place to go.

Within the bureaucracy, we organized and reorganized for greater program effectiveness; we looked for opportunities to write impassioned memoranda to our bosses, hoping to move the situation off dead center and toward negotiation and compromise. But it had to be done with care to avoid giving the impression that we doubted the policy or were seeking to undercut it. In fact, at my level we had no influence, no way of helping the ship of state to change course. All we could do was write memoranda that made us feel better when we went home at night.

I argued in meetings and in memoranda to Unger and Bundy, and occasionally to Secretary of State Dean Rusk, that we were overloading the South Vietnamese government and economy with advice, with goods and services, and with civilian advisers. I argued, too, that by these actions we had taken away any incentive for the South Vietnamese to take charge of their own future. I recommended—to no avail—that we seek to reverse this course.

On South Vietnam's internal political situation, I argued that although we talked to successive South Vietnamese leaders about the need to broaden their domestic political base, thereby narrowing and weakening the political base of the Viet Cong, we did nothing concrete to push them in that direction because we ourselves feared the consequences.

And, finally, near the end of my tour as director of the Vietnam Working Group, I argued that our involvement in Vietnam had, in the end, outstripped any possible national interest we had there.

At the personal level, once in my new job, I did not know where the time went. The hours were long, the pace frantic. One day melted into another, one week indistinguishable from the next. I worked six and a half days a week, and after it was all over realized how little I had concentrated on my family during the two and a half years in that job. Finally, I have no clear recollection of accomplishment or failure, just of work, work, and more work—and of growing doubts about the course we were pursuing in Vietnam.

A letter to my father in November 1965 contains some flavor of those days.

> I feel that we have been less than communicative these past few months. I can only say that my present assignment is really more than a full-time job, and that I hardly see my family let alone find time to sit down and write a letter. I'm not sure that's the way to live, but that's the way I'm living for the time being.
>
> My job, of course, aside from being wholly demanding, is full of interest and frustration. It is the central US foreign policy problem today and is the center of public and official attention, up to and including LBJ. Every day is fast, long and frantic, including mountains of paper, frequent meetings, public speaking, private briefings, out-of-town trips, etc., etc., etc. The week before last I was in Paris for three days, assisting in a presentation on my problem to the NATO Council and in a background press conference. This past week I taped a brief interview for a local radio station and spent two hours briefing a Senator and one hour briefing a Governor. All of this is not to impress you, but to give you a bit of the flavor of a harried bureaucrat. . . .

In Washington it was indeed a different war. Positions became increasingly polarized between "hawks"—those who favored prosecuting the war vigorously—and "doves"—those who favored actively seeking a negotiated solution or just abandoning the effort. The atmosphere in the State Department weighed heavily in favor of unwavering support of the president's policy. If one had doubts about a particular decision or course of action, those doubts had to be presented positively, in the form of suggestions for better achieving the president's objective: a South Vietnam free to determine its own future without outside interference.

Ironically, the positions of hawks and doves—and of the administration in the middle—all ignored the South Vietnamese. The hawks had no confidence in the South Vietnamese ability to fight or to govern, that is, to fight to achieve our objectives, and to govern according to our rules. They therefore wanted to push the South Vietnamese aside, to take over the war, and to win. The doves were contemptuous of our Vietnamese allies for the same reasons: They felt guilty about the U.S. role and wanted us to find our way out of the quagmire on almost any terms. The administration, caught in the middle, chose the most ineffectual path: It tried to fight a limited war, restricted in geography but employing massive resources, against a foe with limited resources but with unlimited determination, drive, and patience. It was, in effect, a war that could not be won as we conceived it.

Eventually the administration, to quiet its dovish critics, began desultorily to explore the prospects for negotiations, but on the basis of a compromise its foe was not interested in. The South Vietnamese, whom we supposedly were trying to help, were consulted less and less and saw their stake in their own country taken over more and more by an outside power.

The meetings, the pressure, and the tension were endless and mounting, and most of the activity at my level was essentially bureaucratic. It had little to do with the prosecution of the war itself. We were deluged by requests for briefings, for information, for analyses, for recommendations, for speeches, for press guidance, for note-takers at high-level meetings, for drafts of instructions to the embassy in Saigon, for agreement or comment on other messages, for policy guidance to our other embassies around the world, and for meetings with foreign diplomats to explain our policy.

Vignettes from the period capture the flavor of working in the bureaucracy on Vietnam: I was surprised one day to get a phone call from Joe Alsop, the well-known, influential syndicated columnist—and noted hawk—with access to the highest levels of our government. Alsop invited me to lunch at the Metropolitan Club, the most prestigious social men's club and watering hole in the nation's capital. I accepted with alacrity, flattered by the attention of this Washington icon. I enjoyed a delightful, expensive lunch on my host, but was virtually unable to break through his slick, self-assured monologue about what we needed to do to lick those communist bastards in Vietnam.

On another occasion Jack Anderson, tabloid-style columnist Drew Pearson's intrepid gumshoe reporter, tracked me down by telephone in Cincinnati, Ohio, where I was to give a speech on Vietnam at a women's college. Anderson told me he had in his hand a copy of a letter I had signed to a concerned citizen commenting on a recent news story to the effect that ESSO trucks in South Vietnam were paying Viet Cong taxes in order to get their petroleum product deliveries through Viet Cong roadblocks to their destinations. Apparently Anderson interpreted my letter as a weak rationalization for allowing such a thing to happen, thereby contributing to the coffers of the enemy that was killing and wounding more Americans every day. Without recalling the substance of my letter (then or now), I assured Anderson that whatever I had said in my letter was based on the best information we had available at the time. Anderson was not satisfied with my bureaucratic reply. He asked me to reveal the name of the superior who had obliged me to sign the letter, saying he would go after him instead of me. I replied that no one had obliged me to sign it, reiterating that it was based on our best information. He kept insisting. I kept repeating my litany. Finally, in exasperation, he gave up. No "exposé" ever appeared.

Perhaps my most searing memory from the period was that of briefing Representative John Moss of California on a now long-forgotten and failed peace initiative that had leaked that morning in the press. Assistant Secretary Bundy had asked me to do the briefing, I have always assumed, because I knew virtually nothing about the initiative. Like a good soldier I carried out my briefing, which the congressman instantly recognized as telling him nothing more than what he had read in that morning's newspaper. His reaction was less than charitable: He said he had understood that I was an expert on Vietnam. I lamely answered that there were many levels of expertise on Vietnam in the State Department. He responded that if that was all I could reveal about this important matter, I should tell Secretary of State Rusk that if he did not call the congressman before Moss left for California that afternoon, he would have to tell his constituents he could no longer support the administration's peace efforts because he could find out nothing about them. Needless to say, Rusk indeed called Moss before the latter left for California. After that phone call Moss knew much more than I ever learned about that peace initiative.

Another hallmark of the era was the resort to gimmicks, best characterized perhaps by a frustrated statement Dean Rusk reportedly made to the effect that "if we have tried a thousand ideas and they have failed, we need to find the thousand and first idea. It may just work." True to this policy guideline, the department hired consultants, academics, and others to ferret out ideas that might work: messages and themes that would persuade the Viet Cong to defect and begin to support the government, studies of land reform and other measures that might enhance popular support for the Thieu government, and advice on—even drafts of—a suitable constitution for South Vietnam. One of these consultants, Henry Kissinger, was sent at Ambassador Lodge's suggestion to South Vietnam to evaluate the state of loyalty and popular support for the South Vietnamese government. I was asked to brief him over lunch. I found his grasp of the situation remarkable for one with so little background in Southeast Asia.

Perhaps the ultimate in gimmickry was "McNamara's fence," a proposal that Secretary of Defense McNamara endorsed for building an elaborate system of electronic barriers along the demilitarized zone at the 17th parallel and straddling the infiltration routes across the Lao and Cambodian borders with South Vietnam.

Most of us working in the Vietnam vineyards in that era did a lot of public speaking: foreign policy conferences, veterans' groups, radio and television talk shows, university forums, public rallies, women's clubs, men's clubs, and church groups. Once in Indianapolis, at a national American Legion convention, I followed Miss America on the program. Somehow I sensed that my audience's minds were elsewhere. Another time, on a local television talk show in San Diego, I was sandwiched between the first woman graduate of the San Diego police academy and a clown act. During my brief interview, my hostess, an unusually attractive young blonde with large green eyes (I still remember!), stumped me with her first question: "Mr. Miller, what do you suppose those young North Vietnamese soldiers are thinking about as they trudge down the Ho Chi Minh Trail?" Not having the faintest idea, I mumbled something about how they probably thought about their families and the unpleasant tasks that lay ahead.

Once, filling in for Bundy at a municipal rally in the main square of Reading, Pennsylvania, I defended the administration's policy on Vietnam. I had been told that ten thousand people were expected. In fact, there were no more than five hundred, including some fifty silent protesters holding up placards with various slogans of the times, calling on the United States to get out of Vietnam, accusing it of war crimes. "LBJ, LBJ, how many kids have you killed today?"

At Stanford University, my alma mater, I met nothing but hostility from the faculty members who introduced me but ended up "holding the coats" of the hawks and doves in the audience who began attacking each other as much or more than they attacked me.

Perhaps my biggest thrill came with a letter from a British diplomat friend, Sir Donald Murray, then serving as Her Majesty's ambassador in Tripoli, Libya, announcing that he and his wife, Margery, had just heard me on the BBC World Service!

It was also during this period that ten-year-old daughter Margaret cried out one day at the dinner table, "Vietnam, Vietnam! That's all I ever hear! I'm sick of Vietnam! Can't we ever talk about anything else!"

It was during this period, too, that late one Sunday afternoon, when I had a few hours of relaxation at home, the phone rang with someone at the other end who was at a meeting debating Vietnam and who wanted to confirm a fact with me. I gave him my answer and hung up. Five minutes later, his opponent called to argue at length about my earlier answer.

It is perhaps no wonder then that years later, a colleague, reminiscing about this period, said he was convinced I was not going to survive the pressure: Each time he saw me he found me more pale, more drawn. It is no wonder, either, that during this period Bundy reportedly remarked to an aide bemusedly, "I don't understand why Miller isn't more enthusiastic!"

Much of my time in this job was taken up with such activities. Some of my time, however, was consumed in the intense interagency competition for resources and influence that had more to do with bureaucratic politics than with the prosecution of the war in Vietnam thousands of miles away. These bureaucratic skirmishes offered me occasional opportunities to express my views on broader questions of the war, even though those views had little if any influence.

In mid-1965, Lyndon Johnson again changed ambassadors in Saigon, replacing General Maxwell Taylor with Henry Cabot Lodge. On his second tour, Lodge took with him this time the so-called Lansdale group—a number of individuals with varied previous experience in Vietnam gathered under the leadership of the fabled General Edward Lansdale to give Lodge advice about how the United States might influence internal political developments in South Vietnam. Lansdale had been an adviser in the Philippines in the Magsaysay era in the 1950s and had been credited with assisting in the defeat of the communist-inspired Hukbalahap rebellion. It was this accomplishment that had made Lansdale the model for the simple, down-to-earth hero in the novel *The Ugly American.* In South Vietnam in the mid-1960s, however, the Lansdale group proved to be just another gimmick overloading the U.S. mission structure, a gimmick that divided authority, confused reporting and analysis responsibilities within the mission, and above all, had no particular inside track to a winning formula.

Washington oversight of the swollen U.S. civilian programs in Vietnam was plagued with repeated reorganizations, ostensibly to achieve greater effectiveness but in reality to try to keep the various government agencies from working at cross-purposes. Each agency was burdened with the normal bureaucratic instinct to acquire more responsibility and influence in the country's most critical foreign policy problem. More responsibility and influence meant more resources and more time in the spotlight and next to the president's ear, and hopefully, more promotions—and correspondingly less for other, rival agencies.

In the continuum of these bureaucratic maneuvers and manipulations, Len Unger created a midlevel interagency committee with representatives from the Departments of State and Defense, the Joint Chiefs of Staff, CIA, AID, the White House, and USIA. Anthony Lake, one of the bright young Foreign Service officers who had served in Saigon when I was there and who had returned to become staff aide to Unger, was the committee's recording secretary.

The decision to form this committee, the Vietnam Coordinating Committee (VNCC), arose from everyone's frustration at the difficulty in effectively coordinating an interagency civilian effort. Yet the memorandum establishing the committee and governing its work was worded vaguely, to avoid endless wrangling over agency responsibilities and prerogatives. Only in this way were the operating agencies, which had the resources, willing to let the State Department, which had primary foreign policy responsibility but few resources at its command, chair the group. The establishing memorandum first made clear that the committee was restricted to civilian programs and had no authority over combat or other strictly military operations. Then it listed the committee's responsibilities as including giving advice to the Lansdale group on internal political developments and dealing both with the "growing pressures on manpower and resources, U.S. and Vietnamese" and with the political and economic implications of growing U.S. force deployments.

The memorandum also created a Working Group Committee, which I chaired, to coordinate lower-level operational problems. It also referred to other VNCC subcommittees on intelligence, psychological operations, economic warfare, and public affairs, noting that they, too, should dispose of "as much Interdepartmental business in their respective fields as possible." [1]

To help focus the VNCC's initial discussion, I circulated a memorandum to committee members, offering an analysis, without solutions, of the problems I saw facing the future of the U.S. nonmilitary effort in South Vietnam. I suggested that U.S. nonmilitary programs were rapidly reaching the point "where they are beyond both the economic and administrative capacity of South Viet-Nam to absorb, and [that] if this apparently spiralling situation continues, it could lead to an upsurge of popular feeling against the American presence to the point of undermining our entire effort."[2]

After the committee's first discussion, it was clear that neither the Defense Department nor the AID representatives wanted to pursue the subject of my memorandum, and that if the State Department insisted on doing so, it would generate much "debate and disagreement." I argued to Unger that the United States was increasingly taking over governmental functions in South Vietnam for itself and, at the same time, "not attacking what remains the essential Communist challenge—gaining control of the country through erosion and subversion at the village and hamlet level."[3]

Inevitably, within a few months, by April 1966, reflecting the bureaucracy's inability to agree and its unwillingness to act together, the interagency coordinating role was moved to the White House under the chairmanship of Robert Komer, a superactivist known around the Vietnam circuit as "Blowtorch." Unger, bowing to the inevitable, disbanded the VNCC in the face of Komer's establishment of the Vietnam Interagency Committee.[4] Inevitably, too, my own committee quickly disappeared. In August, I proposed to call no more committee meetings.

However, I soon had a new vehicle for venting my continuing concerns that our massive programs were choking an inadequate South Vietnamese government apparatus: a report from the U.S. mission in Saigon assessing our nonmilitary programs in South Vietnam. In a memorandum to Len Unger, I argued that the report reflected the mission's inability to make decisions on "roles and missions," as well as the limited success that our civilian aid programs were having in the countryside and in helping the reconstruction of rural social and governmental institutions. I decried our inability to overcome "vested agency interests in their own programs." I pointed out that the mission could not agree on the more permanent local defense force needed to consolidate the security gains initially made by regular military forces and rural development cadre teams: "If more permanent local defense is a police function, then AID and CIA have the supporting role and MACV does not. If it is a paramilitary function, then there is wide disagreement as to whether MACV or CIA and AID are the proper supporting elements."

I also pushed an earlier theme, writing that "we are plying South Viet-Nam with far more nourishment than it can digest," and argued that this process "has become a vicious circle and is in danger of losing its relevancy to the problem, unless we consider an American takeover of South Viet-Nam to be a real solution. The most we can say that we have achieved in the nonmilitary field over the past five years is that we have staved off disaster; and we can see no prospect for doing any more than that in the foreseeable future." Finally, I argued that serious thought should be given "to a gradual reduction of nonmilitary programs, both in number and size, with the objective of reaching a more realistic level of effort within Vietnamese absorptive capacity."[5]

Unger forwarded my views to Komer in the White House that same day and commended it to him in connection with a report to the president that Komer was preparing.[6] A week later Komer replied with controlled irony and sarcasm: "I greatly appreciate Bob Miller's stimulating comments . . . so thought provoking that I would like them explained in more detail. . . ."

Komer professed to agree with me on the mission's inability to clarify roles and missions because of vested agency interests. However, he in effect dismissed the argument by saying that this was why he and Ambassador William Porter had been appointed (Porter had recently been named to coordinate mission nonmilitary programs in South Vietnam on the ground). In other words, this problem would soon go away.

Komer asked for more detail on just which of our programs were overburdening the Vietnamese. He also questioned my assertion, saying that we were

> sending so many more Americans to take over an increasing proportion of the machinery. We have under 2,000 nonmilitary Americans in the official community at present. Even if we doubled this, we could hardly take over from the GVN [Government of Vietnam]. Rather we would be strengthening our advisory role.
>
> I also wonder [Komer continued] about Miller's gloomy conclusion that just because all we have done in the last five years in the nonmilitary field is to stave off disaster (a fair point) there is "no prospect of doing more than that in the near future." If we can generate local security in the countryside, admittedly a difficult task, why need we be so passive if not defeatist?. . .
>
> Miller's last conclusion that we should give thought to gradual reduction of nonmilitary programs is perhaps the most interesting of all. I'd genuinely like to know which ones he has in mind. Otherwise I can't review the picture. . . .[7]

In response, I estimated that local South Vietnamese officials spent up to 50 percent of their time consulting with American advisers, which suggested to me that they did not have time left to do their jobs. I added some specific figures to show that the more we spent on civilian programs, the less we achieved.

> . . . In FY 1963 we allocated $38.1 million for counterinsurgency; in FY 1964, $46.8 million; in FY 1965, $65.9 million; in FY 1966, $160.5 million; and for FY 1967, some $320 million is being proposed, or more than has been allocated in the four preceding fiscal years combined. . . . To carry out the FY 1967 program, a doubling in the numbers of U.S. civilian advisory personnel and a tripling in the numbers of third-country nationals are being proposed; Vietnamese manpower requirements for the new program are estimated at 76,000, and piaster [Vietnamese currency] requirements at nearly 15 billion. This latter figure represents one quarter of the total money supply and, coincidentally, is about the size of AID's initial estimate of the inflationary gap which will be created if the FY 1967 program is adopted. The Mission has since indicated the gap might approach 45 billion piasters which all agree is intolerable.
>
> If one tries to relate these program figures over the past four years to results achieved . . . one might conclude from the figures, erroneously or not, that the program must be almost doubled every year in order to maintain the status quo in the countryside.[8]

Komer's report on "the other war" had of course gone to the president on September 13, 1966. It reflected none of my earlier analysis and could not wait (I presume) for the further comments Komer had solicited.

Meanwhile, Saigon, and in fact all of South Vietnam, continued to be rocked by political turmoil. When Nguyen Cao Ky emerged as prime minister after Nguyen Khanh's leadership had collapsed, he, too, continued to have difficulty in establishing his primacy. Buddhists in central Vietnam conspired with rival South Vietnamese military leaders to challenge Ky's authority. While supporting Ky's efforts to consolidate his hold over the reins of government, U.S. efforts were directed at pressing Ky and others on a path to national elections to establish a truly constitutional government that, we hoped, would act as a strong pole of attraction away from the Viet Cong.

In April 1966, as part of our effort to move South Vietnam toward an elected, constitutional government, the State Department formed another interagency committee to coordinate U.S. views on the process of political development in South Vietnam. In effect, this Political Development Working Group (PDWG) was concerned with drafting a new constitution and preparing for presidential elections, although the group agreed that we had to avoid appearing to be getting involved in the elections or political party development.

Reflecting the deliberations of the PDWG, an instruction was sent to the embassy in Saigon with guidance regarding South Vietnam's preparations for constituent assembly elections that September. The cable indicated that the guidance had served as "the basis for highest level discussions of elections and political development" during Lodge's recent consultations in Washington. The cable set forth nine objectives for the United States, including an election date, avoidance of anti-Americanism, a better image for South Vietnam in the United States, and the election of a constituent assembly that fairly represented South Vietnam's noncommunist body politic.[9]

The Vietnam Working Group at State also tried to wrestle with the issues of a peaceful settlement of the war. In March 1966, Len Unger forwarded a paper to Under Secretary of State George Ball that Unger described as an initial attempt to explore the U.S. position on terms for a settlement in Vietnam should Hanoi show an interest in negotiations. The paper tried to deal with the most difficult issue of the role and status in any settlement of the National Liberation Front of South Vietnam (NLFSVN, or just NLF), the political arm of the Viet Cong. In order to avoid almost automatic resistance to the idea of negotiations with the enemy, Unger was obliged to take a firm line, "believing that such a position reflects the current posture of the United States on the Vietnam question," putting new ideas in the form of "contingency plans" and "fall-back positions," keyed to alternative and less favorable negotiating circumstances. Unger's carefully worded memorandum gingerly concluded that we were also studying the possibility of South Vietnamese military contacts negotiating amnesties for local Viet Cong commanders.[10]

In July, Unger circulated copies of a paper to senior officials in the State and Defense Departments and the NSC. General Maxwell Taylor, by then military adviser to President Johnson, commended the paper to the president. Taylor urged Johnson to press the State Department to come up with a plan for negotiating a cessation of hostilities in advance or as part of the negotiations for a final settlement. Taylor proposed that the plan suggest ways for winning support "for the unpopular positions which we will inevitably be obliged to take and hold throughout the negotiations." Taylor's memorandum to the president reflected his concern that a Communist peace proposal "to stop the bombing and start talking" would catch us by surprise.[11]

By mid-July it was evident that the forthcoming constituent assembly elections would fall short of the nine U.S. objectives sent earlier as guidance to the embassy. A cable to Lodge, drafted by me, revised by Bundy, and authorized by Harriman after clearance with Secretary Rusk, reassured Saigon that we did not expect political miracles out of the September elections but went on to note that there was already widespread skepticism regarding the South Vietnamese government's intentions to carry out meaningful elections.[12] In an internal memorandum I expressed my personal disappointment in the results of the constituent assembly elections and my conviction that any South Vietnamese government that proposed contacts with the NLF, the creation of a legal leftist party, or talks with the NLF would not likely survive for long, nor would a constituent assembly or more permanent legislative assembly that advocated such measures.

I felt we had to find a way to get the political climate of South Vietnam off "dead center," albeit with the greatest care and deliberateness. I thought we needed to encourage assembly members and generals alike to think seriously about how the rank and file of the Viet Cong might be reintegrated into Vietnamese society and how they might participate in Vietnamese political life. In my view, the South Vietnamese could not hope to defeat the Viet Cong or eradicate it completely but had to find a way to absorb them in a noncommunist political framework. I argued that "the objective of this process should be to achieve what we failed to do with the elections for the Constituent Assembly: to persuade the Assembly and the generals, and for that matter all firmly anticommunist elements, that their new constitution should expressly provide for the participation in political life of any and all, save those who try to take power by force."[13]

The department's official reaction to the results of the constituent assembly elections was much more positive than my personal comments were. In a cable to Lodge drafted by Tony Lake and myself and approved by Dean Rusk making the best of a disappointing result, we referred to the "favorable atmosphere surrounding highly successful Constituent Assembly elections" and suggested that the moment was now propitious to open a dialogue with the South Vietnamese government on a longer-range program directed toward the Viet Cong in order to foment divisions and to promote a settlement.[14]

In March 1967, Lyndon Johnson again changed ambassadors in Saigon. This time he appointed veteran diplomat Ellsworth Bunker to replace Lodge. Bunker, formerly a businessman, had held a series of ambassadorships in both Republican and Democratic administrations. Yet another tall, silver-haired patrician, Bunker was widely respected as one of America's top diplomats. But he had no more success than his predecessors had in "managing" the U.S. effort in Vietnam and in bringing it to a successful conclusion.

Johnson planned to announce Bunker's appointment during a summit meeting with South Vietnamese leaders in Guam. Before taking up his heavy new responsibilities, Bunker wanted to visit his wife, Carol Laise, a career Foreign Service officer whom he had recently married and who was then serving as the American ambassador to Nepal. The president provided Bunker with a special aircraft to do so and instructed him to proceed from Kathmandu to Guam to be present at the summit meeting. However, wanting Bunker to waste no time in starting his briefings on Vietnam, Johnson arranged for three briefing officers to accompany him to Kathmandu—William Jorden, then on the NSC staff; Colonel Robert Montague of the Joint Staff in the Pentagon; and myself. Because Johnson was sensitive about his appointments leaking before he was ready to announce them, we were not allowed to tell even our wives where we were going.

The secrecy of the mission was such that, at both our refueling stop at a U.S. Air Force base in Turkey and our stop in New Delhi, where we had to change to a smaller aircraft for Kathmandu, the air base commander and our embassy in New Delhi had been told only to be ready to receive an unidentified VIP party. At the air base, where we landed in the early morning hours, the commander served us breakfast and took us on a tour of the base. The principal tourist attraction was the Quonset hut where U-2 pilot Gary Powers had lived before he took off on his ill-fated reconnaissance flight over the Soviet Union, the failure and exposure of which had scuttled the Eisenhower-Khrushchev summit in Paris seven years before.

In New Delhi, Jerry Greene, the embassy's deputy chief of mission, met Bunker and his party as a courtesy while we changed to the embassy air attaché's aircraft. Bunker had been ambassador to India, where his first wife had died and where Carol Laise had worked for him as political counselor, and Greene did not find it surprising that Bunker would be heading for Kathmandu to see his new wife. But, when he saw me, whom he had known when I had been in the Executive Secretariat and he had been a junior aide to Dulles and whom he knew was working on Vietnam, he knew "something was up." The news of Bunker's new job, which leaked from Washington while we were in Kathmandu, clarified everything.

I stayed in Kathmandu for only forty-eight hours, completed my routine briefing obligations, had a pleasant lunch with Ambassadors Laise and Bunker, along with Jorden and Montague, at the ambassador's residence, and prepared to return to Washington commercially while Bunker and the others continued on to Guam. I was rushing back to Washington to fill in for Unger, who was to accompany the president to Guam. But my last dinner at the hotel did me in. The food was so bad that I had a premonition that I would be ill, and ill I was during the night. The next day I was so sick that I could hardly drag myself and my suitcase to the airport to catch my flight to New Delhi and onward. I decided that I had to recuperate in Athens, staying with my mother-in-law, who nursed me back to health on chicken broth and boiled rice. I arrived in Washington two days late but fully restored to health. So much for the one "secret mission" of my career!

After nearly two years as director of the Vietnam Working Group, and nearly five years in the Vietnam vortex—and weary of the struggle—I sent to Unger my thoughts about Vietnam in the context of the evolving Cold War. Noting that the U.S. objective in Vietnam was "not the defeat of the enemy, but the cessation of its aggression against South Viet-Nam," I argued that the world of 1967 was not the same as the world of 1961, or even of 1965. I pointed to the developing chinks in the Iron Curtain in Europe, the resolution of the Cuban missile crisis, and the ebbing of superpower confrontation in Africa. I noted that in Asia, India had had a taste of Chinese aggression and Indonesia had successfully put down a Communist-supported coup d'état. Finally, I referred to "the startlingly rapid deterioration in Sino-Soviet relations, and now the perplexing internal turmoil within China itself," and concluded that "clearly, the world is more diverse and evolutionary than it was in 1961" and that "the communist world is just not considered to be the monolith it was a few years ago."

I then proceeded to outline what I saw as our "real dilemma in Viet-Nam: [that] our commitment may have outstripped our national interest there." I argued that we could accept far less in a settlement of the Vietnam conflict than we could have in 1961 in terms of our national security; yet, with over 400,000 troops there and thousands of casualties, "we cannot accept too little for our sacrifice." In my view, this dilemma served to polarize public and congressional opinion in favor either of escalation or withdrawal, a trend that I thought would accelerate as the 1968 presidential elections drew nearer. I urged that we start to seek "a satisfactory resolution of the conflict a good 18 months before the elections rather than to let the intensified emotion of the elections determine our course."

I pressed for a deescalation of measures against North Vietnam, including a "gradual reduction of aerial attacks, parallel by parallel, to the 20th parallel over the next few weeks." I said that the next step, "if we found ourselves truly on the path of deescalation," would be to engage in at least preliminary talks with Hanoi.

Then I came to the clincher: "I think subconsciously we wish to avoid facing decisions regarding talks with the Viet Cong [VC] at least until there is an elected, constitutional government in South Viet-Nam. We somehow hope that such a government will quickly attract large numbers of wavering VC followers into a national reconciliation program." I expressed serious doubt that this would occur, arguing that such a government would only likely "be interested in attracting anticommunist elements, and that neutralist or other left-of-center elements will be expressly excluded. Under these circumstances, although the new government will have more legitimacy and therefore be in a stronger negotiating position, it is not likely . . . to attract many new elements."[15]

A month later I prepared another memorandum on the problems of a cease-fire in Vietnam for Unger to send to Averell Harriman, General Maxwell Taylor, and Assistant Secretary of Defense John McNaughton. In an attached study that I had drafted, I sought to flesh out what I thought it would take to interest both sides in a cease-fire, noting that only as the main outlines of the Viet Cong's political future were known and agreed would it be possible for each side to gauge its potential advantages and disadvantages. My study assumed there were two basic elements of a political settlement between Saigon and Hanoi that could make a cease-fire agreement mutually acceptable and workable: "(1) The GVN acceptance into nonsensitive cabinet positions . . . of several personalities drawn from the NLF (e.g., Minister of Health, Social Welfare, Transport, Communications), in return for NLF acceptance of a unified national administration down through province and district level with unrestricted access countrywide; and (2) GVN acceptance of local VC-oriented village and hamlet administration in VC-controlled areas in return for demobilization and disarming of VC forces."[16]

That summer, Len Unger—a quiet, disciplined professional who had performed with distinction for three tumultuous years in the Vietnam pressure cooker (after three years as ambassador to Laos)—left to become ambassador to Thailand. Philip Habib, another career Foreign Service officer, replaced him as Bundy's deputy. Habib came into the job from Saigon, where he had been counselor for political affairs in the embassy there. A brilliant, earthy man, Habib had a rough-hewn physical exterior—and personality—reflecting his humble origins as the son of a Lebanese immigrant grocer in Brooklyn. However, this deceptive exterior masked a generous spirit and a mind of infinite finesse. With a doctorate in economics from the University of California at Berkeley, a gruff, open, and fearless manner, and complete personal integrity, Habib was to become a key figure in the U.S. government's ongoing Vietnam drama, first here as deputy assistant secretary of state for East Asia and the Pacific, then as chief of staff of the Vietnam Peace Talks delegation in Paris, later as ambassador to Korea, assistant secretary of state for East Asia and the Pacific, and finally, under secretary of state for political affairs. After his retirement he was used by successive presidents and secretaries of state of both political parties as a troubleshooting negotiator in the Middle East, Latin America, and elsewhere until his untimely death from heart failure in 1992.

In September 1967, presidential elections were held in South Vietnam, bringing about yet another—and as it turned out the final—leadership transition in South Vietnam. The new leaders lasted eight years, until the final collapse of that tormented country. As discussed above, Nguyen Cao Ky had taken control of the government in 1965 in a bloodless coup d'état, pushing aside a brief and ineffectual experiment in civilian government led by Phan Huy Quat (or "Fanny" Quat as we irreverently called him). Sensing the need for establishing his legitimacy as South Vietnam's leader—and facing repeated challenges from the still-dissatisfied Buddhists in central Vietnam who managed to ally themselves with local military commanders against him, Ky tried to evolve a form of representative government. In the end he became the unintended victim of his own process: Ky expected to continue to lead his country and intended to become the military candidate for the presidency. However, Army head General Nguyen Van Thieu proved to have greater support with the military establishment. In an "eyeball to eyeball" confrontation between the two in a key conference of generals, Thieu won the candidacy of the military forces. Ky was forced to accept second place as Thieu's vice presidential candidate. There was then no doubt that Thieu would win the presidency in a "free and fair" election.

Once again, the United States was made uneasy by this transition of power among the Vietnamese over which, despite our overwhelming influence in military, economic, and financial terms, we really had no ultimate control. We had become comfortable—finally—with Ky, and Thieu was not well known to us at the time. I recall being summoned by Bundy to a meeting with Rusk and McNamara in Rusk's office to discuss this latest political crisis in Saigon. However, I quickly discovered that my "expert analysis" of why Thieu was likely to win the contest (he had the majority of the military leaders on his side because the army was far larger than the air force) was the last thing these frustrated cabinet officers, especially McNamara, wanted to hear.

In the end, like Diem, Big Minh, Khanh, Suu and Huong, and Quat and Ky before him, Thieu became the trusted object of our attention and support. Our deep involvement left us no choice. Thieu proved to be the strongest, surest leader since Diem: He maintained his presidency until the very end—from 1967 until 1975, when North Vietnamese troops marched into Saigon.

That same month, September 1967, the U.S. mission in Saigon sent to

President Johnson a "Blueprint for Viet-Nam," designed to seek the president's endorsement of the report as a "strategy and program of action in Viet-Nam" tied to the South Vietnamese presidential elections that had recently taken place. Ambassador Eugene Locke, Ellsworth Bunker's deputy, was in Washington to obtain that endorsement. I drafted a memorandum for Bundy to send to Secretary Rusk in preparation for a meeting with Locke to discuss the "Blueprint."

By now my comments had become acerbic: Enveloping my views with the bureaucratic "we," I dismissed the "Blueprint" as merely "a compendium of the principal programs already being carried out by all Mission agencies, including measures which [Washington agencies] and the Mission have been anxious to get the Vietnamese to adopt for some time." I noted that it was predicated on the assumption that "victory can be achieved by a continuation and reinforcement of existing policies and programs. It does not take into account our negotiating track, including the contingency of early negotiations, on the contrary, . . . the Mission assumes that a program of victory is the best insurance that Hanoi will be persuaded to negotiate at some point."

The "Blueprint," I wrote, endorsed General William C. Westmoreland's requests for troop increases, "intensification of the bombing of the North, subject only to the risk of a wider war (with no mention of the related problem of civilian casualties)," and "the idea of sending significant forces at least into Laos, and possibly eventually into Cambodia." I argued that the "Blueprint" proposed

> pushing the new GVN to move in too many areas with unclear priorities. We thus find in the "Blueprint" the same tendency that has often beset us in the past, of trying to do too much too soon in relation to the piece of spaghetti we are pushing. Moreover, the Mission has as yet made no effort to cost out the "Blueprint" in terms of the additional requirements for Vietnamese, U.S. and other Free World resources.
>
> We have indicated to Ambassador Locke that underlying our outgoing messages to Ambassador Bunker . . . is the strong conviction that our highest priority effort over the next few months must be devoted to assisting the Vietnamese leaders (1) to develop the institutions provided for under the constitution, (2) to broaden the government's base of support, and (3) to launch an impact program limited to projects that the government is capable of carrying out in the short range. Without progress on these key fronts, the prospects for meaningful progress against the enemy both militarily and politi-

> cally are indeed limited; pushing the new government to proceed on all fronts at once, as proposed by the Mission, could bog the Vietnamese down badly. . . .[17]

By the end of 1967, I had worked on Vietnam for five and a half years without letup. Our labors on the Vietnam Working Group had received some recognition from the administration. In April 1967, I was honored to receive, on behalf of the office I headed, the Department of State's Distinguished Honor Award in a ceremony presided over by Secretary Rusk. Later the same year, my colleagues and I were invited to the White House, along with coworkers from other civilian agencies, to receive from President Johnson himself the Vietnam Civilian Service Medal. These two awards were welcome at least as symbolic recompense for the endless hours we had all devoted to our nation's top-priority foreign policy problem of the era. I was more than ready for a change and was gratified to be assigned to the Imperial Defence College (now the Royal College of Defence Studies) in London for calendar year 1968. My family and I went happily to this "rest and rehabilitation" assignment.

As I left, in early January 1968, there still seemed to be no way out of Vietnam. The war had stabilized, President Thieu was firmly in command, programs in the field seemed to be making progress, the enemy was taking a terrible pounding, both in the South and from our incessant bombardments in the North. But on the home front, resistance to the war was growing, demonstrations were becoming more violent, and doubts about where we were heading were multiplying at senior levels of government. Something had to happen to change an ever more somber prospect for our country. Our Cold War strategy, so successful in Europe with the Marshall Plan and NATO, and even in the Congo where our sparring with the Soviet Union under the United Nations' umbrella had succeeded in preserving a unified nation, had gone terribly awry in Vietnam.

In this unending Vietnam drama, as in a Greek tragedy, there were villains and heroes, and there was the chorus—the rest of us. If John Kennedy had been badly served by those associates who undermined his policy of supporting Diem, he was equally badly served by those who argued that we were winning, or that we had no other choice than the one we were pursuing if we were to preserve the credibility of our treaty commitments and stem the tide of communist expansionism.

When the results of Kennedy's policy—a South Vietnam in political turmoil and with a deteriorating security situation in the countryside—were handed to

Lyndon Johnson, who had been skeptical of the decision to unseat Diem, Johnson found his options sharply narrowed. By then there seemed to be no turning back—neither was there any visible "light at the end of the tunnel." Moreover, Johnson, not about to be defeated, was not interested in solutions or advice that fell short of an American victory.

Looking back on the era, I marvel that my besieged superiors did not send me packing for my views, which raised questions but provided no practical solutions they could use to extricate us from the quagmire. I also marvel at how unrealistic I was in seeking somehow to turn around the American juggernaut that was suffocating South Vietnam and progressively removing its government and its army, and even its people, as irrelevant elements in a war that in the end only the Vietnamese, and not we, could have won or lost. My views were equally unrealistic in thinking that we could move a Vietnam that had been so thoroughly polarized politically on both sides, first by the French Indochina War and then by our own Vietnam War, to see its way clear to a peaceful solution that involved compromise, both in Hanoi and in Saigon.

With the benefit now of more than thirty years' hindsight, the only document of mine that, in my view, stands the test of time is the one in which I argued that our engagement in Vietnam by 1967 had far outstripped our national interest. Had we had the courage to reassess the costs of preserving South Vietnam's right of self-determination in light of the improving prospects for the region in 1965 before we had sent many combat troops to Vietnam, perhaps we might have been able to level off our military and nonmilitary effort in Vietnam and shift our attention to our more genuine treaty commitment to Thailand and our help to the other, newly independent countries in the region—and perhaps most important, to seek an earlier opening to China.

Even that point of view was unrealistic at the time: It was out of keeping with the temper of the American people. It might be interesting to speculate that a Nixon victory over Kennedy in 1961 might have led to an earlier reconciliation with Communist China and to more effective, more decisive military action in Southeast Asia before the American people had tired of the war and its growing casualties. It might be interesting, too, to speculate what the course of history might have been if Hubert Humphrey had defeated Nixon in 1968. But by 1968, it was too late: We already had half a million troops—and mounting casualties—in Vietnam. As the Nixon years demonstrated, to end the war in a way that justified the sacrifices of money and so many of America's youth and that preserved our credibility as it was perceived at the time proved to be an equally impossible task. In the end, it consumed the Nixon presidency as it had destroyed Johnson's. It also leaves open even today the question of whether the course we followed was worth the lingering trauma inflicted on our society—to say nothing of that inflicted by all sides on Vietnam.

Perhaps the more telling speculation would be whether Kennedy, if he had lived, would have had the vision—and the courage—to adjust American policy in Vietnam in light of the mounting tension between the Soviet Union and China, the failures of communist-inspired insurgencies elsewhere in Southeast Asia, and the growing power of Japan in East Asia, rather than to persist in believing that defending a small country ten thousand miles away threatened by a communist takeover was a real threat to America's security. Despite the evidence on both sides of this question, put forward by those who continue to fight the Vietnam war even today, I think Kennedy would have succumbed to the same political pressures of mainstream America at the time that Johnson and Nixon did. Vietnam became America's greatest excess of the Cold War because that was the way America responded to its problems in the 1950s and 1960s.

FIVE

Peace Talks in Paris

FOR ME, 1968 was a year of "time-out" on Vietnam. The commandant of the Imperial Defence College (IDC), Air Chief Marshal Sir Donald Evans, was anxious that the American State Department's Vietnam expert not embroil his decorous establishment in controversial debate on Vietnam. I was only too happy to oblige, and maintained a suitably low profile. Nevertheless, it was still difficult to escape the subject even in the IDC's quiet, staid halls on Belgrave Square in central London. Vietnam kept creeping into our discussions in the corridors and over lunch.

We had arrived in London in early January, and it was bitterly cold and damp. Snow and ice were on the ground, and the wind chill compounded our discomfort. We stayed in a colleague's apartment while he and his wife were on home leave and while we hunted for a suitable apartment to rent for the year. The friend's apartment was barely heated by American standards, and when we were not out looking for a place to live, we were shivering in bed wearing pajamas, sweaters, socks, and anything else that would keep us warm. Watching the curtains move as the wind came around the window frames and into the room did nothing to improve our dispositions.

We were so constantly and miserably cold that we took the first warm apartment we could find, a two-bedroom affair in an old town house that had been converted into apartments. It was small, awkwardly arranged, and unimaginatively furnished but well located on Hans Place behind Harrod's department store near the intersection of Sloan and Pont Streets in Kensington, and only a ten-minute walk to the Imperial Defence College.

Far from the Vietnam cauldron, I soon immersed myself in such issues as the (British) Commonwealth—what it was, what it was not, and what its future would likely be; relations between science and government; and generally, the world as seen through the British perspective. My British colleagues, senior military officers and civil servants, were consumed in 1968 by what they saw as the distasteful prospect of joining the European Common Market (today the European Union). They preferred Britain as it was—or as they nostalgically and unrealistically wanted it to remain. Central to their dream was maintaining the "special relationship" that Britain had enjoyed with the

United States during World War II and that had been strengthened by the personal ties between Roosevelt and Churchill. They saw in the transatlantic tie more than an English-speaking union; they sought to remain apart from Europe politically, economically, and culturally, arguing that maintaining the special tie to the United States was the better and more congenial alternative for their security and economic well-being.[1]

I counterargued that, although Britain remained our closest ally and most trusted friend, the vast power imbalance between us was alone sufficient, to say nothing of our global reach and responsibilities as well, to make the wartime special relationship obsolete and unworkable in today's world. I suggested that history was driving them toward association with Europe and a position toward the United States on a level with that of our other principal NATO allies.

Also present at the Imperial Defence College as students that year were officers and civil servants from many Commonwealth nations—India, Pakistan, Malta, Malaysia, Canada, Australia, New Zealand, Ghana, Kenya, and Jamaica. Although we were all government officials, military and civilian, we were not officially representing our governments. This made our discussions lively, and sometimes heated. The United States, as the world's most powerful country, came in for its proportionate share of criticism, no matter what the topic or geographic region.

So the year in England gave me a chance to "decompress" from my years of frenetic activity on Vietnam and to spend more time with my family. We had ample opportunity to sample some of Britain's delights—to prowl around London; to explore English castles and cathedrals, public buildings, museums, and parks, and to enjoy the theater. We were able, too, to visit the countryside on numerous occasions. A number of our British colleagues had country houses, to which we were occasionally invited on weekends. The English countryside is a joy to experience, with its ancient towns and villages (and their pubs!), winding highways and country lanes, and lush green meadows and forests.

As part of the IDC curriculum, I also visited areas of Europe I had not seen before—West Germany and Berlin, Malta and Italy. I had hoped to see Czechoslovakia and Romania as well, but Soviet troops invaded Czechoslovakia that summer in response to Alexander Dubček's "Prague Spring," and that opportunity was lost. Instead, we had a quickly improvised trip to the Netherlands and to Malta, where the local British commander provided briefings, tours, and a gin-filled picnic aboard his launch.

This idyllic interlude was rudely interrupted in late October by a phone call from Phil Habib, now chief of staff of the U.S. delegation to the Paris Peace

Talks on Vietnam. Following President Johnson's March 31 announcement of his withdrawal from the presidential race, American and North Vietnamese representatives had opened negotiations in May aimed at halting U.S. bombing attacks against North Vietnam as a prelude to wider negotiations to end the war. Habib wanted me to proceed to Paris immediately in anticipation of an imminent announcement of the long-awaited bombing halt and the opening of negotiations with our South Vietnamese ally, the North Vietnamese, and the Viet Cong.

Although my sudden departure from the IDC six weeks before the end of the academic year upset the established traditions of that institution, I was personally pleased to be named as senior adviser to the Peace Talks delegation. While in London I had received another promotion, this time to minister-counselor. I had just passed my fortieth birthday. I left London for Paris with high hopes on November 1, the day the bombing halt and the ensuing prospects for wider talks were announced. Kaity and Margaret joined me at the end of the term, and our son, George, who had been left in the United States in boarding school, joined us for the Christmas holidays. We found a comfortably furnished three-bedroom apartment on the sixth floor of an old apartment building on Avenue Niel in the seventeenth *arrondissement.* With misgivings, we signed a lease for a year, but were reassured by the landlord that if we left sooner, he would adjust the lease accordingly. As it turned out, we stayed nearly three years and were never asked to sign another lease.

The year 1968 had been tumultuous—and tragic—for the United States, beginning with the communist Tet Offensive throughout South Vietnam. On January 31 during Tet, Vietnam's traditional lunar new year celebration, the communists launched a dramatic, daring attack against the American embassy itself in the heart of Saigon, as well as a "carefully coordinated series of attacks [that] exploded around the country like a string of firecrackers."[2] The impact of the Tet Offensive on U.S. public opinion, reinforced by vivid pictures of the carnage every night on television at home in the United States, in the face of regular assurances from U.S. officials that the war was going well, was immediate and negative. Its impact on the Johnson administration and on the unfolding 1968 Democratic presidential primary race was equally dramatic.

Among the Tet Offensive's first casualties in Washington was Robert McNamara, one of the truly tragic figures of America's Vietnam experience. By the time the Tet Offensive occurred, McNamara was a broken man. Recruited by John Kennedy from the Ford Motor Company, McNamara and the group of "whiz kids" he brought into the Pentagon approached Vietnam as they approached their tasks in private industry. McNamara's supreme confidence in quantitative measurements to judge progress in Vietnam cracked as troop levels increased, casualties mounted, more and more resources were squandered, and the situation continued to deteriorate on the ground. From urging Kennedy and then Johnson to commit large numbers of ground troops to South Vietnam, McNamara by 1968 turned deeply pessimistic about the U.S. effort in Vietnam. In effect, he was no longer of any use to Johnson and had to go. Johnson arranged for him to become president of the World Bank.

Johnson asked his new secretary of defense, Clark Clifford, for his recommendation regarding General Westmoreland's post-Tet request for 206,000 more troops. Westmoreland, a spit-and-polish, textbook general up against a definitely nontextbook situation, had badly misjudged the signs leading up to the Tet Offensive. Equally, he badly misjudged the American public's reaction to his soothing statements that the offensive represented the enemy's "last gasp" effort, statements that were in stark contrast to the scenes of carnage in the heart of Saigon and across the country transmitted into America's living room television sets.

In any case, Clifford, who replaced McNamara on March 1, 1968, gave a cautious reply to Johnson's request. However, events were precipitated by antiwar activist Senator Eugene McCarthy, who dared to challenge Johnson in the New Hampshire Democratic presidential primary and came within three hundred votes of winning. This encouraged Bobby Kennedy to throw his hat into the ring in the April 2 Wisconsin primary along with McCarthy. Johnson's advisers predicted defeat unless he came forward with a "peace proposal." By late March, Johnson had let Westmoreland know he would not get his 200,000 troops, which would have required calling for national mobilization—in effect putting the nation on a war footing.

However, it took a meeting of "wise men," including Dean Acheson, Arthur Goldberg, Henry Cabot Lodge, McGeorge Bundy, and others, to persuade the president to forsake his goal of military victory in favor of peace negotiations. The "wise men" were influenced in their views by a briefing they received from Phil Habib, who told them it might take five to ten years more to achieve real progress, given the inefficiency and corruption of the South Vietnamese government. In response to a direct question from Clifford as to what he would do if the decision were his to make, Habib said he would "stop the bombing and negotiate."[3]

The rest is history, as they say. Lyndon Johnson made his peace proposal, and to add credibility to it, withdrew from the presidential race. Both Robert Kennedy, campaigning against Johnson for the presidency, in part on differences over Vietnam as well as over civil rights advocacy, and Martin Luther

King Jr., campaigning for civil rights for African-American citizens, were assassinated. Vice President Hubert Humphrey, classic New Deal liberal and ultimately Johnson's political heir, unable to distance himself officially from Johnson's Vietnam legacy in the American voters' minds, lost the presidential race to Richard Nixon.

Three days after my arrival in Paris, I watched the presidential election returns at the U.S. Information Service's offices in the Hotel Talleyrand, across the Place de la Concorde from our delegation offices in the U.S. embassy. The Hotel Talleyrand had housed the U.S. delegation to NATO, where I had served as a junior officer more than a decade earlier.

Before the night was very far gone, it was clear that Richard Nixon, not Hubert Humphrey, would be our next president. It is generally believed—and was undoubtedly true—that South Vietnam's President Nguyen Van Thieu had devoutly hoped for this outcome, believing that Nixon's conservative, anticommunist credentials would serve Saigon's interests better than Humphrey's openly liberal ones would.

South Vietnamese–U.S. relations had already been strained over the pace and objectives of negotiations with Hanoi. Thieu was deeply concerned that the Johnson administration, anxious to end the war and to ensure Humphrey's election, was ready to sacrifice South Vietnam's interests, indeed its very existence, by agreeing to a coalition government with the Viet Cong and amorphous neutralist elements in South Vietnam before North Vietnamese troops were withdrawn. Whether or not Thieu's delaying tactics contributed to Humphrey's defeat is for historians of American presidential politics to decide.

In the end, events of course did not bear out Thieu's calculations: The domestic pressures on the new administration to end the Vietnam tragedy were as strong or stronger—especially after the Cambodian incursion in May 1970—than they had been on the Johnson administration.[4] In turn, the Nixon administration had ample opportunity to be frustrated by Thieu's obduracy during the negotiations, up to the very last, when Kissinger, against Thieu's determined resistance, was forcing through an agreement with Hanoi at the end of 1972.

I had joined a powerhouse delegation, headed by Averell Harriman and Cyrus Vance, who had both been in Paris since May negotiating the bombing halt/wider talks understandings. Harriman was a veteran Democratic politician-diplomat who had served since the days of Franklin Roosevelt, and Vance was a New York lawyer who had been Robert McNamara's deputy secretary of defense. Phil Habib, delegation chief of staff since May, remained responsible to Harriman and Vance for coordinating all of the work of the delegation.

Lieutenant General George Seignious, the delegation's senior military adviser, was later replaced by Lieutenant General Fred Weyand, who had been a senior Army commander in Vietnam and later became Army chief of staff. Their principal staff person was Colonel Paul Gorman, who later capped an illustrious career as a four-star general and commander of the U.S. Southern Command. Carl Salans, the State Department's deputy legal adviser, became the delegation's legal counsel, later replaced by George Aldrich, another deputy legal adviser for the State Department. William Jorden, former journalist and NSC staff member, was the delegation's press spokesperson. He was assisted and eventually replaced by Harold Kaplan and later by career Foreign Service officer Stephen Ledogar.

Richard Holbrooke, John Negroponte, David Engel, and later James Rosenthal and Peter Collins, all of whom (except for Collins) I had served with in Saigon, were staff members and advisers operating at levels far beyond their junior rank. Negroponte, Engel, Collins, and Rosenthal were Vietnamese language officers and also proficient in French. In addition to providing political analysis and advice, they were used as speechwriters and as note-takers and translators in meetings with the Vietnamese, both allies and adversaries. Alec Toumayan, the State Department's top French interpreter, was also with us for the duration. He was ably assisted by Sophie Porson and Jose de Seabra.

After the bombing halt and Hanoi's commitment to wider talks, the United States sought to maintain the momentum toward the wider talks. We pressed the North Vietnamese to hold the first wider meeting no later than November 6, less than a week after the bombing halt began and earlier if possible. However, the Thieu government declared itself not ready for such an early meeting.

From November 1, 1968, to January 20, 1969, we pursued the elusive goal of agreed procedural arrangements for the wider talks with our Saigon colleagues and Hanoi adversaries. I began my functions as a senior adviser on the U.S. delegation by participating in regular liaison sessions with the South Vietnamese government delegation. I had known the head of Saigon's delegation, Ambassador Phan Dang Lam, in Saigon when he was secretary general of the foreign ministry and the Thieu government's senior professional diplomat. I had also known Lam's chief of staff, Minister Nguyen Van An, in Saigon when as an army colonel, he headed Saigon's liaison mission to the International Control Commission. The role of the commission, composed of representatives of Canada, Poland, and India, had been to monitor compliance with the 1954 Geneva Accords.

Lam was a quiet professional who carried out Thieu's instructions to the letter with great skill. An was an old anticommunist fighter, originally from

North Vietnam, who distrusted American motives almost as much as he hated Hanoi. An was not driven by the desire to find a negotiated solution; his aim was to prevent the weakening of South Vietnam's position at any cost. But he had long since made his own personal accommodation to the inevitable outcome, having taken advantage of his official contacts over the years to place all or most of his numerous children in France, Canada, Australia, or the United States.[5]

As we met endlessly (and separately) with the Saigon and Hanoi delegations in a frustrating effort to overcome the many procedural obstacles to moving on with the wider meetings, Hanoi violated a key understanding of the bombing halt agreement, namely that it would respect the demilitarized zone (DMZ) between North and South Vietnam and not shell major population centers in South Vietnam. This further delayed progress toward procedural solutions. Along with the other members of the delegation, Dick Holbrooke and I spent much time wracking our brains to find solutions that would meet Thieu's concerns for establishing Saigon's legitimacy at the negotiating table without giving the Viet Cong delegation any legitimacy at all, and at the same time meet Hanoi's demands for exactly the opposite result. Holbrooke and I collaborated on so many proposals and messages to Washington that our drafting moniker became "Millbrooke."

We wrestled with every issue that the Saigon delegation raised with us: Saigon wanted its representatives to be the first to enter and exit the conference chamber; it claimed the preeminent position at the conference table on our side; it wanted Harriman and Vance to meet the Saigon representatives at the airport on their arrival and to call on them at their offices from time to time; it wanted pride of place as opening speaker for our side at the first substantive wider meeting; it wanted the U.S. and Saigon representatives to be "cochairmen" of our side; it wanted frequent references to the fact that the Saigon delegation would speak first for our side on matters of "immediate and direct political concern to South Viet-Nam"; it wanted joint U.S.-Saigon delegation press briefings following each conference session with the Saigon spokesperson leading off.[6]

As the entire world watched and became exasperated, we also spent an inordinate amount of time designing shapes for the conference table that would deny Hanoi's claim that the meetings were four-sided while preserving our concept of a two-sided conference—and that both Hanoi and Saigon would accept as such.

As these procedural wrangles went on, Harriman, seeing his chances for bringing peace to Vietnam rapidly disappearing, became increasingly impatient and irritable. His ire was aimed in particular at Saigon's representative in Paris, Ambassador Lam, whose suspicions of U.S. motives and actions he found galling in the extreme but who, in truth, was following the detailed instructions of President Thieu.[7]

Because of our leader's impatience and irritation, we worked up contingency plans: If the Saigon government continued recalcitrant, we would consider holding meetings with the Hanoi delegation and the Viet Cong, without the Saigon representatives present, on "subjects in which the primary interest or initiative could be considered to lie between the United States and the Democratic Republic of Vietnam," such as "common characteristics of US and DRV forces in South Viet-Nam as external military forces." If the Viet Cong were present, we would meet on an "our side–your side basis" and the Saigon delegation would be free to join discussions at any time.

In our contingency planning, we recognized that such talks could at most only achieve a partial deescalation of hostilities, "an important objective in itself," but "we would not be able to get into key subjects such as a political solution, a full cessation of hostilities, international supervision and guarantees in such talks . . . [without representatives of the Saigon government present]."[8]

The dialogue between allies was eventually eased with the issuance of a joint US-GVN statement setting forth agreed "ground rules and arrangements for the new meetings in Paris," which would enable the Saigon government to send its delegation to Paris "to engage in direct and serious talks with the Hanoi delegation, toward ending the communist aggression and the establishment of a just, secure, and guaranteed peace in Viet-Nam."

The statement went on to set forth these ground rules and arrangements: The new meetings would be two-sided, not four-sided; the two-sided meetings would not imply any diplomatic recognition for the Viet Cong; there would be direct talks between Saigon and Hanoi delegations; and the Saigon delegation would play the leading role on our side on all matters of principal concern to South Vietnam. Further, the sole agreements previously reached between the United States and North Vietnam were on the bombing halt and on convening the new meetings. In the new meetings (the South Vietnamese preferred the term "new meetings" to "wider meetings"), the United States and South Vietnam would work "in close cooperation and in close consultation with the Troop Contributing Countries" (the other allied countries with troops in South Vietnam), there was no change in the U.S. opposition to a coalition government in South Vietnam, the United States would not recognize any form of government not freely chosen through democratic and legal processes by the people of South Vietnam, and the imposition of a coalition government would be "in conflict with this principle."[9]

Following the issuance of these statements, Habib and I met with An on November 27 in anticipation of holding such meetings regularly. Habib indicated we wanted to move as rapidly as possible into bilateral talks with the Hanoi delegation to set procedures for the first new meeting between the two sides. This meeting in turn would work out rules of procedure for subsequent, full plenary meetings of the two sides.

On November 30, three days later, An informed Habib he had no instructions allowing him to agree to the procedures we had proposed and that he did not know when Lam would return to Paris. Vance and Habib pressed An, pointing out that they had scheduled a meeting with Hanoi's delegation on Monday, two days later, and needed to confirm that Saigon had agreed to our position. On the basis of information from our embassy in Saigon, Vance and Habib told An they were confident that Saigon had no problem with our position.[10] Gradually we began moving toward procedural solutions, meeting regularly with our Saigon colleagues and then with the Hanoi delegation to gain their agreement with what Saigon and we had finally been able to work out.

That December, Henry Kissinger, President Nixon's designated assistant for national security affairs, had published an article in *Foreign Affairs* magazine assessing the prospects for negotiations on Vietnam. Kissinger's key conclusion was "that in our negotiations we should concentrate on military issues such as cease-fire while leaving the distribution of political power to the Vietnamese parties."[11] I used the occasion of Kissinger's article to press my views on Governor Harriman—views that I continued to hold from my days on the Vietnam Working Group: that we had swamped the South Vietnamese with advice and material goods that they were unable to absorb; that we had been unable to organize ourselves to cope with the problem efficiently; that we had substituted quantity for quality in our approach; and that we had progressively diminished the South Vietnamese incentives to solve their own problems with our ever-growing material support.

I went on to argue that, nevertheless, "the sheer weight of our military might" had brought Hanoi to the negotiating table and to the realization that it could not take over South Vietnam by force. I acknowledged, however, that in return for Hanoi's giving up its ultimate objective of gaining control of South Vietnam, Hanoi would seek to relieve American military pressure on its military and political assets in the South. Having achieved a bombing halt over North Vietnam, Hanoi would now seek the withdrawal of American forces from the South and the insertion of the NLF [Viet Cong's National Liberation Front] in sufficient strength into the body politic of the South to give it the real possibility of gaining control over the weak and divided noncommunist political and military forces within a few short years. I argued that Hanoi would be willing to pay a considerable price to get rid of U.S. forces, but that we did not know whether it would pay the price we demanded. In fact, I said, we ourselves were not sure of our settlement price.

I suggested to Harriman that the new administration would have the task of establishing, working toward, and seeking Saigon's acceptance of this ultimate settlement price. In my view, our settlement price would consist of two basic elements: (1) the withdrawal of all North Vietnamese units and all military and political personnel seconded to Viet Cong units; and (2) a political solution. But I cautioned that for Hanoi to agree to withdraw all of its military forces and personnel to achieve thereby a total U.S. military withdrawal, it would insist on gaining a potentially commanding position in an internal political solution in the South. I went on to say that it was this latter element that we had consistently assured South Vietnam publicly we would not seek to impose, and that we were thus almost wholly dependent on the South Vietnamese for this element of the solution.

I concluded my thoughts to Harriman by recommending that the new administration offer to Saigon that we negotiate together a mutual withdrawal of all external forces from South Vietnam (U.S. and North Vietnamese), and support Saigon fully in its own negotiations with the NLF for a political solution. But, I argued, if the South Vietnamese government took no such political initiatives, we should make it clear to Saigon that the "United States cannot be expected to be inhibited from seeking solutions in its own national interest. If the GVN is not willing to join the meetings in Paris on a reasonable basis, we will seek early discussions with the DRV/NLF [Democratic Republic of Vietnam (Hanoi) and the National Liberation Front (Viet Cong)]. . . ."[12]

I have no idea whether my memorandum influenced Harriman's thinking, but in his memoirs, Kissinger relates that on January 7, 1969, Harriman sent him a personal memorandum setting out what he thought the new administration should aim for in the Vietnam negotiations. According to Kissinger, Harriman favored his "two-track" approach, with the military issues discussed between the United States and Hanoi and the political issues left to the Vietnamese parties. Kissinger notes that Harriman "added acidly that the United States did not 'have an obligation to retain the present government [in Saigon].'"[13]

Toward the end of the agonizing effort to reach agreement with both allies and adversaries on procedural arrangements, on January 12, 1969, I attended my first private meeting with the Hanoi delegation, accompanying Vance and Habib to the North Vietnamese "safe house" in the working-class suburb of Choisy le-Roi. Since the beginning of the private meetings with the North Vietnamese during the bombing halt negotiations, Vance and Habib had gone to extraordinary lengths to protect the privacy of the meetings. On leaving for such a meeting, Vance and Habib would depart the embassy on foot, seemingly for a stroll. The other members of the delegation would head off in another direction on foot, where they were picked up at a prearranged rendezvous spot. Then they would swing by to pick up Vance and Habib. This deception was used for several years, and the press apparently never caught on.

At the January 12 meeting, Vance offered procedural proposals that the Hanoi representatives, Ha Van Lau and Nguyen Van Vy, rejected out of hand.[14] Procedural agreement was finally reached with Hanoi on January 16, but only after another crisis with our Saigon allies and after we asked both the French as our hosts and the Soviets to intervene with Hanoi.

On January 15, at 5:00 P.M., Minister An called to ask me to come urgently to his delegation's headquarters to see Ambassador Lam and to ask Vance to stop the implementation of the procedural agreement reached with the other side. Lam had just spoken to Thieu in Saigon by phone to convey carefully the terms of the procedural agreement that Vance had just reached with his counterpart, Ha Van Lau, on the Hanoi delegation—after full consultation with Thieu's delegation in Paris. According to Lam, Thieu "felt very strongly" that the French government's drawing of lots to determine the order of speaking should not take place at the French Foreign Ministry but at the Hotel Majestic. Lam said Thieu also "emphasized his wish that our public treatment of the new meetings avoid referring to them as enlarged talks."

I told Lam that we fully agreed with the second point but that the first point had been formally agreed between our two governments and worked out with the other side, and we could not now go back on it. Lam said he had conveyed to me the position of his government, and in light of the situation, it would be necessary for Ambassador Bunker to see Thieu immediately, even if they had to be awakened. I agreed to report to Harriman and be back in touch.

Between then and the next morning, Lam and I spoke by phone several times while this issue was worked out with the French and with the Hanoi delegation: There would be no decision by chance, our side would speak first, and the Saigon delegation would speak first for our side. Lam said he would report this agreement immediately.[15]

On January 17, Vance and I met with Lam and his associates to review physical arrangements for the restricted meeting between delegation deputy representatives. Characteristically, Lam went over every detail meticulously, including seeking assurance that Hanoi had agreed to be civil in its address to the Saigon delegation. Uncharacteristically, he ended the meeting by congratulating Vance on the results of these long and tortuous negotiations on procedures, saying they were "satisfactory even if they are not fully satisfactory." He apologized for all the trouble he had caused and wished Vance and Nguyen Xuan Phong (Lam's newly arrived deputy) success in the restricted meeting "so that we can proceed to the substantive meetings."[16]

The long-awaited first "new meeting" on procedural arrangements was finally held at the Hotel Majestic on Avenue Kléber on January 18, 1969, two days before the Nixon administration was sworn in. The meeting was held at the level of each delegation's deputy representative: Cyrus Vance for the United States, supported by Bill Jorden, myself, John Negroponte (note-taker and unofficial Vietnamese interpreter), Alec Toumayan (French interpreter), and a court reporter; and Nguyen Xuan Phong for the Saigon government, supported by Minister An and a press officer. The meeting, with double translations (Vietnamese into French, then into English; English into French, then into Vietnamese), lasted five hours. All procedures were agreed to for the plenary sessions to come,[17] including provision for a circular table "with two rectangular tables for secretarial purposes 45 centimeters apart from the two midpoints of the circular table."[18]

In his memoirs, Henry Kissinger suggests that President Johnson gave away major negotiating leverage with Hanoi by agreeing to a "unilateral bombing halt" in return merely for the opening of wider talks.[19] Kissinger also recounts that Vietnam was "the subject of our [the Nixon administration's] principal mistake during the transition." He argues that Hanoi was anxious to have the procedural wrangles worked out before Nixon took office in order to avoid the risk that Nixon might abrogate the bombing halt in the face of Hanoi's intransigence over getting wider talks started. According to Kissinger, contrary to his advice, Nixon instructed his secretary of state–designate, William Rogers, to authorize outgoing Secretary of State Dean Rusk to urge Saigon to accept the procedural arrangements before Nixon's inauguration.[20]

Conceivably, following Kissinger's logic, Johnson might have relieved some pressure on himself by withdrawing from the 1968 presidential race and initiating the bombing halt negotiations, while at the same time holding out for greater concessions from Hanoi in exchange for an actual bombing halt. Conceivably, too, this might have made Thieu less recalcitrant. Had Nixon still won, with a bombing halt still in question and with Nixon's reputation for decisive action, Hanoi might have come under greater pressure to compromise. But Kissinger overlooks, or at least seriously underrates, the rapidly building pressures from within the Democratic Party to stop the bombing and end the war, to say nothing of its hope to promote Humphrey's election. Surely, dragging out the bombing halt negotiations would have divided the Democratic Party even further.

In any event, January 20 came and went. The changing of the guard took place in Washington and at U.S. delegation headquarters in Paris. Patrician, veteran politician-diplomat Averell Harriman, in his late seventies, left, a disappointed and disgruntled peacemaker. Patrician, veteran politician-diplomat Henry Cabot Lodge, in his early seventies, arrived to take Harriman's place, ready to defend his country's interests in Vietnam once again and far more sympathetic to the plight of South Vietnam than Harriman had been. (Lodge, as indicated earlier, had played a key role in holding the Kennedy administration's feet to the fire on the overthrow of Ngo Dinh Diem five years before, when Kennedy had had second thoughts about proceeding.)

Harriman and Vance—under the watchful eye of Lyndon Johnson in Washington—had carried out a genuine negotiation with their North Vietnamese counterparts to exchange a bombing halt over North Vietnam for Hanoi's commitment to engage in wider negotiations that included the South Vietnamese government (and the Viet Cong). While this achievement was much more limited in scope than coming to a full settlement, it was soon clear that Lodge's brief was a very different one. In his memoirs Kissinger recounts that because of Nixon's deep distrust of the State Department, he "wanted to change the negotiating instructions on Vietnam drafted at State that reflected the approach of the previous administration. But he wished also to avoid a controversy. He therefore asked me to phone Ambassador Henry Cabot Lodge, our negotiator in Paris, to suggest that Lodge send in through regular channels, as his own recommendation, the course of action that the President preferred. Lodge readily agreed. . . ."[21] It was thus clear from the beginning—although not to us in the delegation at the time—that the Nixon administration's concept of the Paris negotiations was a public relations exercise rather than a genuine negotiation.

Cyrus Vance, Harriman's deputy, agreed to stay on for a short transition period. Vance's replacement as Lodge's deputy was Lawrence E. "Ed" Walsh, another New York lawyer but without any experience in diplomacy, no knowledge of Southeast Asia or Vietnam, no understanding of diplomatic negotiation, and little talent for it. (Walsh went on to play a major role as special prosecutor in the Iran-Contra Affair during the Reagan administration.) Walsh's appointment was another clue that the Nixon administration saw little substantive role for the Paris negotiating team. Fortunately, Phil Habib, a veteran career diplomat who enjoyed the confidence of both the Democratic and Republican political leadership, stayed on as chief of staff and heartbeat of the delegation.

At the first, ceremonial new meeting at the Hotel Majestic, the full delegations for both sides (or the four parties) met face to face for the first time. I found myself in the eighth and last seat at the table for the U.S. delegation, preceded by Ambassadors Lodge, Walsh, and Vance, Phil Habib, Marshall Green (whom Nixon had just named assistant secretary of state for East Asia and the Pacific), General Seignious, and Bill Jorden. The meeting's opening ceremonies took place under the glare of full publicity, and the next morning I found that Madame Nguyen Thi Binh, head of the Viet Cong delegation, and I were linked in the same photograph prominently displayed on the front page of *L'Humanité,* the French Communist newspaper. My position in the last seat at the table for the U.S. delegation put me close to Madame Binh, who occupied the first seat for her delegation. The photographer, focusing on her, could not block me out.

It was said at the time that had the parties been placed aboard a battleship in the South China Sea, an agreement would have come about quickly. Paris indeed was a delightful place to negotiate, and our work quickly settled into a frustrating routine. Under our demanding chief of staff, Phil Habib, we continued to wrestle with the issues, hoping that we would find a negotiating formula that Washington would authorize us to put forward and that Hanoi would accept as a basis for genuine negotiation. Habib was tireless in fulfilling his responsibilities. He orchestrated the routine work of the delegation and, at the same time, challenged us all to think deeply about the issues despite the tight policy constraints imposed by Washington.

Phil would spend endless hours, including evenings and weekends, in his office brooding about the war and its continuing anguish, searching for ways to cut through the issues and bring peace to Vietnam and to the United States. He knew that Washington looked to him to provide the best possible professional advice to the delegation's politically appointed leadership—and to keep them from mistakes in judgment, in public statements, and in their recommendations to Washington. He knew, too, that Washington counted on him to instill professional discipline on delegation members to avoid uncontrolled, unauthorized discussions with the press, unhelpful speculation outside the delegation about peace proposals, secret meetings, and so forth. Fortunately for the delegation—and for Washington—Habib inspired such trust, confidence, and respect, even camaraderie, that morale and discipline remained at a high level. And fortunately for Habib, members of the delegation and their wives were experienced, high-quality professionals who knew their responsibilities and carried them out superbly, despite misgivings and frustrations regarding the Nixon-Kissinger approach to negotiations as the war ground on in Vietnam and the discontent grew at home.

Phil Habib also had a very human side. He loved Paris; he loved the restaurants, the French food, the wines. He loved the attention he got from the press, from other diplomats, and from public figures that sought him out for information and views about the United States' number-one foreign policy problem of the day. He also could be impatient with any mediocrity or sloppiness in the performance of his colleagues.

Lodge's opening statement in the first plenary session on January 25, 1969, set forth concrete proposals for negotiations: restoration of the demilitarized zone between the two Vietnams; mutual withdrawals of American and North Vietnamese forces; respect for the territory of Laos and Cambodia, through which North Vietnamese troops passed regularly on their way to infiltrate clandestinely into South Vietnam; essential elements of the 1954 Geneva Accords as the basis for peace; more effective international supervision; and early release of prisoners of war on both sides.

At the same session, the other side insisted the United States initiate serious discussions with the NLF. They declared that their four- and five-point programs had to be taken as the basis for a political solution. Madame Binh, principal spokesperson for the NLF, said that on the basis of its five points it was prepared, with the other parties, to initiate the work of the conference. But, she continued, referring to Lodge's proposals, to raise so-called concrete issues without speaking of ending U.S. aggression could not lead to "correct" solutions. Xuan Thuy, Hanoi's chief representative, said Hanoi had already many times rejected the U.S.'s DMZ proposal. In other words, the other side flatly refused to negotiate on any basis but its own.[22]

This initial exchange set forth the essential elements of each side's position—the one wide apart from the other—which continued, with some modifications, virtually until the endgame in December 1972 and January 1973. Our side sought the withdrawal of foreign forces before a political solution, to be worked out by the South Vietnamese parties themselves, could be put in place. The other side sought a political solution, to be worked out between the U.S. "aggressors" and the "legitimate representatives" of South Vietnam, the National Liberation Front. The withdrawal of foreign forces, by which they meant U.S. forces, would then take care of itself.

As the Paris meetings proceeded week after week, month after month, and even year after year, events took place—on the battlefield, in the United States, in diplomatic activity in key capitals, at the Paris conference table—that affected this "dialogue of the deaf," but nothing materially changed at the negotiating table for nearly four years. Even the secret talks between Henry Kissinger and Le Duc Tho, which were taking place unbeknownst to most of us on the U.S. delegation, got nowhere until they were buttressed by renewed bombing attacks against North Vietnam in December 1972—the so-called Christmas bombing—and by the Soviet Union's diplomatic intervention with Hanoi.

Much of what both sides did during these meetings did not constitute a negotiation but rather a public relations effort. We sought to convince world opinion that we were engaged in a serious effort to end a war that had gone on far too long and for which no real military solution was possible. Hanoi and its NLF subordinates sought to persuade world opinion—especially American public opinion—that American intransigence alone was to blame for the endless war. Nevertheless, real issues were explored, both in the public sessions and in the private bilateral discussions with the Hanoi delegation. As a result of this process, a certain amount of "diplomatic underbrush" was cleared away and some modification in irreconcilable positions did occur. Meanwhile, the war went on and U.S. casualties mounted—as did Vietnamese casualties on both sides.

In February 1969, as part of a European trip at the beginning of his presidency, Richard Nixon paid the U.S. delegation a visit. Lodge, who had been Nixon's running mate in their unsuccessful bid for the presidency and vice presidency against John Kennedy in 1960, formed a reception line in his office to present each one of us to the new president. In the few seconds or so that I made eye contact with Nixon, shook his hand, and exchanged banalities, I had the distinct impression that he was more awkward and ill at ease in meeting me than I was in meeting him.

In March, Thieu offered to hold private and unconditional talks with the NLF on the subject of political settlement; and in April, he made public his six-point "basic solution." Not surprisingly, the NLF labeled Thieu's offer as a "perfidious maneuver" and called for the United States to withdraw and renounce "Thieu-Ky-Huong" (Nguyen Cao Ky was Thieu's vice president and Tran Van Huong was South Vietnam's prime minister) before serious conversations could lead to a settlement.

In April, too, in response to the growing political pressures at home, Nixon ordered the initiation of a "Vietnamization" program—the gradual, phased reduction in the number of U.S. troops in South Vietnam as South Vietnamese forces were able to absorb their functions. These reductions—carefully termed "reductions" and not "withdrawals"—nevertheless showed Hanoi that the United States was in fact withdrawing its forces unilaterally in response to domestic political and public pressure to end the U.S. engagement there. This in turn lessened the pressure on Hanoi to compromise in its demand that the Thieu regime be dismantled before discussion of military issues could ensue.

At the conference table we also began to elaborate on our proposals for mutual withdrawal, saying they "could begin simultaneously and be phased over an agreed period of time." This, too, was roundly attacked by the other side as a subterfuge to avoid the core issue of political settlement.[23]

In that same month, Lodge asked me to accompany Judge Walsh on a so-called orientation visit to South Vietnam. Lodge felt that Walsh was at a disadvantage serving as the deputy head of a delegation negotiating a peace settlement for a country he had never visited. Lodge found that Walsh's lack of knowledge of the issues and of Vietnam made him a liability rather than an asset. Moreover, temperamentally, the two men were unsuited to each other.

Walsh and I flew to Washington for briefings, then on to Tokyo, Hong Kong, and Saigon. In Saigon we had briefings at the embassy and the U.S. Military Assistance Command, then visited each of the four corps areas, whose headquarters respectively were at Da Nang and Pleiku in central Vietnam, and Bien Hoa and Can Tho in the delta. Everywhere, our briefings were optimistic about the military situation—par for the course—but everyone from General Abrams, the commander, on down stressed the continuing need for adequate levels of military assistance to give South Vietnamese forces the wherewithal to resist the pressure from the continuing North Vietnamese assault.

After briefings at I Corps headquarters in Da Nang, Walsh and I flew in a "Huey" turbojet helicopter along the edge of the demilitarized zone dividing North Vietnam from South Vietnam. A violent thunderstorm forced us to land at an isolated "free-fire" base in the mountains a few kilometers south of the DMZ. After a number of nervous moments of watching the flashing red "overload" light on the instrument panel, we were glad to be safely down in friendly territory. While we waited for the storm to pass, we were sheltered in the bunker at base headquarters, surrounded by sandbags placed there to protect against incoming enemy fire—none occurred during our brief visit. It gave Judge Walsh—and me—an immediate sense of the war and the accompanying tensions for American soldiers located close to enemy territory and guns—and waiting for the diplomats in Paris to stop the war.

In II and III Corps, at Pleiku and Bien Hoa, respectively, the same pattern of briefings emerged—optimism laced with concern about South Vietnam's ability to handle North Vietnam alone. In IV Corps, at Can Tho, we were met and hosted by John Paul Vann, the flamboyant, outspoken ex-Army officer then serving as the regional civilian director of Civil Operations and Rural Development Support (CORDS).[24] The delta was the area least threatened by regular North Vietnamese units, but the same estimate of the situation applied there as it did elsewhere in South Vietnam.

What Judge Walsh understood from his visit to South Vietnam I am not sure. Nevertheless, he could now say that he had visited the length and breadth of the country and had a better idea of the situation and the issues at stake than he had had before his trip. Back we flew to Paris via Washington, and Walsh resumed his duties as Lodge's deputy.

That spring and summer a number of developments occurred in rapid succession. At the May 8 plenary session, Lodge identified the U.S. negotiating strategy as following two tracks: Our first objective was a negotiated settlement, but "in the event the other side was not yet ready to negotiate, President Nixon on April 18 had set three factors for the unilateral reduction of US forces. Peace, therefore, could come more rapidly or less rapidly." At the same session, the NLF put forward its ten-point "global solution," which simply rehashed the other side's basic negotiating position: U.S. troops had to be withdrawn "totally, unconditionally and unilaterally"; the South Vietnamese government had to be dismantled; and the United States had to pay war reparations.

In June, Nixon and Thieu met at Midway to agree on and announce the first American troop reduction, kicking off the Vietnamization program. In June, too, the NLF announced the formation of the Provisional Revolutionary Government of South Vietnam. In July, Hanoi released three U.S. prisoners of war, and on July 11, Saigon proposed free elections including the NLF if it renounced the use of force. "With the July 11 proposal by the GVN our side's negotiating position was essentially complete. . . ."[25]

Our public negotiating efforts were supplemented occasionally by bilateral meetings with the North Vietnamese that were kept out of public view. But they all had the same result. I assisted in a number of these meetings held between Henry Cabot Lodge, and later Phil Habib, and Xuan Thuy, the permanent head of the North Vietnamese delegation. The meeting place alternated between Hanoi's site in the working-class suburb of Paris, Choisy le-Roi, and our site in another suburb. We continued to go to considerable lengths to disguise our departures from the embassy.

The secret meetings were professionally more satisfying, and more interesting, than the meetings at the Hotel Majestic. The positions developed for these meetings were more substantial and thus the dialogue more serious. Moreover, it was important to meet Xuan Thuy and his senior colleagues face-to-face in a more relaxed, more informal setting to see if some genuine progress might be possible.

When we met at their site, they were hospitable and personally friendly. Conversation during the tea breaks included personal chitchat about families, individuals' backgrounds and experiences, life in Vietnam, and American pastimes and sports. But the negotiating sessions were all business—and no progress was made on the principal issues. Four private meetings were held in the summer months of 1969, then none in the ensuing fourteen months.

Behind the scenes, however, Kissinger began his own secret meetings with Le Duc Tho, the senior Hanoi negotiator, all with the same results. As they had with the Vietnamization program, domestic political pressures led Nixon to engage Kissinger directly in these secret talks with Le Duc Tho. Yet Kissinger was no more successful than his negotiators in Paris were in moving Hanoi off its stubborn refusal to discuss military issues before the basic political issue was resolved: the prior removal of the Thieu regime.[26]

As Kissinger himself recounts, his first secret meeting was with Xuan Thuy in Paris in early August, Le Duc Tho having returned to Hanoi: "This, as I learned later, guaranteed that little would be said other than the stock formulas that had come to dominate those plenary sessions. For Xuan Thuy was not a policymaker but a functionary."[27]

Kissinger held three secret meetings with Le Duc Tho in Paris between February 20 and April 4, 1970. Kissinger himself assesses his effort as barren. In his memoirs, he notes that at their first meeting Tho

> cut to the heart of the dilemma of Vietnamization. All too acutely, he pointed out that our strategy was to withdraw enough forces to make the war bearable for the American people while simultaneously strengthening the Saigon forces so that they could stand on their own. He then asked the question that was also tormenting me: "Before, there were over a million U.S. and puppet troops, and you failed. How can you succeed when you let the puppet troops do the fighting? Now, with only U.S. support, how can you win?"
>
> From this analysis, Le Duc Tho's conclusions followed inexorably. He insisted that military and political problems be dealt with simultaneously—a position from which he never deviated until October 1972.[28]

After these three meetings were over, Kissinger held to this assessment:

". . . Le Duc Tho could see no reason to modify his demands for unconditional withdrawal and the overthrow of the Saigon government. He would see none until two and a half years later, when the military situation left him no other choice."[29] Nevertheless, Kissinger, feeling the pressure of U.S. public opinion to end the war, continued his fruitless efforts throughout 1970, 1971, and 1972. In December 1972, Nixon resorted to the "Christmas bombing" of North Vietnam to force Hanoi to modify its position and come to an agreement on the withdrawal of external forces without any longer insisting on the dismantling of the Thieu regime. Then, Nixon and Kissinger had major difficulty in persuading Thieu to agree to what they had finally gotten Hanoi to accept.

Ho Chi Minh died in September 1969. In the same month the United States announced a further reduction of 35,000 U.S. troops in South Vietnam—to 484,000. In December, Lodge resigned and left. Walsh followed shortly thereafter, and Habib became acting chief of the delegation. Hanoi accused us of downgrading the talks, and Xuan Thuy boycotted the sessions. That same month Nixon announced yet another troop reduction of 115,000 by April 1970.

So the months came and went. In our delegation the frustration level rose, as evidenced by the ironic humor displayed. We complained that we had thought of everything and it had been rejected. After three intradelegation romances blossomed into marriages, one of the wives coined the delegation slogan "Make love not peace" (a takeoff on the antiwar protest slogan then current in the United States).

Throughout the whole period of the Paris meetings on Vietnam, a steady stream of visitors came to the delegation seeking to meet with senior delegation officers antiwar activists, wives or other relatives of prisoners of war or those missing in action, members of Congress, journalists, foreign diplomats, and others. Many sought our help in gaining access to the North Vietnamese delegation either to get information about loved ones or to get personal impressions of Hanoi's negotiating position. I saw foreign diplomats regularly to brief them on the state of the negotiations. I also saw a few activists and others, but most of our visitors saw the delegation head or Phil Habib.

The year 1970 unfolded as 1969 had. The plenary sessions continued fruitlessly. In March 1970, Prince Norodom Sihanouk was deposed by General Lon Nol in Cambodia, an event that offered the Nixon administration the opportunity to increase its efforts to deal with North Vietnamese infiltration of troops and equipment into South Vietnam through Cambodia. It also led to Hanoi's charges that we were widening the war. In April, Nixon announced another troop reduction of 150,000 over the next twelve months.

In May, Nixon ordered U.S. forces to enter Cambodia to try to destroy North Vietnamese and Viet Cong "sanctuaries" there. This action met with wide public outrage at home. It led to mushrooming antiwar protests that culminated when Ohio National Guardsmen shot and killed four student demonstrators at Ohio's Kent State University. This shocking event engraved indelibly in American minds the image of a young girl kneeling beside a dead student's body, her face distorted with shock, anger, and anguish. The Cambodia incursion also led to the resignation from Kissinger's staff and from the Foreign Service of Anthony Lake and two of his colleagues.

Habib remained acting head of the delegation for many months until the president named another patrician veteran diplomat, David K. E. Bruce, as U.S. negotiator. Bruce arrived in August 1970, and Habib became his deputy. I, who at the beginning could barely find a seat at the table with the U.S. delegation, had gradually worked my way up the pecking order to the third chair, next to Habib, as the months passed and the process became routinized. On a couple of occasions it looked as if I might even be acting spokesperson in Bruce's and Habib's absence, but my big moment never actually came. My rise in the hierarchy in fact reflected less a recognition of my negotiating skill and indispensability than the dwindling hopes and interest placed in these negotiations—both by the administration and by career and political officials.

In mid-September, Madame Binh, the Viet Cong representative, made a new eight-point proposal. As we were walking to our delegation rooms during the break, I casually observed to Bruce that Binh's proposal appeared to be "old wine in new bottles." Bruce was delighted with the phrase and said he would use it with the press after the session. Habib, who had overheard this exchange, glowered at me for putting this idea in Bruce's head, knowing that once the press got hold of the phrase, the United States could well be criticized for not giving the new proposal careful study before rejecting it out of hand.

There was no stopping Bruce, however. In his brief comments to the press after the session, Bruce unfortunately twisted the phrase into "new wine in old bottles." The press was intrigued, and Stephen Ledogar, the U.S. delegation's acting press spokesperson, spent the rest of the afternoon and evening trying to explain to the press that Bruce had misspoken, that we did not see anything new in this Binh formulation.

After two and a half years of this routine, I decided it was time to move. The meetings were devoid of substance, the work of the delegation was devoid of interest and challenge, and I felt that I had been wasting my time for at least a year. Most of us in the delegation—and perhaps even including the delegation heads—had been unaware that Henry Kissinger was doing whatever real negotiating there was, although we gradually understood that we were just a front to keep public opinion satisfied. In any case, we were no closer to a negotiated settlement than we were the day the talks opened. Nevertheless, U.S. casualties were declining and U.S. troops were leaving Vietnam. The situation on the ground was thus not static, even though the end of the Vietnam War was nowhere in sight.

Could the negotiations have been conducted differently, leading to a different outcome and resulting in fewer American casualties? In his memoirs Kissinger rails against the State Department and the U.S. delegation in Paris as having a vested interest in compromise and deluging him and the president with negotiating ideas that served to undermine Nixon's negotiating strategy. Yet, he also ruefully ruminates further about what might have been:

> Time was not on our side, and piecemeal concessions did more to encourage intransigence than compromise. Analytically, it would have been better to offer the most generous proposal imaginable—and then, if rejected, to seek to impose it militarily. Nothing short of this could have produced Soviet cooperation, for in the absence of crisis there was no incentive for a concrete Soviet step. (When a crisis finally developed in 1972, we induced some Soviet cooperation.) If we had offered at one dramatic moment all the concessions we eventually made in three years of war, and if the military actions we took with steadily declining forces over 1970, 1971, and 1972, in Cambodia, Laos, and North Vietnam (even without the last bombing assault) had been taken all together in early 1970, the war might well have been appreciably shortened—though it is hard to tell at this remove whether Saigon would have been ready to carry the burden of going it alone after a settlement. In the face of the domestic turmoil and the divisions within the administration I did not fight for my theoretical analysis. I joined the general view that, all things considered, Vietnamization was the best amalgam of our international, military, and domestic imperatives.[30]

Just as Kissinger bemoaned the fact that (in his view) Johnson undermined Nixon's negotiating leverage by getting too little from Hanoi in exchange for the bombing halt, he found Nixon and himself hemmed in by the same political realities at home that beleaguered Johnson: Just as the prosecution of the war represented mainstream American political thinking at the time, so did the prosecution of the peace. The Nixon administration approached the search for a peaceful settlement the way Johnson had approached the conduct of the war.

Nixon's overriding negotiating priority, as Johnson's overriding war priority had been, was to get all North Vietnamese forces out of South Vietnam along with American forces, so that that country would have a reasonable prospect of determining its own future.

Neither Johnson nor Nixon sought to maintain the Thieu regime in power either through military victory or a political settlement; but each knew that a political solution that gave South Vietnam at least a fighting chance to survive on its own could not be realized as long as Hanoi had major regular forces in the country. Hanoi's overriding military and diplomatic priority, on the other hand, was precisely the opposite: the replacement of the Thieu regime by a weak coalition before North Vietnamese forces withdrew, a coalition that could rapidly be taken over by a Communist regime (which, as indeed happened, would have been quickly submerged under Hanoi's direct rule). Kissinger notes trenchantly in his memoirs: "We were not prepared to do for the Communists what they could not do for themselves. This seemed to us an act of dishonor that would mortgage America's international position for a long time to come. Our refusal to overthrow an allied government remained the single and crucial issue that deadlocked all negotiation until October 8, 1972, when Hanoi withdrew the demand."[31]

For most of his first term in office, to mollify an increasingly restive U.S. public, Nixon thus relied largely on his program of Vietnamization—of gradually withdrawing U.S. forces unilaterally—rather than on a serious negotiating proposal. In Paris at the time, including in the Kissinger–Le Duc Tho secret talks, both sides continued to try to gain at the bargaining table what they had been unable to gain on the battlefield. Whatever soothing effect Vietnamization had on domestic public opinion in the United States while negotiations were essentially stalemated was dramatically ruptured by Nixon's decision to attack North Vietnamese troops and facilities in Cambodia in 1970: This evoked a firestorm of protest in the United States.

Only in January 1972 did Nixon show any flexibility by offering a cease-fire in place—and only then did Hanoi show any sign of easing its demand for Thieu's overthrow. History can never be rewritten, and it is impossible to know what Hanoi's reaction would have been if a more dramatic, sweeping proposal had been made three years earlier. All we can state with certainty, now that we know the ultimate outcome, is that we were not prepared to face the possibility of such an outcome—the loss of South Vietnam—in 1969.

The Kennedy and Johnson administrations had destroyed South Vietnam's independence, the former by encouraging Diem's overthrow in 1963 and the latter by introducing massive numbers of U.S. combat troops beginning in

1965, troops that the South Vietnamese did not ask for and that increasingly made their war an American war. In the end the Nixon administration, while justly critical of its Democratic predecessors for getting the United States into the Vietnam quagmire with unrealistic and badly thought-out goals and objectives, was finally forced to abandon an ally in 1972 when left with no other option—just as Johnson had had no other option but to change course in 1968 after Tet.

Looking back, it is hard to re-create the cold war mind-set that led us into Vietnam. Southeast Asia has made great political and economic strides (despite its financial, economic, and political turmoil in recent years), Vietnam is struggling to catch up, and the only domino that eventually fell was the Soviet Union itself. Ironically, only Nixon, with his impeccable anticommunist credentials, as well as his strategic vision, could have turned us around on Vietnam as he did on China. He was justly praised for his strategic masterstroke in his opening to China. Unfortunately, on Vietnam, where communist forces were still killing Americans in great numbers (as Communist Chinese forces had done in Korea two decades before), Nixon's strategic vision gave way to more conventional political instincts. America's obsessions with a global communist threat and with its own invincibility combined to blur its judgment about how to deal with communist movements that sought to capture the forces of nationalism in newly emerging Asian nations. Now, however, with Vietnam long behind us but with its lessons still seared into the American psyche, perhaps we will be less likely to repeat what Dean Rusk described as his own misjudgments in the remarkable memoir written with his son, that he had underestimated the tenacity of the North Vietnamese and overestimated the staying power of the American people.[32]

Again, looking back, the arguments that kept us from disengaging from Vietnam for far too long—such as the credibility of U.S. security commitments to allies and the need to honor the sacrifices of fallen Americans—need reexamination in light of the trauma that that engagement, coupled with Watergate, wrought on our own society. The harmful effects of those traumas on our society continue to be felt even today: the burden of national debt that so long limited our ability to deal effectively with domestic and foreign policies and programs; the deep mistrust of government and the divisions that continue to infect our body politic; as well as the lingering effects on individuals and families—illnesses brought on by the massive use of defoliants, and the wasting effects of a drug culture that surely was greatly boosted by Vietnam.

On a personal basis, my family and I had enjoyed our life in Paris. We had close friends there; we happily partook—a second time—of the life that Paris and France generally had to offer—restaurants, theater, history, the French countryside, and trips to Geneva, where we had Greek friends who were waiting out the inevitable demise of the Greek military junta in Athens. We continued our summer vacations in Greece, too.

But all this, too, had to end. I began looking for an onward assignment. Phil Habib left the delegation in mid 1971 on being named U.S. ambassador to South Korea, replacing William Porter, another career Foreign Service officer who became head of the Paris Peace Talks delegation. I was appointed deputy executive secretary in the State Department and was replaced in Paris by Heyward Isham, a colleague with whom I had worked earlier on the Vietnam desk. Taking up my new assignment in the summer of 1971 brought me back into the bureaucratic jungles of Washington, this time at a senior level in the office I had served in more than a decade before—the bureaucratic heartbeat of the State Department. Three years would pass before I would find myself dealing once again with the ongoing agony of Vietnam.

Author (far left) shaking hands with President Lyndon B. Johnson at a White House reception honoring civilian U.S. employees with service in Vietnam, August 16, 1967.
WHITE HOUSE PHOTO

Author receiving State Department's Distinguished Honor Award for Vietnam Working Group from Secretary of State Dean Rusk, December 12, 1967.
STATE DEPARTMENT PHOTO

Author (at right holding envelope) behind Cyrus Vance, deputy chief of the U.S. delegation to the Paris Peace Talks on Vietnam, outside the Hotel Majestic, Avenue Kléber, following a procedural meeting with North Vietnamese representatives, January 18, 1969.

USIS PHOTO

Author (seated fifth from right) behind Secretary of State William P. Rogers, head of the U.S. delegation to the signing ceremony for the Vietnam Peace Agreements, at the Hotel Majestic conference site in Paris, January 27, 1973. USIS PHOTO

Author on his way to present credentials to the Yang di Pertuan Agung (king) of Malaysia, June 1977. USIS PHOTO

Author talking to Tunku Abdul Rahman, Malaysia's first prime minister, on the occasion of a courtesy call in Penang, Malaysia, 1978. MALAYSIAN GOVERNMENT PHOTO

Author presenting his credentials to President Félix Houphouet-Boigny of Côte d'Ivoire, October 1983. IVORIAN GOVERNMENT PHOTO

SIX

The Fighting Ends

I RETURNED as deputy executive secretary to an Executive Secretariat very different in 1971 from the one I had left as a junior officer eleven years before. Reflecting the growing complexity of the State Department's organization, the secretariat was larger and more crisis-oriented—in large part a product of the accretions of the Cold War confrontation with the Soviet Union. For example, the practice of having the secretariat's junior officers take turns as the department's duty officer nights and weekends had been supplanted by a twenty-four-hour, round-the-clock Operations Center. The latest communications technology linked the "Op Center" with the White House Situation Room, the Pentagon's National Military Command Center, and the Central Intelligence Agency, as well as with our embassies and consulates around the globe.

The Operations Center had been created after the Cuban missile crisis in October 1962. Dean Rusk found the department woefully ill-equipped to deal with a major international crisis in a nuclear age in which intercontinental ballistic missiles could reach the United States in minutes after launch from the Soviet Union—even faster from Cuba, only ninety miles off our coast.

The executive secretary now served also as a special assistant to the secretary of state and was supported by two deputies. More important, the Executive Secretariat served as the formal channel for State Department communications with the National Security Council staff in the White House and with other government departments and agencies. Informal communication with the NSC staff and the other departments and agencies continued on a daily basis at lower levels throughout the department, which could not conduct its business otherwise. However, bureaucratic discipline required that formal communications, such as briefing papers and policy recommendations, be transmitted through the executive secretary to ensure that the department spoke with one voice in the name of the secretary of state. William P. Rogers occupied that office when I took up my functions midway through Richard Nixon's first term.

The executive secretary's responsibilities had become difficult, thankless, and even onerous because Richard Nixon and Henry Kissinger, his powerful national security adviser, managed foreign policy directly from the White House. If the Cuban missile crisis had led to the creation of the State Department's Operations Center under the direction of the Executive Secretary to enhance State's role in foreign policy crisis management, the deepening Vietnam crisis, coupled with Nixon's own predilection for personal control over foreign policy, led to the diminution of State's role and the augmentation of Henry Kissinger's national security operation in the White House.

As a result, during the Nixon-Kissinger era, the Executive Secretariat assumed an ineffectual watchdog function. It sought—largely in vain—to protect and preserve the secretary of state's prerogatives as the president's first adviser in foreign affairs, even though the president did not cooperate. Thus, much of the time and energies of the executive secretary and his deputies were expended on enforcing discipline within the department to ensure that the Foreign Service and the bureaus it staffed did not undermine the secretary of state by conveying views orally and in writing directly to Kissinger's staff without bothering to inform the secretary or to seek his approval.

It was a losing battle, and the territory then lost has never been fully regained. Everyone in the department knew where power and authority lay, and everyone sought to influence policy—and to enhance his or her own career in the process—by responding to requests from the source of power, the National Security Council staff in the White House. The most we were able to accomplish was to get the NSC staff to funnel its requests for views and recommendations formally through the secretariat so that we could insist that those views and recommendations be formally transmitted back to the NSC staff through us. In many cases, the substance of those views and recommendations had already been passed informally to the NSC without waiting to see whether the secretary of state approved or not.

The formalities of the system brought me into frequent telephone contact with Kissinger's deputies, General Alexander Haig (who became White House chief of staff at the time of Nixon's resignation and Ronald Reagan's first secretary of state) and later Brent Scowcroft (who became George H. W. Bush's national security adviser). I recall receiving phone calls from Haig in particular, then a brigadier general. While he was conveying requests or instructions over the phone calmly and clearly, often in the background I could hear Kissinger's guttural German accent impatiently ordering him to "get the hell off the telephone—ve've got vork to do!"

On a daily basis, then, to us in the secretariat the enemies appeared to be more domestic than foreign, with Henry Kissinger leading the pack. Kissinger, brilliant, egotistical, and obsessed with power, its attributes, and its rewards, only too readily responded to a president who was determined to isolate his secretary of state and control policy from the White House. In contrast, Secretary Rogers refused to descend into the mud pits to slug it out with Kissinger.

Only history (and not just Henry Kissinger's memoirs) will tell where the national interest really lay in those years. Every day we expended much of our energy on tactical skirmishes rather than on important matters of principle and policy. In any case, it was a fascinating, fast-paced two years that led me to conclude that much of the taxpayers' hard-earned money is spent on elaborate bureaucratic structures aimed more at defending and promoting bureaucratic empires and concepts than at promoting the national interest—however that is defined.

I did not see Secretary Rogers in person very often. My first contact with him had been during my earlier service as a junior secretariat officer, when Rogers was Eisenhower's attorney general. One weekend while I was acting as department duty officer, I had picked up a ringing phone and heard the voice on the other end of the line identify himself as Bill Rogers. As he stated his business, now long forgotten, my mind raced to recall if I knew who Bill Rogers was. Happily, in the nick of time, the name clicked!

In January 1973, Rogers included me on his delegation to Paris, where he signed the Paris Agreements on Vietnam, the culmination of five years' negotiation with Hanoi. Kissinger had done the negotiating, leaving the ceremonial signing to the secretary of state—a telling example of the Nixon-Kissinger approach to foreign policy and of Rogers' acquiescence in it.

After nearly a decade of involvement in the Vietnam conflict, in Saigon, Washington, and Paris, I could hardly absorb the sight at the signing ceremony: the American secretary of state rubbing elbows with Madame Binh, the head of the Viet Cong delegation, a delegation we had refused to address directly since 1969 and an entity we had rightly considered to be wholly subservient to Hanoi. Even more startling was the sight of the heads of the two bitterly opposed South Vietnamese delegations, Saigon and Viet Cong, chatting amiably over glasses of champagne and hors d'oeuvres. To be sure, Phan Dang Lam, the head of the Thieu delegation, looked as if he were chewing on a lemon, but he appeared friendly at least.

The executive secretary and his deputies passed their days immersed in the high-level trivia that needs to be attended to so that the nation's foreign policy can be conducted smoothly and without misstep. Phone calls from Haig or Scowcroft informed us that the president would (or would not) see a particular foreign official or dignitary. We processed paper going to and from the White House and other foreign affairs agencies with information or recommendations for action. We conveyed to the interested departmental bureaus and offices decisions by the White House or the secretary of state that required follow-up and implementation, whether policy actions or agreed invitation lists for state dinners. We controlled the distribution of sensitive telegrams and other documents; and we coordinated arrangements for meetings and trips by the secretary and other "seventh floor" principals (the deputy secretary and the under secretaries). The days were long, the pressure intense.

In these Executive Secretariat jobs, we were expected to stay only two years. After I returned from the signing ceremonies of the Paris Peace Talks on Vietnam, I began to think about moving on. Theodore Eliot, the executive secretary, told me that Secretary Rogers had recommended me to Fred Iklé, the incoming director of the Arms Control and Disarmament Agency (ACDA), to be his assistant director for international affairs, a position usually filled by a career Foreign Service officer. Assignments outside the State Department were not unusual: Foreign Service officers were regularly detailed to the Department of Defense and to other foreign affairs agencies for tours of duty, but it had so far never happened to me.

The position was a presidential appointment, requiring Senate confirmation—an attraction and a challenge in itself. As I looked into it further, I discovered that at the beginning of his second term (and before Watergate descended upon him), President Nixon had acceded to congressional pressure to "purge" the upper levels of ACDA of the dedicated arms controllers who allegedly pursued disarmament as an end in itself. These "softies" were to be replaced by "hardheaded realists" who would keep U.S. interests foremost in mind and negotiate arms control agreements only if those interests were served. The liberals in the Congress who had been instrumental in establishing ACDA, such as Senators Hubert Humphrey and Edmund Muskie, accused Nixon of a cynical move to block, or at least greatly slow down, progress in arms control negotiations with the Soviet Union.

Fred Iklé, fresh from the Rand Corporation, enjoyed a reputation as a brilliant strategic thinker on defense issues. He replaced Gerard C. Smith, who had long been associated with arms control and disarmament. Iklé was looking for a new team to support him, and I briefly became a member of that team.

A strange little man oddly ill at ease with himself and his new surroundings—not unlike Nixon himself—Iklé hired in rapid succession a new deputy director, Owen Zurhellen, a career Foreign Service officer and an old Asia hand, to replace Philip Farley, another long-standing arms control expert; myself, as assistant director for international affairs, to replace James Leonard, another career Foreign Service officer and China specialist; and Admiral Tom

Davies, Robert Buchheim, and Paul Wolfowitz, all as assistant directors of the agency's scientific and technical bureaus.[1]

Before accepting me for the position, Iklé invited me to lunch for an interview. The lunch was an awkward affair, with Iklé having little familiarity with—or regard for—the Foreign Service and diplomacy, and with me having little background in arms control issues. Nevertheless, my nomination went forward to the Senate from the White House—but not before I was quizzed by a White House personnel officer about whether or not I was a Republican, to which I replied that I was a civil servant. I had a perfunctory hearing before the arms control subcommittee of the Senate Foreign Relations Committee. I was quickly confirmed and took up my new responsibilities in the fall of 1973.

I looked forward to the new assignment. It would get me involved once again in European security matters, where I had started out. My responsibilities covered, in effect, all of the international discussions and negotiations on arms control issues—comprehensive nuclear test ban, chemical weapons ban, nuclear-free zones, and most of all, as it turned out, the Mutual and Balanced Force Reduction (MBFR) negotiations about to get under way in Vienna between NATO and Warsaw Pact members. One of my principal functions would be to chair the interagency backstopping committee that reviewed the progress in the MBFR negotiations and worked out agreed instructions to our delegation in Vienna—under the watchful eye of Henry Kissinger's all-seeing, all-pervasive NSC structure.

Since his triumphant rout of George McGovern in the presidential election a year before, Nixon was sinking deeper and deeper into his Watergate quagmire, while our long Vietnam nightmare was inching toward its ultimate denouement, and in Europe, the Cold War continued to evolve. As part of this evolution, and while conducting separate bilateral Strategic Arms Limitation Talks (SALT) aimed at limiting each side's arsenal of nuclear weapons, Washington and Moscow had agreed to two other negotiations, one conducted by a thirty-five-nation Conference on Security and Cooperation in Europe (CSCE), which Moscow had long pressed for; and the other by the MBFR talks between NATO and the twenty-three Warsaw Pact nations, sought by NATO.

The two negotiations were related to, but not dependent on, each other—except in the broadest sense (had, for example, the Soviets pressed ahead on the CSCE negotiations and stonewalled on MBFR, NATO would probably have stonewalled on CSCE). In CSCE, the emphasis was on human rights, free movement of peoples, and so-called confidence-building measures, such as exchanges of information on military maneuvers and troop movements. In

MBFR, the focus was on actual force reductions on both sides of the central European front.

Both negotiations lasted for years, and in the end were only resolved in the context of the reunification of Germany, the disintegration of the Soviet empire, and the end of the Cold War.

I found the subject matter fascinating and important. But it soon became clear to me that ACDA was at best neutral ground between the State and Defense Departments, and at worst a doormat for both agencies. ACDA had no real policymaking authority of its own, and the only people who wanted it to have such authority were "arms controllers" in the Congress like Humphrey and Muskie. The secretaries of state and defense, however, and especially their principal lieutenants, were perfectly content to let ACDA coordinate and staff arms control questions up through the NSC mechanism to the president, and to coordinate and staff the implementation of policy decisions—all provided State and Defense representatives looked over ACDA's shoulder each step of the way.

ACDA was thus the natural choice to chair the MBFR backstopping committee, as the relatively weak referee over the much more powerful State and Defense interests. Nevertheless, like all such decisions in the bureaucracy, the decision to give the MBFR coordinating task to ACDA had itself been hotly contested. Jonathan "Jock" Dean, a colleague, longtime central European specialist, and committed arms controller, was already serving as a special assistant to Deputy Secretary of State Kenneth Rush dealing with MBFR preparatory issues. Dean argued strongly that the State Department should control the MBFR backstopping function and machinery—presumably under his direction and with an augmented staff. To be sure, Iklé argued equally strongly for ACDA to play this role on the grounds that any other decision would contravene ACDA's legislative mandate. Dean countered that Secretary Rogers and National Security Adviser Kissinger had already decided that the MBFR backstopping function should be carried out under the aegis of the Under Secretaries' Committee chaired by the deputy secretary of state, in whose office Dean was placed.

The new executive secretary, Thomas Pickering—who has since had a spectacular career, capped by his appointment in 1997 by President Clinton to be under secretary of state for political affairs—took Iklé's side. Pickering argued that the department had higher priority needs for its scarce resources and that ACDA was just as much under the foreign policy direction of the secretary of state as Dean would be in the deputy secretary's office. In the end,

Pickering and Iklé prevailed, ACDA got the coordinating function, and Dean was awarded the consolation prize as deputy U.S. MBFR negotiator in Vienna.[2]

Despite the serious limitations—and frustrations—of working in an essentially weak agency, we did some useful work during my brief stay in ACDA. We made progress on a threshold nuclear test ban, on a chemical weapons ban, and on moving forward the U.S. position favoring ratification of the Treaty of Tlatelolco, which established a Latin American nuclear-free zone without infringing on our right to free passage of nuclear-powered naval vessels or vessels carrying nuclear arms. On MBFR, we at least got the negotiations launched and helped clear away some of the negotiating underbrush.

The MBFR negotiations, however, rapidly bogged down over the issue of how to define the forces on both sides to be included in the negotiations. NATO insisted that the Warsaw Pact include its vast paramilitary forces. The Warsaw Pact resisted. The other major issue that could not be resolved centered on the disparities of major equipment on both sides. Soviet conventional forces vastly outnumbered NATO forces—and the distance to the central front from Moscow was infinitely closer than the distance from Washington. NATO therefore demanded asymmetrical reductions from the Warsaw Pact to make up for these disparities, to which the Soviet Union refused to agree.

The battle lines were drawn from the beginning in Vienna: The Soviets demanded equal reductions in order to maintain their numerical advantage; the West demanded asymmetrical reductions to overcome the Soviet advantage. The Soviets wanted air and nuclear forces included in addition to ground forces, and they wanted a single-stage reduction. The West wanted ground forces only and reductions in two stages.

Early in 1974, I visited Vienna and a number of NATO capitals to consult on MBFR issues and to get a better sense, firsthand, of the negotiating environment and the views of our delegation and of our key NATO allies. I arrived in Vienna, my first stop, on a Sunday afternoon. Jock Dean had sent word to the airport, via a junior officer, that I was to meet him in the Vienna Woods outside the city for a chat and a brisk walk in the snow. Though I ruined a pair of shoes, not having been prepared for a snowy "walk in the woods," it was a pleasant afternoon that ended up in a *heurigen,* a local bar with wine, cheese, and song. Jock had made sure that I had his point of view before I plunged into my round of meetings and consultations the following day. From Vienna I went to Rome, Paris, Brussels, Bonn, and London, where I met officials in the respective foreign ministries and embassy colleagues for discussions and exchanges of views. In Brussels I called on General Andrew Goodpaster, then supreme allied commander of NATO forces in Europe.

When I returned from my consultations, I had a better idea of the negotiating atmosphere, the issues, and the attitudes toward the negotiations in the national capitals I visited. However, it was already clear that neither the East nor the West was motivated toward early compromise on these intractable issues. After a year of ACDA, and of dealing with Fred Iklé's temperament and personality, I therefore jumped at Phil Habib's offer to become his deputy assistant secretary of state, at first responsible only for the Indochinese states of Vietnam, Laos, and Cambodia and later for all of Southeast Asia. Habib had just been named assistant secretary of state for East Asian and Pacific affairs by Kissinger (who by now had achieved his ambition of becoming secretary of state).

So I rejoined the State Department's Bureau of East Asian and Pacific Affairs in late summer 1974, as the war in Vietnam, Laos, and Cambodia headed toward its denouement. Richard Nixon had resigned the presidency in disgrace over Watergate earlier that summer, to be succeeded by his vice president, Gerald Ford, who had been appointed in place of Spiro Agnew, who himself had earlier resigned the vice presidency in disgrace for having taken bribes as governor of Maryland.

Before Watergate destroyed his presidency, Richard Nixon had altered the global strategic landscape with his dramatic opening to China. Only a president with Nixon's impeccable anticommunist credentials could have engineered such a move. Had a Democratic president—Kennedy or Johnson—tried it, Nixon himself would have led the attack in opposition.

Nixon's historic visit to Beijing in 1972 was perhaps the defining act of his presidency in foreign affairs. It foreshadowed the end of China's twenty years of isolation and, in one master stroke, realigned the Cold War's bipolar standoff into a triangular strategic balance among the Soviet Union, China, and the United States. Its other principal effect in Southeast Asia was at last to reduce the Vietnam War's import from constituting, in U.S. eyes, a major confrontation between the United States on the one hand and the Soviet Union and China on the other, to what it might have been all along: a regional postcolonial contest between nationalist and communist forces. Accordingly, the impact of America's defeat in Vietnam, when it finally came, was commensurately reduced.[3]

In the three years since I had left the Paris Peace Talks on Vietnam and been away from any responsibility for Vietnam, the Paris Agreements on Vietnam had been signed, remaining U.S. troops withdrawn from South Vietnam, and U.S. prisoners of war returned from both North and South Vietnam. Despite the changing strategic backdrop described above, the war and the domestic turmoil surrounding it continued. The Congress grew progressively resistant to the administration's repeated requests for military and economic assistance to enable Thieu's government in South Vietnam and Lon Nol's government in Cambodia to go on defending themselves against the unremitting pressure of North Vietnam and its Cambodian allies to bring those countries under communist domination.

Assistant Secretary Habib asked me to be responsible for following Vietnam, Laos, and Cambodia. Along with the desk officers for these three countries, I became immediately absorbed in calculating how many days' supply of ammunition Cambodian government forces had left. Our other immediate major preoccupation was whether North Vietnamese forces would try to complete the conquest of South Vietnam in their coming 1975 spring offensive.

On Cambodia, everyone knew it was touch and go—that there was a direct correlation between the number of days' supply of ammunition left to the Cambodian forces and their ability to go on fighting without further U.S. supplies. On South Vietnam, the general consensus was that North Vietnamese forces could—and would—very likely take South Vietnam's two northern corps areas, I and II; but with continued U.S. assistance, Thieu's forces would be able to hold on to most of the country's two southern corps areas, III and IV, including the southern highlands, the Mekong Delta, and the Saigon metropolitan area, which together contained some 60 percent of the population and the preponderance of the country's rice-growing areas. This was an optimistic estimate of the situation. In the back of our minds, though, lurked this question: How long could South Vietnam survive if U.S. aid were cut off for good?

To help me make up my own mind on these questions and to get an updated, firsthand sense of things, I persuaded Habib to let me go to South Vietnam, Cambodia, and Laos for a few days in late October 1974. My last visit to the area had been from Paris with Judge Walsh five years before.

In Saigon I stayed with Graham Martin, our ambassador. Like Jock Dean in Vienna, he wanted to be sure I got the right slant on things. Hence his invitation to stay at his residence. A veteran career Foreign Service officer and a secretive, brooding, manipulative man, Martin was controversial both among his colleagues and with the press. He sought to ensure that only he, the chief of mission, had access to all available information—or at least that he made everyone else believe that only he had all the information on which to base decisions and make recommendations to Washington. And Washington, especially Henry Kissinger—similarly secretive and manipulative—counted on Martin's methods to keep the sprawling U.S. mission under tight discipline and away from a restive and skeptical press. This led to complaints within the mission, which found their way into the press, that Martin was suppressing Foreign Service reporting in order to tell Washington what it wanted to hear. Kissinger is reputed to have said of Martin, "I know he's a son of a bitch, but he's our son of a bitch!"

Martin invited me to attend a meeting of his Country Team, the heads of all the U.S. government agencies that made up the U.S. mission. It was an eerie experience. Martin led the discussion. No one was allowed to raise any issue unless it had been precooked with Martin in advance. In one sense, Martin was right: It was too late in the game for free debate. The only issue was, How was it all going to end? That issue depended on another question: How long could the U.S. Congress be persuaded to support the Thieu government's resistance to North Vietnam's unremitting pressure? The opening to China had been a vital strategic move, but it only set the stage for the endgame in Vietnam.

In each of the four corps areas I visited, briefings by both Vietnamese and American officers were, as always, upbeat, optimistic, and positive. The enemy was formidable, but South Vietnamese forces, with our assistance, were up to the task of defending against them. The object of the briefings was to persuade the visitor from Washington that continued American assistance was vital to the South Vietnamese cause, that the cause remained important to America's security, and that North Vietnam was in egregious violation of the Paris Agreements on Vietnam it had signed less than two years before. Above all, the briefings were meant to convey to Washington that there was still a game and that the game was worth the candle.

The briefings had their desired effect on me. I came away believing that the situation in South Vietnam was tenable even though some territory was likely to be lost to Hanoi's forces in the anticipated spring offensive of 1975. Despite the fact that the question was in the back of everyone's mind, including mine, I did not actually contemplate the possibility that U.S. aid might be entirely cut off as soon as it actually was—less than six months later. Neither did I consider South Vietnam's total psychological dependence on that aid. South Vietnam had depended for so long on U.S. aid and the United States was so accustomed to giving it that the possibility of its end was literally unthinkable—even to think it would have seemed disloyal to the policy, so indoctrinated had we become despite our doubts.

From Saigon I went to Phnom Penh in Cambodia. Here the atmosphere was markedly different. Phnom Penh was a city under siege, and the U.S. embassy was a principal target. In March 1970, neutralist Prince Norodom

Sihanouk, Cambodia's venerable chief of state since 1954, had been deposed while out of the country by anti-Communists Lieutenant General Lon Nol and Prince Sirik Matak.

At the Geneva Conference of 1954, Sihanouk had managed, unlike the leaders of Vietnam, to resist partition of his country into Communist and non-Communist zones. Since then, by masterfully steering his weak, vulnerable country between the Scylla of anticommunism, represented by France and the United States, and the Charybdis of communism, represented by the Khmer Rouge, North Vietnam, and their powerful sponsors, China and the Soviet Union, Sihanouk had kept Cambodia intact and unified.

However, as the Vietnam War grew in intensity, North Vietnamese forces used eastern Cambodia with more and more abandon as the southern end of the Ho Chi Minh Trail—the principal infiltration routes from North Vietnam to South Vietnam. In response, U.S. forces attacked these supply routes in Cambodia with increasing ferocity and increasing frequency. Nixon's dispatch of thirty thousand U.S. troops into Cambodia in late April 1970, and the resulting public outrage in the United States, had led the Senate to prohibit further incursions into Cambodia by American ground troops after June 30, 1970 (the resolution failed in the House). Nevertheless, U.S. planes continued to bomb North Vietnamese installations in eastern Cambodia. As this pressure grew, Sihanouk found himself increasingly pushed out of his neutral position and toward the position of his powerful Communist neighbors. After Lon Nol and Sirik Matak took charge, Cambodian Communist forces inevitably stepped up their attacks against the Cambodian government and its American sponsors.

When I arrived in Phnom Penh in October 1974, John Gunther Dean, a Harvard classmate and old friend, had been ambassador there for six months. He had previously served in Vietnam, Laos, and France, as well as in West Africa. He was thoroughly familiar with Indochina, its history, and its problems. His French was impeccable, his courage unflagging, and his loyalty to his political leaders in Washington constant. Dean's deputy chief of mission, Robert V. Keeley, was also an old friend. Keeley, with long experience in Africa and in Greece, had known Dean from their previous service together in West Africa. He had not served in Southeast Asia before, but he was fully experienced in complex third-world problems further complicated by Cold War pressures.

The embassy in Phnom Penh was under regular rocket attack. That, plus the deteriorating situation throughout the country—the growing Khmer Rouge attacks on provincial towns, its rocket attacks on Phnom Penh itself, and the Cambodian government forces' dwindling supplies of ammunition—placed Dean, Keeley, and their mission under almost intolerable pressure. The tension in the embassy was palpable, yet under Dean's and Keeley's calm, controlled leadership and example, the staff went quietly and professionally about its business. It was a performance literally under fire, one that the Foreign Service takes for granted when faced with it but that is little understood or appreciated by the public at large.

During my visit, Dean and Keeley made sure that I was briefed on the precariousness of the situation, that I called on appropriate Cambodian officials, and that I was able to get into the field, an experience that brought me closer to physical danger than I had been since the bombing of the embassy in Saigon nine years before. But, unlike Martin in Saigon, Dean and Keeley made no effort to skew their appraisals with false optimism or attempts at thought control.

We flew by helicopter to Kampong Chhnang, some sixty miles north of Phnom Penh at the southern end of Cambodia's great lake, the Tonle Sap, where the Khmer Rouge had carried out an attack a day or two before. The helicopter was filled with Cambodian military officers, Bob Keeley, and myself. On the way, the senior Cambodian officer, a brigadier general, decided we should land on a *phnom*—a hill—where a large Buddhist temple and statue had been attacked some days before by the Khmer Rouge.

We landed and inspected the temple, which indeed had been badly damaged. Then we were informed by the pilot that our aircraft was too full to take off vertically and that there was not sufficient clearance to take off horizontally. So he took half of us and deposited us in an open field a thousand yards away, while he went back to pick up the other half of the party. That was one of the longest fifteen or twenty minutes of my life, standing undefended in an open field in insecure territory. Bob Keeley said later that in his mind he kept seeing the headlines in the *Washington Post:* "Senior State Department and Embassy Officials Lost in Cambodia!" Happily for all of us, there was no untoward incident and the rest of the trip was uneventful. In fact, I remember little about the trip other than the incident I have just recounted.

From Phnom Penh I went on to Vientiane, Laos, where I stayed with Charles Whitehouse, then ambassador to Laos and another old Foreign Service friend. Laos, the smallest and weakest of the three Indochinese states, had been part of French Indochina and had suffered the same fate as Cambodia and Vietnam: It was caught between a determined, ruthless Communist onslaught directed from Hanoi and the determination of France, and later the United States, not to let Indochina slip behind the "bamboo curtain." At the Geneva Conference in 1954, a tripartite government had been established for Laos, with anticommunist, neutralist, and procommunist elements. By 1961, when

John Kennedy was inaugurated, the Geneva arrangements for Laos had come unraveled. Eisenhower and Dulles had given full support to the anticommunist elements under General Phoumi Nosavan, which led the procommunist Pathet Lao, under the "Red Prince," Prince Souvanouvong, to step up their pressure against the other factions. On Inauguration Day in 1961, Eisenhower told Kennedy that Laos would be his most pressing crisis and that the United States should respond vigorously to the mounting communist pressure, even if it meant sending U.S. troops.

Kennedy instead called for the reconvening of the Geneva Conference to restore the original terms of the 1954 agreement for a three-party government. At the same time, he sent a battalion of U.S. Marines to northeast Thailand to strengthen his bargaining position. And finally, with the assistance of Averell Harriman, his negotiator in Geneva, Kennedy threw U.S. support to Prince Souvanna Phouma, the head of the neutralist faction of the Lao government, abandoning Eisenhower's policy of supporting Phoumi Nosavan, the head of the anticommunist faction.

By the time of my brief visit in late 1974, Souvanna and the United States had become fast allies, with Souvanna relying on unstinting U.S. support against the growing pressures of the Pathet Lao and North Vietnam, while at the same time carefully maintaining his neutralist position. The United States had a huge mission in Vientiane—over eight hundred Americans, including families—in this tiny country of three million people. However, during my brief stay in Vientiane, Laos resembled nothing so much as a peaceful, mythical kingdom of the mysterious East.

Whitehouse took me to a local festival in Vientiane's main square, where traditional music and dances took place and where, by the end of the evening, the whole crowd was participating. Under this delicately Asian and Buddhist facade, and under a carefully orchestrated outward position of neutrality, Souvanna and a series of tough, skilled American ambassadors from G. MacMurtrie Godley to William H. Sullivan and Charles Whitehouse collaborated in a determined effort to blunt the Communist advance. Accompanied by Whitehouse, and in keeping with the delicate balance within the Lao government, I went through the motions of calling on Phoumi Vongvichit, a doctrinaire Communist Pathet Lao cadre serving as deputy foreign minister.

On my last night in Vientiane, I attended a dinner Whitehouse gave for the Lao defense minister, Sisouk na Champassak. The Australian ambassador appeared in Lao national dress, adding to my impression of a never-never land unluckily caught up in a nasty and bloody Cold War struggle.

I returned to Washington and wrote my trip report—a trip report I would be embarrassed to read today. I said Cambodia was on the ragged edge—it was clear that if friendly forces were deprived of ammunition, they could not survive for long. On Vietnam, I was more optimistic. I said that the situation appeared to be salvageable. In all four corps areas, the South Vietnamese appeared to be confident, well supplied by the United States, and ready to withstand North Vietnam's onslaught, if and when it came. At most, according to my briefings, some ground might be lost in the coming spring fighting season in the two northern corps areas, but the bulk of the population, at least in II, III and IV Corps, could be protected.

My report was circulated within the State Department and probably went over to the Pentagon, too. By the time it was distributed throughout the bureaucracy, a congressional cutoff of aid was much more likely than when I had left a few weeks before. James Bullington, a young officer on the Vietnam desk who had served in Vietnam after me and who was married to a Vietnamese national, bluntly told me I was wrong about Vietnam. He said that if the Congress cut off aid, South Vietnam would be gone in six weeks. He asked for authorization to make his own appraisal on the spot. Habib agreed to let him go. When he returned, after talking not just to American officials, but to Vietnamese friends and relatives, he confirmed his earlier gloomy view that the cutoff of U.S. aid would mortally wound what remained of South Vietnam's morale. I had seen the Vietnam glass as half full, not contemplating an early cutoff of our aid; Bullington saw the glass as half empty as the aid cutoff became a clear and even likely possibility. We circulated his report, but reports from the bowels of the State Department at that stage of the game had little impact. Our political leaders could see for themselves, from the growing determination in the Congress to stop aid to South Vietnam altogether, that the endgame was near.[4]

On January 28, 1975, the Ford administration requested from the Congress a supplementary military assistance appropriation of $300 million for South Vietnam and $222 million for Cambodia. As the Congress declined to act, or debated giving much smaller amounts, the administration warned of the dire consequences of the Congress's failure to act. As it became clear in February and March that the Congress was unwilling to continue appropriations for a losing—and unpopular—cause, the Republican administration was determined to establish that it was the Democrat-controlled Congress that was responsible for the collapse of South Vietnam and Cambodia. At a news conference in mid-March, President Ford reiterated that the survival of noncommunist governments in Cambodia and South Vietnam was vital to the security of the United States. He noted further that uncertainty over the American commitment to Cambodia had led the Thai government to request the withdrawal of all U.S. troops from Thailand and the Philippine government to decide to review its relations with the United States.

On April 2, the State Department announced the decision to begin the evacuation of Americans from Cambodia. On April 12, that evacuation was carried out. John Gunther Dean's picture on the cover of *Newsweek,* with bowed head and the American flag folded under his arm as he boarded his evacuation helicopter in Phnom Penh, poignantly captured the moment. That same day the president's press spokesperson, Ron Nessen, reiterated the president's continuing support for more military assistance for Cambodia and South Vietnam.

The tragedy in Cambodia for those Cambodians who had placed their faith in the Americans and who either could not or would not come out with us, was no less than for those in South Vietnam. But the collapse of South Vietnam occurred over a period of several weeks, starting in Hue in the north and moving like a tidal wave south to Da Nang, with scenes of panic as Vietnamese tried to clamber aboard American planes and helicopters sent in to pick up Americans and Vietnamese employees of the U.S. consulate and other U.S. government agencies. The tidal wave continued southward along the coast as the withdrawal, and panic among Vietnamese, grew, until North Vietnamese tanks pushed through the gates of the presidential palace in Saigon on April 30, 1975, and completed Hanoi's decades-long goal: the conquest of South Vietnam and the reunification of the country. With that, the U.S. embassy completed its evacuation of American employees and other Americans and as many Vietnamese employees and their families as they could—by helicopter from the roof of the embassy.[5] Suddenly it was over, the burden was lifted from America's shoulders if not from its psyche, and the aftermath began.

In those final weeks, while the Ford administration and the Congress were publicly wrangling over the fate of Cambodia and South Vietnam, in the bureaucracy we quietly turned our efforts to the myriad problems associated with the coming collapse. Without acknowledging either to ourselves or to others that the game was finally lost, we began evacuation planning. We began, too, to plan for the anticipated "bloodbath" of revenge by the North Vietnamese against the South Vietnamese population, as well as for ways to handle the estimated one million refugees that would try to escape the bloodbath any way they could—mostly by boat out to sea. We began to worry about the huge quantities of American weapons and equipment that would fall into the hands of the enemy. In the back of our minds, many wondered if there would be a search for scapegoats—for those who were responsible for losing South

Vietnam, as happened after China fell to communism nearly thirty years earlier.

Much of our contingency planning took place very quietly but at an accelerating pace. We did not wish to contribute to South Vietnam's collapse by telegraphing our evacuation planning. Graham Martin in Saigon was particularly sensitive to the danger of panic among the general population and of enraged Vietnamese troops attacking evacuation planes, or the embassy itself, out of a sense of abandonment and betrayal. Martin, in his reports from Saigon and during his visits to Washington as well, railed against the defeatism he detected in the bureaucracy and in particular in the State Department, arguing that it was contributing to the Congress's negative attitude toward appropriating more aid. Back in Saigon, he resisted requests for information to help us with our evacuation and refugee planning—for the numbers of Americans, third-country nationals who worked for us, and loyal Vietnamese employees and families to be evacuated. He also argued that perhaps he should plan to stay behind with a small staff in an effort to begin to build a relationship with the new masters of the country as a means to prevent the worst from happening.

As the days went on, the pace of high-level meetings picked up. By the end, Henry Kissinger was holding daily meetings in the White House Situation Room with the secretary of defense, James Schlesinger; the chairman of the Joint Chiefs of Staff, General George Brown; the head of the CIA, William Colby; Phil Habib, and a few others. Behind the principals sat staff officers like me, ready to follow up on the decisions taken each day. The atmosphere of these meetings was somber and realistic.[6] There was no effort to hide the grim realities about to befall South Vietnam. Everyone was conscious of the gigantic responsibility that all of us in Washington bore to do everything possible to save American lives, as well as the lives of the thousands upon thousands of Vietnamese who had depended on us for so long. Deep in our hearts, we knew that the tragedy of South Vietnam's downfall was the compounded tragedies of millions of people in that war-torn country—people killed in war on both sides, people killed in retribution, people driven from their homes and their country to escape retribution and forced to make their way to resettle in unfamiliar lands and unfamiliar cultures. These people in effect had believed in the same cause we had espoused for so many years, but they increasingly lacked the conviction to fight a war that the United States, through ill-conceived policies and programs and monumental miscalculation, progressively took away from them and made its own.

As we tried to plan quietly for the evacuation of Americans and for the anticipated huge refugee outflow, the Congress sought to exercise its constitutional function of holding hearings on the coming catastrophe. Senator Edward Kennedy, chairman of the Senate Judiciary Committee's Refugee Subcommittee, called hearings on April 8, 1975, four days before Phnom Penh's evacuation, and as refugee flows from northern South Vietnam began to gather momentum. I accompanied Daniel Parker, AID administrator, who was Senator Kennedy's principal witness.

In his opening statement, Kennedy summed up his point of view: "For too many weeks, our Government has stood paralyzed, as events rapidly overtook whatever small decision our Government was making to assist the millions of orphans and refugees and war victims in South Vietnam and Cambodia. But this is not a time for paralysis in our Government. This is a time for bold actions by the President. It is a time for new initiatives to fully meet our obligations to the people of Indochina. It is a time to admit our past mistakes and misplaced priorities, and a time to finally use the immense resources of our country to help bring peace and relief to the people of Indochina."

Brief excerpts from Parker's opening statement convey the drama unfolding in South Vietnam at the time: "Before the March offensive, the Government of [South] Vietnam had over 265,000 refugees and war victims. As of April 7, 1975, 310,000 new refugees have been registered; 93,000 more have been sealifted by 20 U.S. vessels, and approximately 40,000 more by 70 other vessels. We estimate another 150,000 refugees are still moving into and in the areas controlled by the Government of [South] Vietnam. . . . An estimated 750,000 refugees are not within these figures. Many are still moving in coastal and river craft, private vehicles, and on foot, into and within areas controlled by the Republic of [South] Vietnam, or have settled with relatives or friends. In sum, the Government of [South] Vietnam's refugee burden has been more than doubled, and may soon be tripled. . . ."[7]

Kennedy pressed for information on our contingency plans for evacuating Americans and Vietnamese. He turned to me to supplement Parker's generalized answers. Both Parker and I were reluctant to discuss such plans in a public committee hearing because of its potential impact in South Vietnam and also because Kennedy's hearing came on the eve of a National Security Council meeting on the subject. I fell back on Kissinger's press conference statement of a few days before to the effect that we were considering a range of options.[8]

When the final evacuations of Americans came from both Cambodia and South Vietnam, Phil Habib and I and numerous others spent nights in the State Department's Operations Center to monitor the evacuations' progress, hoping against hope that no disaster would occur. We were relieved that both evacuations went relatively smoothly and with minimal loss of life. We were then able to turn our attention to the massive effort of rescuing and resettling the thousands of refugees escaping both overland to Thailand and by sea to the other countries of Southeast Asia.

Laos soon followed Cambodia and South Vietnam, but with a peaceful rather than a violent transition. With Hanoi now moving to consolidate its hold over a reunified Vietnam, and the Khmer Rouge in power in Phnom Penh, a triumphant Pathet Lao rapidly pushed aside the fragile three-party government in Vientiane. The new Lao authorities summarily ordered the American embassy, some eight hundred strong, to reduce its numbers, including U.S. Marine guards, to twelve. To emphasize that it meant business, the Pathet Lao leaders organized mass demonstrations by howling mobs outside the U.S. embassy and the U.S. aid mission. Under these tense conditions, the chargé d'affaires ad interim, Christian Chapman, calmly oversaw the orderly evacuation, largely by surface transport across the Mekong River into Thailand, of hundreds of American employees and their families. Once again, mercifully, while the evacuation was carried out under duress, it proceeded without incident. I still remember discussing evacuation moves with Chapman by phone from Washington with the noise of the howling mob through the receiver in my comfortable, air-conditioned Washington office.

Our embassy and consulates in South Vietnam and our embassy in Phnom Penh were gone, and our relations with those countries severed, as our enemies, the new Communist masters, took over and consolidated their positions. But we in the East Asia bureau of the State Department favored trying to keep a small embassy open in Vientiane. The completion of the Communist takeover in Laos was more gradual and more peaceful. We thought it would be useful to have a listening post in the newly Communist areas of Indochina, which would also serve as a symbol of our willingness to begin building a relationship with the new masters of Indochina. We had been encouraged that the new Lao authorities had not ordered us to close the embassy entirely, only that we reduce its size drastically. A new American ambassador to Laos, Galen L. Stone (another old friend who had served mostly in Europe but who had had a tour in Vietnam), had been named. However, with the advent to power of the Pathet Lao, the drastic drawdown of our embassy numbers, and the general hostility toward the United States, Stone's appointment was canceled and we kept our representation in Vientiane at the chargé d'affaires level.[9]

The outpouring of refugees from all three Indochinese countries, but in greatest numbers from South Vietnam, occupied an increasing amount of our time. Innumerable other problems also clamored for our attention. A high-level interagency task force was thus created to deal solely with the refugee problem, which required coordination among a great number of federal agencies, state authorities, nongovernmental organizations, United Nations agencies, and foreign governments. The immensely talented and energetic Julia Taft, whose husband, William H. Taft IV, was then the Defense Department's legal counsel and later its deputy secretary, was chosen to head the task force. Bob Keeley, fresh from his evacuation from Phnom Penh, became her deputy.

Their task was infinitely complex: to coordinate the shipping necessary to rescue thousands of refugees from the sea, often in rickety, unseaworthy boats; to persuade the nations in the region to give at least first asylum to the thousands of refugees arriving on their shores and overland; to persuade other nations to accept thousands upon thousands of refugees for permanent resettlement in their countries; to coordinate our own massive refugee resettlement effort with our military authorities, state governments, nongovernmental organizations, and community groups—churches, schools, and public service organizations—which arranged the resettlement of individual refugees and their families in communities all across the country.

The East Asia bureau was thus relieved of overall responsibility for the refugee effort, although we continued to participate in the diplomatic efforts to persuade other countries to provide first asylum and permanent resettlement.

Within a few days after the final evacuation of Phnom Penh and Saigon in April 1975, and thus of the dramatic close to this agonizing chapter of our failed Vietnam policy, we in the East Asia bureau began to examine what the shape of a post-Vietnam policy toward East Asia might be, including new policies toward Vietnam, Cambodia, and Laos. The United States continued to have a strong position in East Asia. But would it hold? Would the Congress and the American people continue to support major military forces deployed in the western Pacific in the wake of Vietnam, or would we turn inward and want to wash our hands of the region where we had suffered so much trauma?

The countries of East Asia, whether they had been allied with us or had remained studiously neutral throughout the Cold War and the Vietnam conflict, were also concerned about U.S. intentions. As they feared a general U.S. withdrawal, they saw looming ever larger the presence of China, in whose shadow they lived; of the Soviet Union, whose forces were ever more active in the western Pacific; and of Japan, whose brutal occupation of all of Southeast Asia during World War II had left bitter memories and concerns about a resurgence of Japanese militarism should the U.S. presence diminish greatly or disappear altogether.

In 1967, at the height of the Vietnam War, five Southeast Asian nations (Thailand, Malaysia, Singapore, Indonesia, and the Philippines) had formed an Association of Southeast Asian Nations (ASEAN) to encourage the coordination of economic and trade policies and to provide a forum for political discussion and consultation. The grouping was not a security pact—it expressly eschewed security discussions. It was also expressly neutral toward the superpowers, despite continuing bilateral Thai and Filipino security ties with the United States.

ASEAN succeeded where at least two earlier attempts at regional associations had failed—MAPHILINDO, with Malaysia, the Philippines, and Indonesia; and ASA, an earlier Association of Southeast Asia. President Sukarno's disappearance from the Indonesian scene in 1965 and 1966 had paved the way for ASEAN to succeed where its predecessors had failed. Sukarno's successor, General Suharto, ended the period of confrontation with Malaysia. The five neighboring Southeast Asian nations put aside their many differences and disputes—border disputes, harboring insurgents against each other, ethnic and religious differences—and aimed instead to concentrate on their common concerns and needs for stability and economic growth.

The outside world was skeptical that the ASEAN experiment would work. The Soviet Union was suspicious that ASEAN was SEATO in a new form, and a devious American machination in another guise. Gradually we all welcomed the fragile experiment, supported it, and offered it our cooperation. Fortunately, the ASEAN nations themselves were cautious about moving too far too fast. They had too many differences among themselves that had to be worked out, and they were unwilling to align themselves with any outside power for fear that their new unity would founder on the shoals of the Cold War. They therefore kept the United States at arm's length and deflected our offers of cooperation. Nevertheless, we began to understand that this new arrangement offered the prospect of becoming an element of stability and prosperity in the region, capable of resisting any further threat of communist expansion in the area arising from the U.S. defeat in Indochina.

Continuing U.S. interests in the region, then, called for continuing U.S. engagement there rather than a precipitate withdrawal. Although the end of the Vietnam War led to a drawdown of our wartime force buildup in the region, we sought to maintain our security commitments from Korea and Japan in the north to Taiwan, the Philippines, and Thailand in the south. We sought also to maintain a military presence in those countries, except for Thailand. And we sought gradually to develop our new and growing ties to China. In sum, we would remain fully engaged in East Asia and in the western Pacific, but in an environment in which we aimed to make our new relationship with China a positive strategic factor both in East Asia and globally, and in which ASEAN's new but tenuous unity could be encouraged and supported on ASEAN's rather than on U.S. terms.

We set forth the continuing basic U.S. interest in East Asia in a memorandum to Secretary Kissinger on May 6, 1975, barely a week after Saigon's evacuation was completed: "to prevent any potentially hostile power or combination of powers from dominating the area." The memorandum went on to note that, since 1969, we had already begun "adjusting our posture to accommodate trends in the area, a domestic mood favoring retrenchment, and limitations on our resources."[10] The enunciation of the Nixon Doctrine in 1969, whereby the United States would continue to provide strategic protection for the region, but would look to the countries of the region themselves to fight their own battles on the ground; Nixon's opening to China in 1972; the completion of the withdrawal of U.S. forces from South Vietnam in 1973, following the signing of the Paris Agreements on Vietnam; and South Vietnam's final collapse in April 1975—all were part of this adjustment process.

The Habib-Lord memorandum expressed the belief that "an immediate objective of United States policy in East Asia—regardless of what we ultimately determine to be our proper role—should be to restore confidence among the governments of the region in the constancy of our fundamental policies." At the same time, it noted, "We do not look upon our policies toward individual East Asian countries, or our general stance in the region, as immutable. Therefore, while we may wish to stress in the short term the continuity of our Asian role, we should not forfeit our ability to revise our approach as circumstances may warrant."[11]

This last statement proved prescient. Even as we sought to plan for the future, events occurred that flowed from the debacle in Vietnam, which, though beyond our control, demanded our immediate attention. Just as we were beginning to react to the new realities, other countries were doing so as well.

On the morning of May 11, 1975, I had just arrived in the office around 8:00 A.M. when Lloyd M. ("Mike") Rives, the country director for Cambodia, informed me that the Pentagon had received an urgent message from the U.S. embassy in Jakarta that an American vessel, the *Mayaguez*, had been stopped in the Gulf of Thailand and boarded by Cambodian Khmer Rouge forces. Details were not yet available, but apparently the defense attaché's office in the embassy in Jakarta had monitored an urgent radio message from the ship and had relayed the message to the Pentagon's National Military Command Center.

I immediately briefed Owen Zurhellen, acting assistant secretary in Habib's absence, who was about to go to Secretary of State Kissinger's morning staff meeting. Characteristically, Kissinger reacted angrily to this obvious bad news, furious that he had not been informed earlier. Zurhellen had been sandbagged by circumstances. I had received the first information about the *Mayaguez*'s capture literally minutes before the secretary's staff meeting and had briefed Zurhellen on what sketchy information we had as he left for the meeting. In accordance with normal crisis procedures, Kissinger should have been alerted to the ship's capture by the Operations Center, which in turn would have been notified by the Pentagon's National Military Command Center, the recipient of the original urgent message from Jakarta. For some reason, this had not happened. Under the circumstances, the only thing worse that Zurhellen could have done was *not* to have alerted the secretary to the incident.[12]

In any event, the crisis quickly escalated to the level of the president and the National Security Council. While the incident was being handled thus way above my level of responsibility, over the next few days and weeks I found myself testifying on the facts of the incident and on the U.S. government's diplomatic response to it before House and Senate committees in both open and executive sessions. I was joined in those sessions by Morton Abramowitz, a Foreign Service officer then serving as deputy assistant secretary of defense for international security affairs, who testified on our military response to the *Mayaguez*'s seizure.

The facts of the incident were difficult to piece together. It was equally difficult to understand what the motives of the Cambodians were in capturing the ship or how to deal with the crisis that the capture provoked. Was it an effort by a hostile Khmer Rouge regime to continue to humiliate the United States, rubbing salt into the still-festering wounds of our defeat in Indochina? Or was it simply a misplaced initiative of a local Khmer Rouge commander against what he perceived to be the trespassing of foreign shipping in Cambodian waters?

All we knew for sure at the beginning was that the office of the *Mayaguez*'s agent in Jakarta had gotten a report from the ship that it was being boarded by armed Cambodians. The information was given to the U.S. embassy in Jakarta, which conveyed it urgently to Washington agencies. At first, we believed the ship was heading into port at Sihanoukville, but later we found that it had been stopped off the island of Koh Tang about thirty miles off the Cambodian coast.

The National Security Council met promptly, following which President Ford issued a brief statement declaring that the action was one of piracy. The president demanded the return of the crew and the ship immediately and instructed the State Department to do everything possible to achieve this goal. Carrying out this instruction, we sought through diplomatic channels to convey the president's demand to the Cambodian authorities but had no way of confirming that the message had gotten through. The Chinese refused to convey the message, so we attempted to deliver it directly to the Cambodian embassy in Beijing. It was returned through the regular mail. Direct communication in Phnom Penh was impossible since all Western embassies had by then withdrawn. We asked the secretary general of the United Nations to try to communicate with the Cambodians. He had no more luck than we had had.

Meanwhile, with U.S. air cover, we sought to prevent the Cambodians from disembarking the crew and taking them into Cambodia proper. This action led to the destruction of three Cambodian patrol craft and damage to four others. Nevertheless, the Cambodians managed to get some of the captives off the ship and into Sihanoukville. The National Security Council continued to meet to consider further action. In addition to providing aerial reconnaissance, the U.S. Navy dispatched a number of surface ships to the scene, including two aircraft carriers, the *Coral Sea* and the *Midway.*

With still no reaction from the Cambodians, the president authorized a rescue mission from U.S. Marine elements stationed in Thailand. One of the helicopters loaded with marines crashed in Thailand, killing all aboard. After the operation was under way, Washington became aware that Phnom Penh radio had announced, in a Cambodian-language broadcast, that the Cambodian authorities were prepared to release the ship, but there was no mention of the crew.

After the matter was finally resolved with both the crew and ship released, and after numerous casualties were incurred on both sides, the responsible congressional committees continued to examine the executive branch's conduct during the crisis. Abramowitz and I, with appropriate staff, were called to the Hill several times to give testimony. The committee members were particularly interested in our internal procedures for responding to such a crisis, the decision-making process employed to resolve the crisis, and whether or not adequate consultations with the Congress had taken place. We were unable to satisfy them on any count since we had not been involved in the National Security Council deliberations. The Congress therefore continued to seek the testimony of senior officials who actually had participated in the NSC meetings. They kept getting Abramowitz and Miller until, finally, the deputy secretaries of state and defense, Robert Ingersoll and William Clements, were offered up to them. I accompanied Ingersoll when he appeared before a subcommittee of the House International Relations Committee.

It was a sad and embarrassing hearing, reflecting the diminished stature and authority of the State Department in the Kissinger era. Ingersoll, the second-ranking official in the department, acknowledged that he had been no more than an observer at the NSC meetings and, implicitly, that Henry Kissinger, then both national security adviser and secretary of state, dominated the meetings. Quite properly, he refused to divulge the substance of the NSC discussions, adding to the committee's growing frustration.

Finally, the Congress ordered the General Accounting Office (GAO) to investigate the entire incident. The GAO, after interviewing all concerned and studying the relevant records, concluded that there had been certain lapses in internal procedures in the State Department. They found that the department should have issued a formal Notice to Mariners that commercial ships should avoid the coastal waters in the Gulf of Thailand after the end of hostilities in Vietnam and Cambodia and the takeover of those countries by authorities unfriendly to the United States. The Congress and the GAO focused particularly on the fact that prior to the *Mayaguez*'s capture, Korean and Panamanian vessels had been stopped in the same waters.

The GAO noted that the Bureau of East Asian and Pacific Affairs was responsible for following developments in the region, the Bureau of Economic and Business Affairs was responsible for issuing Notices to Mariners, and liaison between the two bureaus had been inadequate.

The GAO also found that the original emergency message reporting the seizure and boarding of the *Mayaguez* had been received in the department's Operations Center by an inexperienced and junior watch officer, who did not understand the significance of the message and put it aside. Notification of the secretary of state and other responsible senior officials was thus delayed.

The real problems with the incident lay much deeper. The United States had just ended, unsuccessfully, a long and draining war with Vietnam and Cambodia. The nation's nerves were raw, and we saw the seizure of the *Mayaguez* by the new Communist rulers of Cambodia as one more hostile act against Americans. We discovered only later that the *Mayaguez* was not even flying an American flag and that the Cambodians thus were probably not even aware they were stopping an American ship.

Moreover, because the new rulers virtually isolated themselves from all contact with Western nations after their victory in Phnom Penh, communication with them was all but impossible. Therefore, the absence of any response to our messages demanding the release of the ship and the crew, in addition to the refusal of Cambodia's new friends, such as China, to convey messages, added to our sense of the crisis resulting from a deliberately hostile act. This communications gap was compounded because Phnom Penh's announcement of its willingness to release the ship was issued in Cambodian: It took time to capture the message, translate it, and bring it to the attention of Washington decision makers. By then the rescue mission had been launched, and the casualties suffered.

The seizure of the *Mayaguez* also fed the Congress's frustration at not being adequately consulted by the administration on the use of military force and in effect being stonewalled: The administration sent witnesses who, like Abramowitz and me, were not privy to the proceedings of the NSC meetings where the decisions to use force were taken or who, like Deputy Secretary Ingersoll, sought to protect the privileged nature of such deliberations.

As a postscript to the loss of Cambodia, Prince Sihanouk came to the General Assembly in September 1975 to claim Cambodia's seat in the United Nations. Sihanouk had been deposed five years before by Lon Nol and had remained in exile during the intervening years. Now, as head of the Khmer Rouge authorities, he came to New York in triumph. According to UN protocol, the United States, as host country to the United Nations, had an obligation to offer him at least minimal protocolary courtesies on his arrival. Kissinger decided that I, as a deputy assistant secretary of state for East Asian and Pacific affairs, was the suitable official to send to New York to greet Sihanouk on behalf of the United States government. I was senior enough not to offend Sihanouk, yet sufficiently low in the State Department hierarchy not to imply formal recognition of the new Khmer Rouge regime in Phnom Penh.

Off I went to New York to carry out my assignment. Accompanied by Ambassador Franais Kellogg, protocol officer for the U.S. mission to the United Nations, I met Sihanouk and his wife, the strikingly beautiful princess Monique, at planeside. Sihanouk could not have been more gracious in expressing his appreciation for the courtesies extended to him by the U.S. government. We then proceeded to the airport's VIP lounge, where a large crowd of Communist and third-world diplomats and journalists greeted him with great enthusiasm and applause. Sihanouk walked to the waiting microphones and launched a bitter tirade against the United States for all of the crimes he alleged it had committed against his country. After some inner hesitation, I decided not to stalk out of the room in protest but instead to complete the task I had been assigned as official greeter.

As the end of the Vietnam conflict drew near, and in the wake of the Nixon opening to China, the Thai and Philippine governments began to reassess their ties with the United States and generally to reorient their foreign policies. Even before South Vietnam's collapse, the Thai indicated that they wanted our forces removed. The *Mayaguez* affair, during which we used U.S. Marines based in Thailand to attack Cambodian forces and installations without consulting the Thai, reinforced the Thai resolve to rid themselves of the U.S. military presence, a presence that was becoming an embarrassment and an obstacle to repairing their relations with their neighbors in the post-Vietnam environment.

Both the Thai and the Filipinos also wanted to end their SEATO link with the United States. SEATO—the Southeast Asia Treaty Organization—had for some years been pretty much a dead letter, even though its secretariat continued to exist in Bangkok and regular ministerial meetings were still held. Although the Kennedy and Johnson administrations used the SEATO treaty's codicil extending its protection to South Vietnam, Laos, and Cambodia as part of their rationale for the U.S. engagement in those countries, none of the other SEATO members felt obliged to interpret their SEATO obligations as requiring their participation in the Vietnam conflict. Pakistan had effectively withdrawn from active participation in SEATO activities some years before.

Faced with the inevitable, and perhaps recognizing that in the post-Vietnam era SEATO would be an unwanted encumbrance for us as well as for the other treaty partners, we acquiesced in the dismantlement of the SEATO machinery. However, we persuaded the other members, including the Thai and Filipinos, to keep the Manila Treaty, the underlying pact that had led to the creation of the SEATO machinery. Both Thailand and the Philippines had bilateral security arrangements with the United States in any case, which remain in place today along with the seven-nation Manila Treaty.

After the collapse of our efforts in South Vietnam, Cambodia, and Laos relieved us of our military burdens there, Habib asked me to add the rest of Southeast Asia to my Indochina responsibilities. We were immediately faced with Thailand's desire to put distance between itself and its unsuccessful American ally. In March 1975, as South Vietnam's fate was only a matter of weeks away, Kukrit Pramoj became prime minister of Thailand on a platform of seeking the withdrawal of "all foreign forces" within eighteen months. A month later, the wrongful arrest outside a U.S. military base of a disgruntled Thai employee of a U.S. NCO club fanned the flames against the foreign military presence. The *Mayaguez* incident another month later further strained U.S.-Thai relations.

Because of the continuing unsettled conditions in the region, Washington had hoped to maintain at least a residual military presence in Thailand, perhaps as many as three thousand troops and access to air bases.

Thailand was willing to negotiate the conditions under which we might keep that number of troops, but set a deadline of nine months—March 1976—for us to reach the agreed reduced troop presence. The conditions they posed caused the Pentagon great anguish because of the repercussions they would have on our base agreements around the world. We knew that countries from the Philippines (with whom we faced a base-renewal negotiation the following year) to Greece and Spain were watching closely to see what concessions the Thai could extract from us.

In the end, despite warnings from our chargé d'affaires in Thailand, Edward Masters, and later from Ambassador Charles Whitehouse, Washington's inability to reach rapid agreement between the State and Defense Departments on what concessions we were prepared to make led the Thai to lose patience. They shortened the deadline to six months while we continued to wrangle both among ourselves and with them. Finally, the Thai refused to accept our final position on criminal jurisdiction over U.S. military personnel who broke Thai law while off duty. The Thai would not give up their insistence that such off-duty crimes were subject to Thai law and the Thai justice system—and punishment in Thai jails. The Pentagon could not accept that because of the implications it held for U.S. forces around the world—and because of the inevitable domestic public and congressional reaction at home.

One senior Thai official, Anand Panyarachun, was the key figure who held his government steady on course in the face of heavy U.S. negotiating pressure. Anand, who had been the Thai ambassador in Washington and, much later, twice became caretaker prime minister, was secretary general of the Thai Foreign Ministry at the time. An educated, sophisticated, and intense Thai nationalist, Anand understood that in the unfolding post-Vietnam era, a continuing U.S. military presence in his country would be at best an embarrassment, and at worst an obstacle to building new relationships with Thailand's Communist neighbors, Laos, Cambodia, and Vietnam.

Thanks to Anand's single-minded vision—and to our own recognition that we could no longer rely on the military muscle we had had for so long in the region—the U.S.-Thai relationship was no longer burdened with the myriad irritations occasioned by a large U.S. military presence. U.S. forces left Thailand as the Thai had requested, leaving behind only the noncombat military elements attached to the embassy—the Defense Attaché's Office and the military assistance group.

In December 1975, the Indonesian government intervened in East Timor with military force to incorporate the small, former Portuguese colony as an integral part of Indonesia. East Timor had been virtually abandoned the year before by a Portuguese government wracked by internal instability after a leftist coup. Woefully unprepared for independence, East Timor was itself torn apart by a civil war among Marxist, pro-Indonesian, and pro-independence factions. The Indonesian government, which had had a close call with a Communist-inspired coup a decade before, was not about to allow a Marxist regime to take power in its midst.

According to a well-documented account, Indonesian president Suharto informed President Ford and Secretary Kissinger, then visiting Jakarta, on the eve of the East Timor takeover.[13] Ford and Kissinger reportedly raised no objection but asked that U.S.-provided equipment not be used. The question of whether such equipment was or was not used plagued the U.S. government for the remainder of my stay in the East Asia bureau. When we received reports that it was, the United States quietly suspended arms shipments to Indonesia for several months in an effort to avoid a formal congressionally mandated cutoff of aid to Indonesia.

Meanwhile, our base agreement with the Philippines came up for renewal in 1976. Our stalwart ally, Ferdinand Marcos, had also been bitten by the nationalist bug but in a different way. Marcos claimed that the Philippine alliance with the United States, and especially the major American bases there, entailed a growing risk of making the Philippines a target for a hostile China or Soviet Union. Therefore, the United States should pay heavily for putting the Philippines at such risk. He therefore demanded that we pay "rent" for our bases in the amount of $1 billion.

But other issues were involved as well, issues that occupied midlevel officials like myself in both governments. The massive U.S. base facilities in the Philippines were an important legacy of the colonial relationship between our two countries. In addition to our two major bases, Clark Air Force Base and Subic Bay Naval Station, we had numerous other bases, as well as communications facilities, bombing ranges, and more. The Filipinos pressed us to return to them any base facilities that we no longer needed post-Vietnam. They sought to establish at least nominal Filipino military control over the remaining bases, arguing that anything less was a derogation of Philippine sovereignty. And, as in Thailand, they sought Philippine jurisdiction over U.S. military personnel who committed crimes while off duty.

William H. Sullivan, our ambassador to the Philippines, asked me to come out to Manila for a careful and detailed survey of all our facilities to gain a better understanding of the issues involved and of the compromises he thought the United States should be prepared to make in the new post-Vietnam environment.[14]

Out I went for ten days. Accompanied by an embassy political-military officer, Michael Connors, I visited all major facilities and was briefed in detail as to their continuing importance to the U.S. strategic position in the western Pacific. In the end, however, it was Ferdinand Marcos's greed that determined the failed outcome of the negotiations, not U.S. intransigence or a high Philippine sense of nationalism.

Marcos sent his highly respected foreign minister, Carlos P. Romulo, to Washington for the negotiations with Henry Kissinger. Once the negotiations were under way and Kissinger saw where they were headed, he directed us over a weekend to put together a package of military, economic, financial, and technical aid that would incorporate all existing programs and add a dollop here and there to amount to $1 billion for the coming fiscal year. Marcos instructed Romulo to turn it down as insufficient, saying that he preferred to wait for the incoming Carter administration, which he was sure would be more generous. (It was not.)

One of our more puzzling issues was what attitude we should adopt toward the victorious Communist regimes in Hanoi, Phnom Penh, and Vientiane in the wake of the failure of our decades-long policy of opposing communism there. Immediately after the fall of Saigon and Phnom Penh, we had placed embargoes on all trade and financial transactions with a unified Vietnam (the embargoes had applied to Communist North Vietnam since 1954) and Cambodia as "enemy states" as authorized by the Trading with the Enemy Act of 1917 and the Export Administration Act of 1969. These embargoes by a Republican administration were seen by the Democratic-controlled Congress as vengeful acts taken in defeat. Subcommittees of the House and Senate Foreign Affairs and Foreign Relations Committees summoned the administration to explain itself, and the administration sent me as their witness.

Accompanied by legal and economic advisers from the State Department, I explained that the Trading with the Enemy Act authorized the president to take such steps; that we felt it was prudent to deny financial and strategically important goods and assets to the hostile new regimes; and that doing so would allow us to monitor their attitudes toward us. The Democratic representatives deplored the actions as ones that would take years to retract (in the event, the embargoes lasted nearly twenty years). I stuck to the administration line. In the House subcommittee, the frustrated members tried to elicit my personal view on whether the action was wise or not. I declined to be drawn into a discussion of my personal views, stating that I thought I could be more useful to the committee by explaining the administration's reasons for taking the step. Happily the chairman sustained my demurral.

Aside from general relief that the war was finally over and the bitter aftertaste of defeat, two factors influenced the Ford administration's attitude toward the new and victorious Communist-controlled states of Indochina: the countervailing pressures of the organizations insisting on a full accounting of our dead and missing personnel in Southeast Asia and those of liberal and humanitarian groups for humanitarian aid to help "bind the wounds of war." The first set of pressures, generally issuing from those who had favored the U.S. engagement in Vietnam, ensured that the United States would not move quickly to establish normal diplomatic relations with Hanoi or Phnom Penh even though the new authorities of both claimed their nations' seats at the United Nations. There they were treated by the U.S. government as the other Communist states had long been treated: Their movements in the United States were closely restricted to New York City and its surroundings, unless specific permission was granted to go further afield.

In response to the second set of pressures, generally issuing from those who had opposed the war and sought ways for the United States to make restitution for the destruction it had caused, the State and Commerce Departments established procedures under the trade and financial embargoes whereby humanitarian aid groups could apply for licenses to ship limited amounts of humanitarian supplies, and later of agricultural goods, to the former enemies. In general, the Ford administration took the position that responsibility for helping Vietnam and Cambodia recover from the destruction of the war had passed to the Soviet Union and China, the backers of the new Hanoi and Phnom Penh regimes. However, the Ford administration was prepared to make limited exceptions for specific humanitarian aid projects. Democrats in the Congress found this position spiteful, driven by the bitterness of defeat rather than by a more generous desire to help heal the wounds of war. Again, I found myself testifying before the relevant congressional committees to explain the administration's position.

In late June 1976, I was asked to accompany Nelson Rockefeller, during his brief term as President Ford's appointed vice president, on a trip to Southeast Asia, Australia, and New Zealand. Rockefeller had been invited by the Australians to give a speech in Sydney on the occasion of Australia's celebration of the American bicentennial. It was decided that he should visit a number of nations en route, beginning with France, then on to Iran to see the shah, and then to Malaysia, Singapore, Bali in Indonesia, Australia, and New Zealand, returning to the United States via Tahiti, Los Angeles, and New York—a round-the-world tour.

For his meeting with the shah, Rockefeller was accompanied by Ambassador Alfred L. "Roy" Atherton, assistant secretary of state for Near East and

South Asian affairs. I met the party in Tehran for the rest of the trip, with Atherton returning home from there. I arrived in Tehran just in time for the shah's farewell reception for Vice President and Mrs. Rockefeller on Kish Island in the Persian Gulf, to which I flew from Tehran in the U.S. military attaché's plane.

The shah was in the process of building a plush resort on Kish Island and received the Rockefellers there, even though construction was still under way. His farewell reception was held in a sumptuous pavilion and attended by senior members of the shah's entourage, his wife, the shabanou, and their sixteen-year-old heir to the Peacock Throne. I was presented to the shah and was struck by his slight build and seemingly shy manner. In contrast, the shabanou seemed a much more self-possessed and positive presence. The young prince was more like his father, quiet and shy.

After spending the night in solitary splendor in my own luxurious cabana, where I noted the huge television set was not yet hooked up, I joined the vice president's party for our departure to Kuala Lumpur, Malaysia. Traveling with Nelson Rockefeller and his wife was a pleasant duty. He was not a difficult taskmaster. We briefed him and left him alone as he desired. In his party were two or three collaborators from his political life, including a speechwriter. He was also accompanied by Captain (later Admiral) Jonathan Howe, his military aide.

On arriving in the steamy tropical capital of Kuala Lumpur, a gathering of Malaysian government officials greeted us and whisked us into the Hilton Hotel for our brief stay. While in Kuala Lumpur, we became aware of the Rockefeller penchant for collecting mementos by the gross from each of his stops along the way. At the Hilton, he and his wife became enamored of the hotel's attractive, locally made wastebaskets and asked to buy two dozen. The hotel management could not find any wastebaskets to match, so they sold them two dozen out of the hotel rooms themselves!

The Malaysian prime minister, Hussein bin Onn, entertained the Rockefellers at a splendid dinner in the state guest house. Here I met a number of Malaysian officials whom I got to know well when I later returned to Malaysia as ambassador. When the time came for the exchange of toasts, Rockefeller rose and toasted the health of the Malaysian president, caught himself, and in a typically American gesture not so appreciated elsewhere, put his arm around the prime minister's shoulders and said, "I mean the king!" So much for my briefings.

Rockefeller spoke to Kuala Lumpur's American community at the ambassador's residence. As the cavalcade was leaving the hotel for the residence, I was a minute late in coming down. I saw that the cavalcade was ready to leave and rushed around the car to jump in quickly. Instead, I fell into a storm drain, badly twisting my ankle. In excruciating pain and fearing I had broken my ankle (which I had not), I got in the car and off we went. The police outriders leading the cavalcade turned off the broad Jalan Pekeliling onto the wrong narrow residential street. Understanding they had made a mistake, they obliged the entire cavalcade to turn around on the proverbial dime, ruining a few beautiful, well-trimmed lawns in the process.

Then off to Singapore, where Rockefeller had a meeting with Prime Minister Lee Kuan Yew, the forceful, cerebral, outspoken head of that tiny island state. On then to Bali, where the Indonesian government feted Rockefeller with another banquet.

Next stop Canberra, where Rockefeller was met by a few noisy anti-Vietnam protesters while visiting Australia's military museum. Rockefeller duly delivered his Bicentennial speech in Sydney, the central purpose of his entire trip, then on we flew to Wellington, New Zealand. Another brief stop, another black-tie dinner (in an increasingly crumpled tuxedo), and we began the long journey across the Pacific to Los Angeles, broken by a twenty-four-hour stopover in Tahiti. Before landing in Tahiti, our VIP Boeing 707 did a flyby, at five hundred feet, of the spectacularly beautiful Bora-Bora coral reef island. The flyby was dramatic, and we got a close-up view, but it was somewhat unsettling to experience that huge aircraft being brought so low and so close to the emerald green hills of Bora-Bora.

In Tahiti, the Rockefellers once again went through the local market, scooping up local mementos by the gross, leaving the local merchants marveling at their good fortune. Our brief stopover was also marked by a picnic aboard a motor launch from which there was literally no escape from the tropical sun and thus from a monumental sunburn.

We returned to Washington in time for the massive celebration on the Mall of our bicentennial Fourth of July. Half a million people gathered there on that beautiful sunny day to celebrate peacefully the end to the Vietnam War and to the divisions it had created in our society and our body politic. It was a truly emotional experience, uplifting in its symbolism and reassuring in its calming effect.

Jimmy Carter defeated Jerry Ford in November 1976. Carter named Cyrus Vance secretary of state, and Vance chose Richard Holbrooke as his assistant secretary of state for East Asia and the Pacific. I had been in three Washington assignments for a total of six years and began to hope for an appointment as ambassador. Also, while I had known Vance some years before at the Paris

Peace Talks on Vietnam and would have been happy to serve him in Washington, both Dick Holbrooke and I were uncomfortable about my continuing as his deputy since he was ten years my junior and had been far junior to me when we both had served in Vietnam some fifteen years before. So it was clearly time for me to seek my fortunes elsewhere.

When the wheel of fortune stopped, it pointed to Malaysia, not the most important country in Southeast Asia from the standpoint of U.S. interests but a complex and interesting one nonetheless. Our relations were good but not close. A former British colony, Malaysia had chosen a neutral path after independence. It was too prosperous to receive traditional U.S. aid—although it did have some 150 Peace Corps volunteers. It was also officially a Muslim country and government, and although moderate in outlook and in policy, it often sided with its fellow Muslim states against Israel and the United States.

I left the East Asia bureau in March 1977, well before my appointment had been approved by the White House. While I waited, somewhat anxiously, for the nomination to be nailed down, I studied the Malay language, as well as Malaysia's history, politics, and economics. At Easter, my nomination still not pinned down, my family and I went to Mexico for a ten-day vacation. Our children by then were in university, and we wanted to have a family vacation together before Kaity and I went off to Malaysia some ten thousand miles away and they returned to university.

Off we went to Mexico City and the Yucatán. One afternoon, returning to our modest hotel in Mérida in the Yucatán after a day's sightseeing, I found a two-day-old phone message from Phil Habib, then under secretary of state for political affairs. I caught him just as he was leaving the office for the airport to go to Algiers, as I recall. Put off by my taking two days to return his phone call, Habib shouted, "Miller, aren't you interested to know that the president wants you to be his ambassador in Malaysia?!" I knew Phil well enough to take his bluster with equanimity and explained that I had just gotten the message. Phil calmed down and said that I'd better "get back to Washington and go to work!" We finished our ten days' leave and returned to Washington, ready to face a new chapter in our lives.

The Vietnam War (if not its trauma) was finally behind us—and behind me personally. Nearly fifteen years had passed since I had been posted to Saigon. Except for brief periods in other assignments, Vietnam had almost totally absorbed my attention over those fifteen years: the turmoil leading to the end of the Diem regime; the decisions to bomb North Vietnam and to send combat troops; the superficial wounds I had sustained in the terrorist attack against the embassy in March 1965; the growing frustration the war provoked at home inside and outside the government and the mushrooming protest movement at home and abroad; the painful process of starting negotiations for a way out; the prolonged negotiations themselves; and finally, the agonizing collapse of South Vietnam.

Making peace in Vietnam had proven to be as frustrating as making war had been. In making both war and peace the United States woefully underestimated a wily, tenacious, and determined, if primitive, enemy. Taking ultimate victory for granted, the United States had no strategic plan—no clear idea of where it was going and what it could realistically accomplish either in waging war or in negotiating peace. During the war, it had no idea of an alternative leadership to Diem, no means of preserving or restoring internal political stability in the vacuum that followed the coup against Diem that it had encouraged, and no clear strategy for winning militarily. In our frustration, we progressively pushed aside the South Vietnamese, whose war it was, and took ever more responsibility for prosecuting it, thereby rendering defeat inevitable.

Even when we finally sought a way out of the quagmire, our room to maneuver was constrained by pressures to get negotiations going to end the fighting and bring U.S. troops home; and the negotiations themselves were prolonged by our belief that somehow we could achieve at the negotiating table what we had failed to achieve on the battlefield, and that abandoning South Vietnam would betray our commitments to allies around the world and the memory of the thousands of American troops who had fallen in Vietnam. In the end we did abandon South Vietnam to its fate because we finally had no other choice. Vietnam, truly, was America's last great excess of the Cold War.

Throughout this entire process the U.S. government—and the American people—were progressively rent by division and passionate disagreement about what we were doing in Vietnam and why. Each president from Eisenhower to Nixon found his freedom of action constrained by the decisions of his predecessor, by the Cold War mind-set of the time—a mind-set that lumped together all Communist challenges around the world into one global conspiracy against the West—and by his own unwillingness to risk political defeat domestically by challenging that mind-set. Each president surrounded himself with like-minded advisers—dissenters were marginalized because they offered less attractive alternatives from a domestic political point of view. The rest of us in the bureaucracy did our jobs, nursed our growing doubts, wrote our memoranda, and were glad, finally, when it was over. A few resigned; some made dramatic gestures of protest (such as Daniel Ellsberg, who leaked a set of highly classified documents to the press—the so-called Pentagon Papers); and some managed to get the ear of highly placed officials, if to little avail. Meanwhile, our course in Vietnam was pursued inexorably, taking down two presidents in its path. In retrospect, there must have been a better way, and all of us share responsibility for not finding it. Even after the Tet Offensive of 1968, which triggered Johnson's withdrawal from the 1968 presidential race and his initiative to seek a way out through negotiations, we made peace the way we made war—slowly, haltingly, and ineffectually.

Now, in Malaysia, I would have to deal with a major aspect of the aftermath of America's Vietnam excess—thousands upon thousands of "boat people" fleeing South Vietnam in rickety, unseaworthy boats to Malaysia's shores and those of neighboring countries in search of safety and new lives. As it turned out, this was the single most demanding problem I had to deal with during my three years in Malaysia.

PART III

Beyond Vietnam

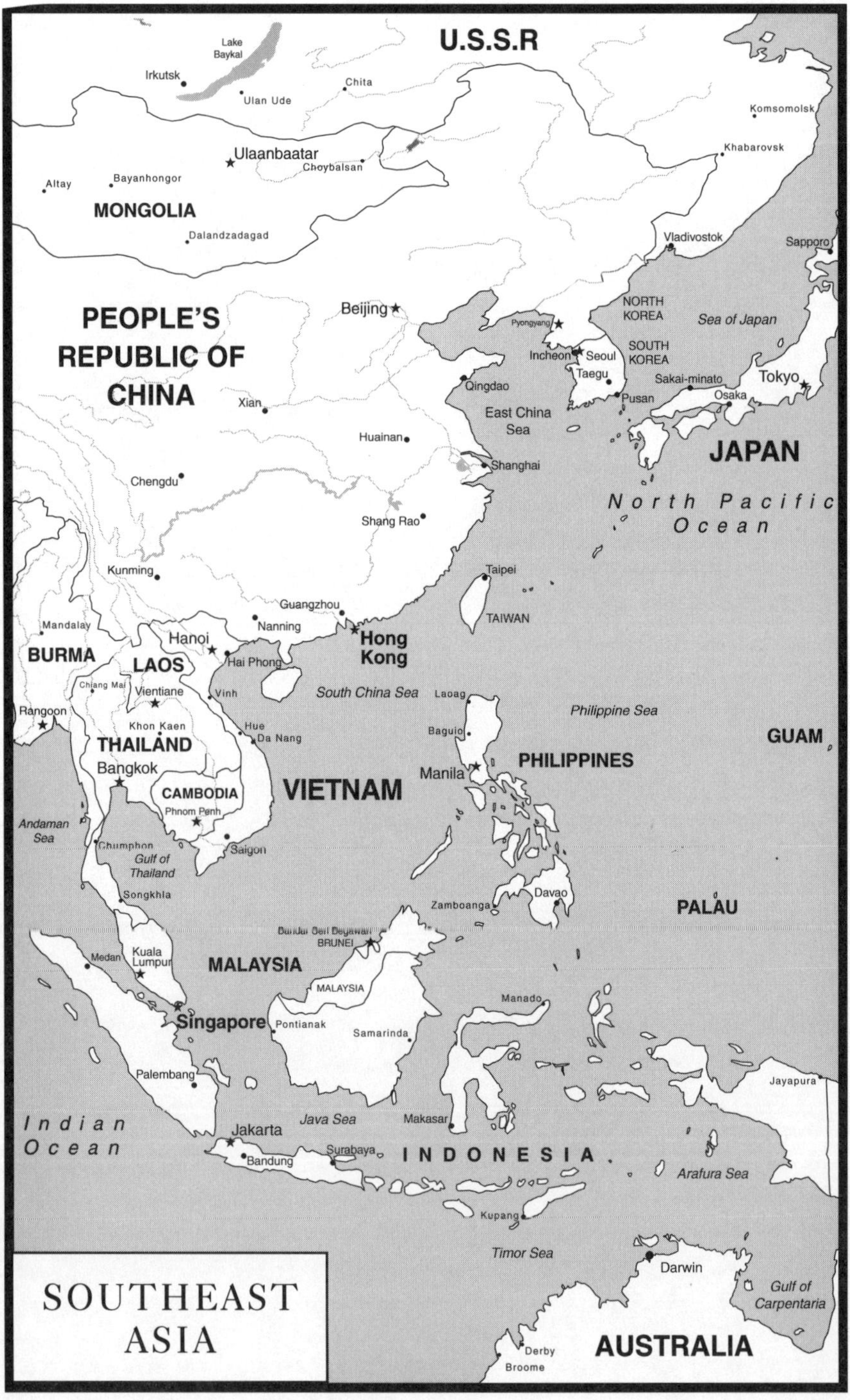

SOUTHEAST ASIA

SEVEN

Aftermath

TO BE APPOINTED an ambassador, the president's representative to a foreign government, is an honor. For a Foreign Service officer, it can be the capstone of a career. I was forty-nine years old and pleased to reach this goal at a relatively young age.

After leaving the East Asia bureau, I immersed myself in preparations—studying the Malay language, reading the Malaysia desk files, as well as books and articles on Malaysia, talking with people who knew Malaysia. I knew little about Malaysia other than what I had picked up from my responsibilities regarding Southeast Asia in the previous three years and from my brief visit there with Nelson Rockefeller. I had also accompanied the new Malaysian ambassador, Zain Azraai, when he called on President Ford to present his credentials. Zain, a career diplomat, had been a special assistant to the prime minister at the time of the Rockefeller visit. His appointment to Washington had already been announced. Unusually handsome, with piercing black eyes, a halo of flowing black hair, and a carefully trimmed beard, and resplendently dressed for the occasion in the traditional Malay dress, Zain cut a fine figure in the Oval Office. President Ford was gracious during the brief ceremony, although he gave the impression he was not sure whom he was receiving, or where Malaysia was, until he referred to his notes.

Malaysia was a small, relatively prosperous, newly independent nation, a former British colony and now a member of the Commonwealth. It had achieved its independence through negotiation and not through bloodshed. It was the world's top producer of tin, rubber, and palm oil. We were content that it remained more or less in the British sphere of influence.

After its own successful thirteen-year struggle against an internal communist insurgency, Malaysia had chosen to remain neutral in the great Cold War struggle, keeping its distance from both the United States and the Soviet Union. In fact, it was promoting ZOPFAN—a proposal for making Southeast Asia a Zone of Peace, Freedom, and Neutrality, free of even the transit of nuclear weapons and nuclear-powered vessels. We found this awkward, unrealistic, and incompatible with our security commitments in the region, even in the post-Vietnam world. Nevertheless, the Malaysians did not press the concept but kept it alive as a long-term goal. This made it acceptable to us.

The United States was Malaysia's most important market. Malaysia, too, looked to the United States to protect it from the threat of communism, even though Malaysia refused to align itself directly with us in that struggle. Finally, Malaysia looked to America, among others, as a source of educational and technical assistance—Fulbright programs, the Peace Corps, student scholarships, and so on.[1]

My predecessor, Francis Underhill, advised me to take a hobby to Kuala Lumpur, arguing that I would not be kept busy enough with my official activities. In the Foreign Service, Malaysia had a reputation of being a good place to serve—a tropical garden spot still basking in the old British colonial aura of spacious villas with verandas and ceiling fans, servants and amahs, well-manicured lawns, clubs for golf and tennis, and hill stations at nearby Fraser's Hill and the Cameron Highlands where one could escape the oppressive heat from time to time.

Malaysia was beginning to come more to our attention however. Growing numbers of Vietnamese boat people were landing on Malaysia's beaches, and Malaysia was assuming a prominent role in the Association of Southeast Asian Nations (ASEAN), which was gathering momentum as a regional grouping. It was also of increasing interest to American business. Exxon and Shell had found sizable deposits of oil and natural gas there, and high-tech firms—Texas Instruments, Intel, and others—were building factories and employing a low-cost workforce of highly trainable young Malaysians for their computer-chip and other assembly lines. Also, Malaysia was quietly responsive to the Defense Department's overtures for periodic ship visits and other forms of occasional cooperation between our armed services, including the sale of military equipment.

My Senate hearing was a formality for the same reason—Malaysia was not controversial either in our foreign policy or in our domestic politics. I was confirmed promptly and planned to arrive in Kuala Lumpur in sufficient time to present my credentials to the king—the Yang di Pertuan Agung (paramount ruler)—in time also to be able to host the traditional Fourth of July reception at our residence. I had a round of calls to make in Washington before departing, both in the State Department and in other agencies that had programs and interests in Malaysia and that had elements in the embassy there, such as the Defense, Agriculture, and Treasury Departments, the Peace Corps, and the Drug Enforcement Agency. In New York, through the Business Council for International Understanding (BCIU), I arranged a program of meetings with

U.S. firms operating in Malaysia. And, in the tradition of diplomatic courtesies, Ambassador Zain and his wife, Dawn, gave Kaity and me a memorable dinner with friends to send us off to their country.

Finally, I was sworn in, with Kaity holding the Bible and with our children, George and Margaret, present, as were a few close friends and Ambassador Zain. The ceremony was held in Phil Habib's office, with Phil presiding. I invited Dick Holbrooke, since he not only was an old friend but also would be my immediate "boss" as assistant secretary of state for East Asian and Pacific affairs. Characteristically detained by many higher-priority demands, Dick rushed in just as the ceremony finished. He invited Kaity and me to meet with him in his office. During our brief meeting, Dick took phone calls, summoned aides, and generally was not focusing on the new ambassador to Malaysia and his wife. We took our leave and expressed the hope that he would visit Kuala Lumpur (which he eventually did).

I had one key management decision to make before departing: to choose a deputy chief of mission, the person who would act in my absence and who would be my most important counselor. My predecessor had already departed Kuala Lumpur, as had his deputy, Robert Dillon. (Frank Underhill was retiring, and Dillon was going as deputy chief of mission to Ankara, Turkey.) The political counselor, Frank Bennett, was also leaving a month after my arrival and after getting me settled in and introduced around.

One of the few prerogatives remaining to an American ambassador at the time was the right to choose a deputy, rather than just leave it to the department to decide. The person at the top of my own list was James Rosenthal. We had served together in Vietnam, on the Vietnam desk, and at the Vietnam Peace Talks. Also, he was director of the newly combined Vietnam, Cambodia, and Lao desks at the time I was deputy assistant secretary. He and his wife, Britta, were good friends from our days together in Vietnam. In addition to being fellow political officers, Jim and I had spent the night in the naval dispensary together after the Saigon embassy bombing in March 1965, having our face wounds stitched up—a special kind of bonding. We did not always agree, but I valued his invariably good advice and sound judgment and trusted his integrity and honesty completely. Fortunately, it was a good career move for Jim, and the timing was right for him.

We were a good team, and our collaboration lasted two years. Jim then jumped at the chance to move to Manila as deputy chief of mission of one of the biggest American embassies in the world. I was reluctant to let him go, but could not stand in his way. He and Britta thrived there.

For my third and final year in Kuala Lumpur, I chose Lyall Breckon as my deputy. Lyall and his wife, Claire, had served with us in Vietnam and had also served in Thailand. I felt the same way about Lyall as I had about Jim; our collaboration was equally fruitful.

Although I could have turned down candidates for other positions in the embassy if I had felt strongly about it, I accepted the people sent by the agencies they worked for. Their quality was almost uniformly high. It was a good embassy, one I was comfortable with, one that I felt carried out its tasks well and effectively in the U.S. interest.

Arriving in Malaysia in mid-June 1977, we were immediately caught up in a swirl of activities—presentation of credentials to the paramount ruler and calls on the prime minister and his cabinet ministers. I learned that one minister, Paul Leong, minister for primary industries (who later became a good friend) was convinced that I was a member of the Secret Service because he remembered seeing me get off the plane as a member of Nelson Rockefeller's party the previous year!

I also held meetings and receptions to meet the embassy team and their families, the American business community, the dean of the diplomatic corps, and my other diplomatic colleagues. Preparations for the Fourth of July reception needed my review and approval. Also, tradition in Kuala Lumpur held that all ambassadors should call on each of the nine hereditary sultans and four appointed governors of Malaysia's thirteen states. This gave Kaity and me the opportunity to travel to every corner of the country, including Sarawak and Sabah on Borneo in East Malaysia, and provided fascinating insights to the history and culture of the Malays and their predominant religion, Islam. This travel also proved important in giving us a grasp of the extent and variety of American activity throughout the country, including business enterprises, Peace Corps projects, and liaison with educational institutions.

Our residence in Kuala Lumpur was an old, spacious British colonial villa surrounded by a large tropical garden that bordered on the Royal Selangor Golf Club. Its household staff of Chinese, Malays, and Indians was a mirror image of Malaysia as a whole, with its ethnic and religious diversity and tensions.

A central fact of modern Malaysia was—and continues to be—its delicate ethnic balance among its 47 percent Muslim Malay plurality, its large 37 percent Chinese minority, and its small 9 percent Indian minority. The Malays were indigenous (*bumiputra,* or "sons of the soil"), while many of the Chinese and Indians were descendants of Chinese and Indian workers brought in by the British in the nineteenth century to work in the tin mines and on the rubber and oil palm plantations.

In 1969, less than a decade before we arrived there, ethnic tensions between Malays and Chinese had erupted into violence and bloodshed, leading to the resignation and retirement of Tunku (Prince) Abdul Rahman, Malaysia's "George Washington" and first prime minister. Although the Malays by constitutional fiat controlled the country's government and politics, the Chinese by instinct, initiative, and business sense controlled the economy. The race riots of 1969 led the Malaysian government to establish its New Economic Policy, a massive affirmative action program aimed at lifting the economic status of the economically disadvantaged Malays and reducing the economic, financial, and commercial power of the Chinese community.

Another central fact of Malaysia was (but by now has been largely overcome) that its enviable prosperity as a world-class producer of primary products—tin, rubber, and palm oil—was highly vulnerable to the price swings of its products in the world market. When prices were down, the economy suffered and unemployment surged, which heightened ethnic tension. It also affected Malaysian-U.S. relations. Because the United States was Malaysia's biggest market, Malaysian authorities tended to blame the international price swings on mysterious market manipulators in London, New York, and Chicago.

This issue was one of the mainstays of the North-South dialogue in and out of the United Nations—the dialogue between the industrialized "have" nations of the Northern Hemisphere and the developing, mostly newly independent "have-not" nations of the Southern Hemisphere. The United States, as the leading and most powerful "have" nation, was the principal target of the dissatisfaction of the "have-nots."

The United Nations had created the United Nations Conference on Trade and Development (UNCTAD) to deal with the issue. UNCTAD was divided into two blocs, the G-7 (Group of Seven) industrialized nations (the United States, the United Kingdom, Germany, France, Canada, Italy, and Japan) and the G-66, the developing nations. Over the years, the major producers and major consumers of a number of primary products, like tin, rubber, coffee, and cocoa, had worked out elaborate agreements for regulating and moderating the effects of price swings on the producing economies. These agreements included provisions for price ceilings and floors that if reached and passed called for market intervention of one kind or another by the great consuming nations—either buying into or selling from the accumulated stockpile of the product.

These agreements were never very effective and each time they came up for renewal were the subject of difficult and protracted negotiation. Finally, UNCTAD came up with the concept of the Common Fund, which sought to combine several such agreements under one overall fund to allow for greater flexibility by operating each individual fund in a bigger pot. But the Common Fund negotiations themselves were difficult and protracted because consumers and producers continued to have very different perspectives.

During my tenure in Malaysia, however, the principal issue I had to deal with was the massive, uncontrolled flow of Vietnamese boat people across Malaysia's beaches on the east coast of the Malay Peninsula as well as in East Malaysia on Borneo. For the Malaysians, in particular the Malay-dominated government, this uncontrolled flow represented a threat to Malaysia's national security and to its delicate racial balance (to Malays the Vietnamese are indistinguishable from Chinese; many of the boat people were indeed of Chinese origin). In Malaysia's eyes, the United States was to blame for this situation: It had not only created the problem by engaging in a lengthy and bloody war from which Malaysia had wanted to stay far away but worse, had lost that war, causing thousands upon thousands of refugees to flee to escape the consequences.[2]

In September, three months after Kaity and I arrived in Kuala Lumpur, Prime Minister Dato Hussein Onn and his wife, Datin Suhaila, went to Washington on an official visit. Following the prevailing practice at the time, we accompanied them and participated in the visit. It was an indispensable opportunity to get better acquainted with both the prime minister and his wife and get firsthand a feeling for U.S.-Malaysian relations at the highest level, as well as a chance to meet President Carter and Vice President Walter Mondale. Especially for smaller countries that do not occupy much of the president's or secretary of state's attention, an official visit obliges the bureaucracy to review carefully all aspects of our bilateral relations and to highlight problems and opportunities for improving them through top-level discussions. For the Malaysian leader, the visit offered the chance to appraise the new U.S. president face-to-face, to get a sense of U.S. policy in the region post-Vietnam, and to get directly across to the president and other senior U.S. officials Malaysia's point of view and its concerns about U.S. policy and actions.

Jimmy Carter received Hussein Onn in the White House Cabinet Room. Both leaders were surrounded by aides, which on the Malaysian side included Foreign Minister Tengku Ahmad Rithauddeen and Ambassador Zain Azraai. On the American side, the vice president was present, as were Assistant Secretary Holbrooke, myself, and aides from the National Security Council staff.[3]

The discussions, which probably lasted an hour or so, were unremarkable; but they served the always useful diplomatic purpose of focusing the president's attention, however briefly, on a friendly country, if in this case one not vitally important to U.S. interests. The meeting demonstrated that the United States cared about Malaysia, gave Hussein Onn the opportunity to develop at least briefly personal rapport with the free world's most powerful leader, and gave him the added cachet at home of a face-to-face meeting with the U.S. president. My meeting the president in person was useful, as I was after all his personal representative in Malaysia. One impression I got from that meeting confirmed Jimmy Carter's reputation for mastering his briefing book. He rarely looked at it, yet knew in detail the subjects to be treated.

Vice President Mondale gave Hussein Onn an official luncheon in one of the small dining rooms on the State Department's eighth floor—another pleasant but hardly memorable occasion, capped by the exchange of informal, generalized remarks and brief toasts.

My most lasting impression of the visit was offered by the prime minister's return hospitality—dinner in Blair House, across Pennsylvania Avenue from the White House, where Hussein Onn and his party were the guests of the U.S. government. Official visits to Washington are carefully calibrated with elaborately worked out protocol. The Hussein Onn visit was not a state visit and therefore did not call for a formal White House dinner hosted by the president. The luncheon by the vice president suited the occasion in terms of U.S. protocol. However, the highest-ranking American official to attend the prime minister's dinner at Blair House was Assistant Secretary of State Holbrooke—high ranking perhaps in the State Department but quite junior in rank to represent the U.S. government at a dinner given by the head of a friendly government in Washington. My wife and I were present, but no secretary of state, no national security adviser, nor even an under secretary of state.

Since the ranking American guest was so junior, the prime minister delegated his hostly toasting duties to his ambassador, Zain Azraai. Just as Ambassador Zain rose and began to speak, a waiter approached Holbrooke and whispered in his ear. Holbrooke left the table and took a telephone call in another room. By the time he returned, Zain had finished his gracious toast, and no American response was delivered. The dinner thus ended on a slightly unfinished, uncertain note. I remembered Nelson Rockefeller's gaffe in Kuala Lumpur a year earlier when, as Hussein Onn's guest, he toasted "the president of Malaysia," covering his embarrassment with a chuckle and a friendly arm thrown around the prime minister's shoulders. As far as I could tell, this evening's slight never affected Hussein Onn's attitude toward the United States or the Carter administration. Perhaps it, and the earlier Rockefeller incident, only confirmed his impression that they were dealing with a slightly bar-

barian superpower. In any case, I doubt that Hussein Onn's successor, Mahathir bin Mohamed, would have been so forgiving, based on his reaction to similar slights, real or imagined.

Fortified by my participation in discussions of U.S.-Malaysian relations at the highest level, I returned to Kuala Lumpur to resume my new responsibilities. Southeast Asia was still adjusting to America's defeat and exclusion from Vietnam, as well as to its gradual normalization of relations with Beijing. Before going to Washington, I had attended, along with the other members of the diplomatic corps, ASEAN's ceremonial tenth anniversary meeting of heads of government. Hussein Onn hosted Lee Kuan Yew of Singapore, Ferdinand Marcos of the Philippines, General Suharto of Indonesia, and General Kriangsak of Thailand. ASEAN, still a fledgling and, in American eyes, amorphous regional association, was clearer in declaring what it was not than what it was. It was not a regional security organization, specifically eschewing discussion of security issues; it was thus not the linear descendant of SEATO, the creature of the United States. Neither was it a body for formal political consultation since two of its members, Thailand and the Philippines, retained security ties with the United States, while the other three embraced nonalignment in one form or another. So what it professed to be was a regional grouping of neighboring states that sought to develop economic and commercial ties with each other and, as it became possible, to lower trade barriers against each other and with the outside world. The very vagueness of its purpose, confusing and bemusing to the outside world, turned out to be the secret of its slow and tentative accumulation of self-confidence and strength.

The outside world, accustomed to the confrontation and bipolarity of the Cold War, tended to give short shrift to a regional grouping with unclear aims whose members were relatively small (except for Indonesia), newly independent members of the international community. Moreover, the members had little to recommend themselves to one another. Each of them had historic antipathies for the others—tribal, cultural, or colonial. Ever since their independence, their relations hardly suggested much in the way of peace and friendship. Under Sukarno, Indonesia had virtually gone to war with Malaysia. Singapore had broken away from Malaysia in less-than-friendly circumstances. Malaysia had territorial disputes with Thailand and the Philippines and exchanged charges with them of harboring subversive elements aimed at overthrowing established neighboring governments.

No self-respecting Western political analyst was willing to predict much of a future for an entity with so many strikes against it. Yet, its cautious, step-by-step, lowest-common-denominator approach gradually took hold and began to gather forward momentum. Below the surface, ASEAN had a number of elements in its favor. All of its members, without exception, had had experience with communist subversion and insurrection against struggling, newly established independent governments. All of them had successfully withstood these onslaughts and viewed the communist victory against America in Vietnam as an ominous portent for the region. They all had a powerful interest in banding together against what they saw as a common threat; and their common solution in the wake of the resounding American failure in Vietnam was to seek accommodation and friendship rather than confrontation.

The United States, Europe, Japan, and other members of the noncommunist world had every interest in seeing ASEAN succeed, to prevent what had happened in Vietnam from spreading beyond Cambodia and Laos. Even as they doubted its prospects, they were eager to befriend ASEAN and do what they could to nurture its fragile existence. The Soviet Union, whose ally, Vietnam, had succeeded so spectacularly against the United States, remained suspicious of ASEAN, convinced that the United States was behind it as another way to confront communism in the region. During a tête-à-tête luncheon discussion, the Soviet ambassador was clear in voicing such suspicions to me. Later on, when his government decided that it, too, should get on the ASEAN bandwagon, the ambassador denied that he had ever been negative on the subject.

China was more ambivalent from the beginning. In addition to its historical enmity toward Vietnam, China considered continued Soviet-Vietnamese collaboration in the region inimical to its interests. China therefore sought to cultivate good relations with ASEAN and its individual members.

ASEAN's policy toward the outside world was simple: It sought to befriend everyone who would be friendly to it. Gradually it began inviting other governments to its annual foreign ministers meetings for "dialogue" sessions outside the formal ASEAN sessions. All those invited, including the United States, responded positively. On the first occasion of a ministerial-level ASEAN-U.S. dialogue in 1979 in Bali, Indonesia, Secretary of State Cyrus Vance convoked U.S. ambassadors to ASEAN countries to Bali for internal U.S. consultations. It was at this meeting that the ASEAN foreign ministers started what has become a tradition at such dialogue sessions: a musical evening at which every ministerial participant is expected to perform solo. Vance could only be persuaded to do so if accompanied by his ambassadors, so I found myself along with my colleagues from other ASEAN countries singing with the secretary of state an old American favorite—"You Are My Sunshine"!

At the same time, each ASEAN country was adjusting its own bilateral relations with China and Vietnam. As a member of the diplomatic corps in Kuala Lumpur, I shook hands with both Prime Minister Pham Van Dong of Vietnam and Prime Minister Deng Xiaoping of China on their respective arrivals (September and November 1978) at Kuala Lumpur's Subang International Airport on state visits, sealing Malaysia's normalization of relations with both countries. I also attended state dinners in their honor, hosted by Prime Minister Hussein Onn. Gradually, the rifts caused by the Cold War and the confrontations of the superpowers were being closed.

However, the problem that continued to absorb most of my attention, because of its threatened negative impact on U.S.-Malaysian relations and its potential to destabilize the ASEAN region, was the mushrooming, uncontrolled arrival of thousands upon thousands of Vietnamese refugees. Dubbed the boat people, they poured across Malaysia's beaches and those of the Philippines, Indonesia, and Singapore, seeking asylum from the new Communist masters in Vietnam. The inevitably lagging response of the international community, including that of the United States, to this human tragedy led Malaysian authorities on occasion to resort to extreme measures to try to solve the problem alone or to dramatize their insistence that the international community drastically step up its efforts to remove the refugees from Malaysia. Local authorities on Malaysia's east coast more than once sought to prevent often overloaded and unseaworthy refugee boats from landing, or the boats would actually be pushed—or towed—back out to sea. These tactics sometimes resulted in the accidental drowning of some refugees, which attracted negative publicity for Malaysia in the world's media. This in turn irritated U.S.-Malaysian relations even more.

The most celebrated case of apparent Malaysian callousness in this regard was that of the *Hai Hong*, a dilapidated, rusting freighter out of Hong Kong with more than twenty-five hundred Vietnamese refugees aboard in shocking conditions of overcrowding, undernourishment, disease, and filth. The *Hai Hong*, with its cargo of human castaways, appeared off Klang, the west coast port for Kuala Lumpur, only twenty-five miles away.[4] The Malaysian government got the world's attention—and ours in particular—by announcing that the ship would be towed out to sea to prevent the refugees from landing in Malaysia. As the terrible conditions aboard ship became known, the world press's reporting evoked outrage that the Malaysians could be so inhumane. I received a phone call from Dick Holbrooke in the middle of the night saying, in effect, that he had just come from Secretary of State Vance's office and that Vance's instructions to me in no uncertain terms were that I was not to allow the ship to be towed out to sea. I told Holbrooke I would do my best.

The next morning, at my request the prime minister, flanked by his flamboyant, acerbic minister for home affairs, Ghazalie Shafie, received me to discuss the issue. After impressing me with the seriousness of their intent not to allow the refugees to land on Malaysian soil, and my impressing them with the serious repercussions in the international community of the inhumane act of turning away sick and helpless people in flight for their lives, we came to a practical solution: Malaysia would allow the ship to dock if the United States would guarantee that the refugees would be processed for resettlement on board the ship and then be taken direct to the airport for onward flights to their resettlement countries. Mentally crossing my fingers that Washington and the rest of the international community would support the arrangement, I gave my guarantee. Happily, the arrangement held and was carried out, and the dramatic case of the *Hai Hong* became history.

The other celebrated case in which the world's attention was again focused negatively on Malaysia occurred when then Deputy Prime Minister Mahathir bin Mohamed was quoted in the world's press to the effect that if refugees kept pouring across Malaysia's beaches, and if the response of the international community continued to be inadequate, Malaysia might have to shoot the refugees.[5] This brought more headlines around the world and more statements of outrage from public figures and from governments. A visit was hastily arranged of a joint congressional select committee headed by the late congressman Benjamin Rosenthal to look into the refugee problem in Malaysia, and presumably to read the riot act to Mahathir. When the committee arrived, word came that Mahathir would see them immediately. We went directly from the airport to Mahathir's office (thereby causing consternation at the residence, where Kaity had to put on hold the scheduled luncheon for the delegation and members of the embassy staff). Mahathir immediately disarmed the group by saying the press must have misunderstood him when he had said "we might have to shoo the refugees away." Another public affairs crisis was thereby quickly consigned to history's dustbin, even though no one—perhaps including Mahathir—has ever been quite sure what he actually did say.

Throughout these high-profile events the international response to Southeast Asia's refugee crisis gathered momentum. The countries of Southeast Asia, including Malaysia, were persuaded, with varying degrees of success and enthusiasm, to fulfill their international humanitarian obligations as members of the United Nations to serve as states of first asylum. Countries around the world, including principally the United States, Canada, France, Australia, and New Zealand, undertook programs of permanent resettlement. The United Nations High Commission for Refugees (UNHCR) coordinated these national efforts establishing refugee reception centers, holding centers, processing centers, and so on. National nongovernmental organizations (NGOs) worked to find resettlement opportunities for individual refugees and their families—in all, a monumental, costly, and largely successful international effort.

During my nearly three years in Malaysia, from 1977 to 1980, over 120,000 Vietnamese refugees poured across Malaysia's beaches alone. Nearly 90,000 were resettled elsewhere, including over 50,000 in the United States. To highlight the American refugee effort to the Malaysian public, we organized a well-publicized departure ceremony at Kuala Lumpur's Subang International Airport for the 30,000th refugee and his family departing Malaysia for the United States. In August 1977, shortly after I arrived in Malaysia, fewer than 200 refugees per month were being resettled in the United States from Malaysia. By late 1979, more than 5,000 refugees per month were leaving Malaysia for the United States.

The diplomatic effort to accomplish this feat was considerable, but it never could have been done without the dedication and hard work of our embassy's refugee coordinator and his staff, who actually saw to the implementation of what diplomacy had agreed to. Joseph Gettier, a young, tough-but-oh-so-gentle AID employee with the face and build of a boxer, the heart and soul of a missionary, and the drive and managerial and diplomatic skills of a CEO of a major corporation, overcame every obstacle to accomplish his mission: to increase the outflow of refugees from Malaysia to the United States. When he needed my help, my door was always open to him.

Before refugees could leave for the United States, they had to be identified and interviewed to determine their eligibility for refugee status under American immigration law and regulations; they had to be given physical examinations; individual sponsors had to be found for each refugee family resettled in the United States, a task undertaken by the numerous NGOs under contract to the U.S. government; and, finally, plane reservations and specific travel plans had to be made for each refugee.

All that was the easy part. Gettier and his staff also worked tirelessly with the Malaysian and UNHCR authorities and other diplomatic missions to establish camps with adequate living and sanitary facilities that met internationally established criteria for first-asylum countries for the mushrooming numbers of refugees pouring into the country. This was not an easy task. The Malaysians, understandably, were totally unprepared for such an influx of what were for them illegal immigrants, and they resented having to provide even temporary facilities for them. They also were fearful that this influx would upset their delicate internal racial balance. Moreover, the great influx of refugees occurred on the east coast of peninsular Malaysia, one of the most, if not the most, traditional Malay Muslim regions of the country, and a region where the moderate, middle-of-the-road Malaysian government faced its most determined militant Muslim opposition. The Malaysian government's solution to this potentially troubling domestic political problem was to designate an uninhabited island off the east coast, Pulau Bidong, as its principal refugee reception facility. Increasing numbers of refugees were placed on the island, at first with wholly inadequate living and sanitary facilities. The refugees themselves had to slap together primitive sleeping quarters and trench-type toilet facilities. The outside world was critical of Malaysia's seeming callousness toward these hapless victims of war, and that increased Malaysia's resentment and resistance.

Gradually these problems were resolved, thanks in large part to the skillful, tireless, and sensitive work of Joe Gettier and his staff. But other problems remained: problems with the NGOs and with the local UNHCR staff, interagency problems within the U.S. government, and problems of accelerating the resettlement countries' intake procedures. Even dealing with our government presented its own difficulties. As Washington kept the pressure up on countries in the region to let the refugees in, improve their facilities, and so forth, these countries kept pressing Washington and other capitals to increase and speed up their intake. In Washington and elsewhere, budgetary, organizational, bureaucratic, and federal-state tensions, as well as domestic politics, created obstacles to increasing the intake as rapidly as needed. U.S. behavior in this regard affected not only the behavior of the first-asylum countries but also of other resettlement countries, which faced their own budgetary and domestic political obstacles. Only by giving a pacesetting example could the United States hope to obtain cooperation from first-asylum and resettlement countries alike adequate to the challenge. This was a message that I and my colleagues in other countries of Southeast Asia had to keep hammering away at with Washington, which was absorbed in its own difficulties.

Little by little, momentum gathered, and by late 1979 the Southeast Asian countries began to see some light at the end of the tunnel. The numbers of refugees leaving for permanent resettlement elsewhere were up, programs were running smoothly, and the volume of new refugee arrivals was tapering off; but the conditions of post-Vietnam Southeast Asia continued to be fragile.

When the Carter administration came into office in January 1977, it had the firm intention of normalizing relations with the new Vietnam. Both Secretary of State Cyrus Vance and Assistant Secretary Richard Holbrooke were convinced that normalization would contribute to the security and stability of Southeast Asia and begin to integrate Vietnam into the Southeast Asian body of nations. But it was not to be for nearly fifteen more years.

Vietnam demanded, as a price for normalization, the $4.7 billion in "reparations" that the Nixon administration had secretly offered (as aid, but without consultation with the Congress) as part of the agreements ending the war in 1973. By the time the Vietnamese had dropped this unrealistic condition, late in 1978, it was too late. Vietnam's relations with the Khmer Rouge regime in Phnom Penh were deteriorating. In December 1978, its patience exhausted by repeated cross-border incursions by Chinese-supported Khmer Rouge forces, Vietnam invaded and occupied Cambodia. Vietnam's action came only weeks after it had signed a treaty of friendship with the Soviet Union, and only days after the United States and China announced that they were normalizing their diplomatic relations and exchanging ambassadors. To Hanoi it was clear that the United States was giving priority to repairing its relations with China over taking the same action with Vietnam.

China became alarmed at what it saw as a Soviet-Vietnamese outflanking action threatening its southern border. In February 1979, fortified by its renewed relations with the United States and Deng Xiaoping's recently completed visit to Washington, China attacked Vietnam across their common border "to teach Vietnam a lesson."[6]

Vietnam's actions made it impossible for the United States to proceed with normalization and gave ammunition to National Security Adviser Zbigniew Brzezinski, who preferred to annoy the Soviet Union by completing the normalization of relations with China. Complicating U.S. consideration of the Vietnam normalization issue, as it did for the next fifteen years, was the widespread belief in the United States that Vietnam continued to hold hundreds of U.S. prisoners of war that they had been committed to release with the signing of the Paris Peace Agreements in 1973 that ended the U.S. military involvement in Vietnam.

Clearly, the Cold War was not yet over in Southeast Asia. More than ever, the region was divided by a "bamboo curtain" between Communist Vietnam, Laos, and Cambodia—all dominated by a reunified Vietnam of nearly 70 million people—and noncommunist ASEAN. Moreover, Vietnam's strike against Cambodia placed strains upon the fragile cohesion of ASEAN. Thailand, ASEAN's "frontline state," now faced Vietnamese troops on its border—a border that had long been ill-defined and contested. The Thai government, historically inclined to "bend with the wind" to defend its independence and no longer certain of its security link to the United States, looked to China as an anchor to windward to protect it from Vietnam. Indonesia and Malaysia, on the other hand, both having suffered from internal subversions supported by China, saw Vietnam as a useful regional counterweight to China. Unlike Thailand, they were not directly threatened by Vietnam—except by its refugee outflow—and did not want to give China an excuse for again meddling in the region.

As for Vietnam, it was doing what came naturally—seeking to dominate its weaker neighbors on its western borders—a fact obscured by the Cold War and inadequately understood by the United States when it had deepened its involvement there in the 1950s and 1960s. For two thousand years, Vietnam first had fought for its independence from China, which it achieved in A.D. 939. Then it began expanding its own territory south and westward, overrunning and destroying the Cham empire and driving the Khmer empire back from the South China Sea behind its present-day borders. Only the arrival of the French colonizers in the mid-nineteenth century stopped Vietnam's advance against much smaller, much weaker Cambodia and Laos. Now that Vietnam had finally disposed of the Americans, it was on the march again, provoked by a Cambodian Communist regime that sought Chinese support against the hated Vietnamese.

Fortunately for all, including the United States, and despite their differences over Cambodia, the ASEAN nations attached high priority to maintaining their own unity, as well as their friendship with all nations. In the end, this policy prevailed and the strains within ASEAN were kept within bounds. Indeed, ASEAN cohesion in the face of Vietnam's invasion and occupation of Cambodia eventually proved to be a key factor in negotiating Vietnam's withdrawal, a UN-sponsored peaceful solution, and national elections that restored a legitimate government to Cambodia. In the wake of the collapse of the Soviet Union, ASEAN cohesion subsequently led to the entry of Vietnam, Cambodia, and Laos into ASEAN as full-fledged members and to removal of a final vestige of the Cold War from Southeast Asia.

One area that has continued to cause some stress in U.S.-Malaysian relations concerns other Arab-Israeli issues. Malaysia, by its constitution and the plurality of its population, is a Muslim country headed by a moderate Muslim government. Malaysia's domestic politics, which include active fundamentalist Islamic elements, obliges the government to side with Islam against its perceived enemies. This led Malaysia to oppose some aspects of U.S. policy in the Middle East and South Asia. When our hostages were taken in Iran in 1979, pictures of the Ayatollah Khomeini appeared overnight in Malay villages across the country. Vague threats against me as the American ambassador were made, which the embassy security officer and the Malaysian police took seriously enough that they gave me a team of bodyguards for a few days.

One incident in particular demonstrates Malaysia's different perspectives and sensitivities in this area. At the height of the refugee crisis, a delegation of the prestigious International Rescue Committee proposed to visit Malaysia and other first-asylum countries in the area to gain a firsthand view in the field. One of the delegation members was to be Rabbi Marc Tannenbaum, a distinguished and active member of the American Jewish community. Malaysia, as it invariably did, warmly welcomed the delegation's visit but said that Rabbi Tannenbaum would not be welcome. When I pointed out the unfortunate impression this act of discrimination would create in the United States, the foreign minister, Tengku Rithauddeen, alluded to the delicate situation that then existed between the Malaysian government and the state government of Kelantan. Kelantan is one of the centers of traditional Islam and at the time, Kuala Lumpur and Kota Baru, the capital of Kelantan, were engaged in a struggle for control of the state government. The Malaysian government was concerned that the visit of a high-profile American Jewish rabbi, active in Zionist causes in their eyes, could be used against them in their efforts to assure continued moderate direction in Kelantan. Rithauddeen added that he was sure the United States would not want to see radical forces gain momentum in Malaysia. In any case, despite my remonstrances and Washington's displeasure and embarrassment—and despite Rabbi Tannenbaum's understandable irritation—Malaysia remained adamant and Tannenbaum stayed away. Rithauddeen assured me that the rabbi would be welcome at any other time.

Some two months later, Washington said Rabbi Tannenbaum had renewed his request to visit Malaysia. I reminded Rithauddeen of his commitment, and Tannenbaum was welcomed with open arms. The crisis with Kelantan had passed, and the time was more propitious.

Malaysia's internal politics—including its economic policies—were interesting to observe, analyze, and report on. Also, the American embassy was blessed with an excellent staff, especially political officers Scott Butcher, who spoke fluent Malay, and Joseph Snyder, who spoke Chinese. The political section was fortunate to have Martha Morrow, a junior Foreign Service officer on her first assignment who had been a Peace Corps employee in Malaysia earlier and who spoke both Chinese and Malay.

Malaysia's basic social contract, embodied in its constitution, guaranteed control of the government by the Malay plurality and full participatory political rights for the large Chinese minority and the small Indian-Tamil minority. This political formula, worked out in negotiation with the British at independence, was designed to resolve, or at least cover over, Malaysia's "fatal flaw": endemic ethnic, cultural, and religious tension between, on the one hand, the indigenous Muslim Malays and, on the other, the nonindigenous Chinese—who are Buddhist, Confucianist, animist, or Christian—and the mostly Hindu Indians. Although the Malays were guaranteed political dominance, the Chinese controlled the economy, a situation that heightened potential tensions between the two groups.

Malaysia's New Economic Policy (NEP), instituted after the bloody race riots in 1969 that led to Tunku Abdul Rahman's retirement, was still in its infancy while I was in Malaysia. The NEP's central provision required that by 1991, business enterprises had to have one-third Malay participation in management, in the workforce, and in equity ownership. Great skepticism abounded both among Malaysians and in the diplomatic corps about the NEP's prospects.

By the time I arrived in Malaysia, Tunku Abdul Rahman's successor, Tun Razak, had died, Hussein Onn was prime minister, and Mahathir bin Mohamed was deputy prime minister and in charge of the NEP. Mahathir was a tough taskmaster and determined to make the NEP work (and, incidentally, to oblige foreign investors essentially to abide by the same rules). He was also determined to diversify Malaysia's economy, making it less vulnerable to the international price swings of its key primary products.

Mahathir was clearly Hussein Onn's heir apparent. Shortly after I left in March 1980, Mahathir became prime minister when Hussein Onn resigned in ill health. Behind Mahathir were two second-tier challengers: Dato Musa Hitam, minister of education, from the state of Johor, and Tengku Razaleigh, minister of finance, from the state of Kelantan. As it turned out, neither made the final cut and Mahathir remained in office. The real challenge for our political section was to alert Washington to younger political "comers" who had the potential to become leaders in the future. One such "comer" was Anwar Ibrahim, who until their falling out, was Mahathir's deputy prime minister and heir apparent. At the time, Anwar was a young Muslim student-activist who had spent time in prison for his radical political views. In our effort to maintain contact with all elements of the political spectrum, both to appraise their potential for leadership and their attitudes toward the United States, our political officers stayed in touch with Anwar, as well as many others, and were consistently impressed with his intelligence, conviction, drive—and essential moderation.

Those members of the government and senior civil servants with whom I maintained contact I found accessible, knowledgeable, and for the most part, highly professional, even though inevitably we could not agree on every issue. The two I was most uncomfortable with were Mahathir and the home affairs minister, Ghazalie Shafie. Mahathir was controversial even among his own colleagues and compatriots. Like Anwar Ibrahim, he had been the "Peck's bad boy" of his generation. He had written a book called *The Malay Dilemma,* which was unsparing in its criticism of the Malay leadership at the time and the Malay penchant for complaining about the more dynamic Chinese instead of doing something about it. Mahathir's book offended the prime minister at the time, Tunku Abdul Rahman, and its author was banished for some years to Singapore. Mahathir was also accused of not being a true Malay (he had a Muslim Indian father). A reserved man with a reputation for a sharp tongue (which he was inclined to use too liberally), he often made his interlocutor uncomfortable. At the same time, Mahathir was a man with a vision for his country, determined to make it economically developed and independent of Western political and economic domination, and still in power at this writing.

I also found Mahathir to be a man of his word. The newly formed American Business Council, officially established in 1978 with my encouragement, invited Mahathir to address its first scheduled business luncheon. In his speech, Mahathir outlined the New Economic Policy and invited American firms to participate actively in Malaysia's development—provided of course that they were prepared to play by Malaysia's rules. Mahathir went on to invite any American firm that found discrepancies between what he had told them that day and their actual experience in dealing with the Malaysian bureaucracy to come see him and "he would straighten things out." On at least one later occasion, an American businessman sought to take advantage of Mahathir's offer when he found that lower-level Malaysian officials were giving him what he considered to be treatment inconsistent with Mahathir's stated policies. Mahathir received him (and me) and promised to straighten out the matter at hand. The American businessman later expressed to me his satisfaction that the matter had indeed been resolved.

Ghazalie Shafie was something else again. Flamboyant, boisterous, and garrulous, he possessed an acerbic wit and tongue and loved to use them to put his visitors down. As minister for home affairs (internal security), he was directly responsible for carrying out Malaysia's refugee policy. Despite his often brusque and loquacious tactics as a tough negotiator, Ghazalie was reliable in carrying out his side of any bargain struck with American officials.

In the midst of all these activities, we received frequent official visitors, entertained them, and took them on their official calls: members of Congress, State Department and other U.S. government officials, and sometimes other public figures (including my older brother, Keith H. Miller, a former governor of Alaska). An arriving congressional delegation, informed of the death of former senator, vice president, and presidential candidate Hubert Humphrey, held an impromptu memorial service on the residence terrace before beginning our official briefing. Joan Baez, well-known American folksinger and anti–Vietnam War activist, came to give a concert to benefit Vietnamese refugees. Her sellout performance was a success, and afterward we gave her a reception at our residence. She made a big hit with Minister Ghazalie Shafie, her host for the occasion. Richard Celeste, then Peace Corps director, came to inspect refugee facilities and to explore the possibility of using Peace Corps volunteers in the refugee effort.

Sandwiched between these activities were Kaity's and my calls on the sultans and governors of all of Malaysia's states. Traveling to the various states, making these calls, visiting American facilities and activities—and seeing the beauty of the Malaysian countryside—added depth and dimension to our Malaysian experience.

The sultans and their palaces seemed to be an anachronism in a modern age—royalty at the state level, with its own traditions and pomp and circumstance. To call on the sultans and their wives required a certain protocol—hats, gloves, and stockings for the wives and dark business suits for the ambassadors. Yet to survive in a modern age, the sultans have to represent something more than tradition and history. In effect, they constitute an important Malay institution, political, social, and religious, which offers yet another Malay and Muslim bulwark in a multiethnic and multicultural society.

The sultan of Johor, in his eighties then, offered us a tour of his palace and his collections of costumes and of silver and gold, and then invited us to lunch. One memento of America that he obviously prized was a signed photograph of Jack Lord, the actor who starred in the television series *Hawaii Five-O.* The governor of Penang entertained us at dinner, during which unseen and silent servants concealed behind curtains swung back and forth a giant *punkah* over our heads to keep us cool.

After a hot and dusty train ride for seven hours through dense, majestic jungle to Kelantan, one of the most traditionally Muslim of Malaysia's states, I asked for a cold beer at the guest house and immediately realized I had committed a blunder. Also in Kelantan, I visited my first Vietnamese refugee camp. I looked forward to the visit with some trepidation. I was not sure how the refugees would receive the American ambassador representing the country that had let them down and led to their actual plight as refugees. To my surprise, I was received with great applause when I greeted them with my few words of Vietnamese. Many of the refugees of course hoped to be resettled in the United States, so despite whatever feelings they had about the past, they were looking to the future.

In Trengganu, on the east coast south of Kelantan, we drove along a coastline of vast white-sand beaches dotted with coconut palms. Here I visited Pulau Bidong, the island refugee center that became Malaysia's principal holding center for refugees being processed for resettlement. Conditions there when I visited were already overcrowded and primitive. They spurred us to step up our programs to remove refugees from such living conditions (which improved over time), but the island center served Malaysian purposes in isolating the refugees from the general population.

In Sarawak, on the island of Borneo, we visited a longhouse (a traditional tribal village with many family habitations under one long roof) some forty miles outside Sarawak's capital, Kuching. At the end of the road we were greeted by the headman, his family, and other notables, all dressed in traditional costumes, which were supplemented for the women with Playtex bras to conform to modern tastes. We were led on foot into the jungle along a stream for another twenty minutes or so to arrive at the longhouse. There we were received with great ceremony, which included drinking a strong wine *(tuak)* from a common coconut half shell passed around among us and joining in the ceremonial dancing.

Aside from official travels, Kaity and I made our own excursions. Our favorite, which we repeated many times, was to drive on Friday night to Port Dickson on the Strait of Malacca, an hour and a half southwest of Kuala Lumpur, and stay the night at the beachside Si-Rusa Inn, an old, somewhat rundown hotel managed by Indians. On Saturday we would drive further south to Malacca, one of Malaysia's most historic towns, for a day of sightseeing, souvenir hunting, and good eating. Malacca was converted to Islam in the late fourteenth century by a Javanese prince fleeing his rivals in Java. It was visited by Chinese admiral Cheng Ho with his fleet in the early fifteenth century and was captured by the Portuguese in 1511 as they pushed their explorations eastward after Prince Henry the Navigator had rounded the Cape of Good Hope. Then the Dutch took it from the Portuguese in the seventeenth century, and the British took it from the Dutch early in the nineteenth century in exchange for British enclaves on the island of Sumatra. Today, Malacca still bears the traces of each of these layers of civilization and culture. It remains a fascinating place to visit.

On Saturday evening we would return to the Si-Rusa in Port Dickson, spend the night again, and return to Kuala Lumpur on Sunday afternoon.

When Kaity and I returned to the United States on home leave in the fall of 1979, I learned in Washington that Ben Read, the under secretary of state for management, had his eye on me for a senior management job in the department. I was not keen on a management job, but it was at the level of an assistant secretary—another step up the career ladder and one I needed if I ever expected to be promoted to the rank of career minister. I had passed my fiftieth birthday in Malaysia and had not received a promotion for ten years (they get harder to come by at the top of the ladder in any case!). I also had always made it a practice to go where wanted and needed. So in March 1980, we said our farewells in Kuala Lumpur and headed back to Washington, where I had been named director for management operations in the State Department—a title so mysteriously bureaucratic and meaningless that I had little idea what I was getting myself into.

In any event, I left Malaysia with a sense of personal and professional satisfaction. Malaysia was not and never had been, by itself, crucial to U.S. interests; but it was part of a resource-rich region that when captured by Japan early in World War II, served as a principal cause of war between Japan and the United States. Moreover, America's war in Vietnam had been fought in large part because of the perception, yet again, that U.S. security would be threatened by the Communist takeover of the region.

I thus left Malaysia feeling that under my stewardship of the American embassy in Kuala Lumpur, U.S.-Malaysian relations had prospered and grown: U.S. investment increased; U.S.-Malaysian trade and defense cooperation had grown; and the problem of the large influx of Vietnamese refugees into Malaysia, so unwelcome there, had been contained, in terms of both U.S.–Malaysian relations and the region's stability.

I also left feeling that I had acquitted myself well as the president's representative in Malaysia, having made the transition from carrying out only State Department and Foreign Service responsibilities to managing the entire breadth of U.S. government interests in Malaysia. The latter responsibility is a very different one from the former; some colleagues make it successfully, but others do not. I felt that I had.

Finally, I left knowing my task had been made easier by an embassy staff that overall was superb, especially my deputy chiefs of mission, Jim Rosenthal and Lyall Breckon, and the embassy's refugee coordinator, Joe Gettier. The entire staff performed in a highly professional manner, reflecting great credit on the United States of America.

Perhaps my most permanent mark on the embassy itself was left on the design of a new chancery building. For many years, including those we spent in Malaysia, the American embassy had been housed on the top three floors—the twelfth, thirteenth and fourteenth—of a high-rise office building in the main business district of Kuala Lumpur. Two years before I got there, the Japanese Red Army, a radical terrorist group, had attacked and held our consular section on the twelfth floor for several days by commandeering the elevators. This experience highlighted the unsatisfactory security position of the embassy in the modern age of terrorism. In addition, a destructive fire in a brand-new and, happily, as-yet-unoccupied high-rise office building a block away underscored our vulnerability to fire as well. Our building was too tall for fire rescue equipment to reach us, and the roof of the building would not hold a helicopter for rescue purposes. While I was there, I refereed a constant disagreement between the embassy security and administrative officers, the former arguing that we had to keep closed and locked the doors to the stairway exits for security reasons, and the latter arguing to keep them open in case of fire.

The Japanese Red Army attack brought authorization from the State Department to buy land for a new, stand-alone chancery, followed by authority to design the new building. During my tenure, we inspected many land parcels and finally settled on one on Jalan Pekeliling (Jalan Tun Razak today) near the ambassador's residence. The disadvantage of that piece of land was its location next to a Shell gas station that must have been a moneymaker because we were unable to persuade Shell to give it up.

After the land was purchased, the department engaged the prominent Washington architectural firm of Hartman and Cox to design and build the new chancery. The basic parameters required that the building fit in with the architecture of the city, yet meet the U.S. government's toughening requirements for building security. Hartman and Cox, after careful study, came up with a design for the building that had, in my layman's view, a heavy, awkward roof. After consultations with me, the architects in effect redesigned the building into an attractive combination of traditional local lines with provision for controlled access that met the department's minimum security requirements. Today the building stands in Kuala Lumpur as an attractive addition to the city's skyline.[7]

EIGHT

Last Assignments, Retirement, and a Return to Vietnam

WHEN I RETURNED to Washington in March 1980, the Cold War was in its waning stages. The Vietnam conflict was over. Our relations with China were gradually overcoming decades of mutual suspicion and distrust and slowly gathering positive momentum. China and the United States were even beginning to cooperate on some of the Cold War's remaining legacies in East Asia. Together they worked to bring about the withdrawal of Vietnamese forces from Cambodia and to promote a UN-sponsored national election to choose a new, representative government there. Even on the Korea Peninsula, where U.S. and Chinese Communist forces had fought each other three decades earlier, China and the United States sought to lessen tensions between the two Koreas. Ronald Reagan, who came into office in January 1981 favoring Taiwan and denouncing China as an enemy of the United States, changed his tune and visited China in 1983 as part of his effort to isolate the Soviet Union.

For its part, the Soviet Union was bogged down in its own "Vietnam" in Afghanistan, and Chinese and American views coincided again, aimed at ending the Soviet campaign there. Internally, the Soviet Union was under great stress. Brezhnev had died in 1982, and he was succeeded briefly one after the other by two old and ailing men, Konstantin Chernenko and Yury Andropov. Andropov died in 1984, and his chosen successor, Mikhail Gorbachev, came to power in 1985 and changed history. Gorbachev saw that the Soviet economy could not continue to support the Soviet empire in the manner to which it had been accustomed since the end of World War II. He introduced the twin policies of glasnost (openness) and perestroika (restructuring), designed to open up the political system and restructure the economy. Under his leadership, Eastern Europe began to slip out from under Soviet control.

Although deeply suspicious of Gorbachev's motives and intentions, the Reagan administration, which during its first term had denounced the "evil empire" and launched its Strategic Defense Initiative, sought to initiate a process of détente through a series of summit meetings and strategic arms negotiations. Despite the Reagan administration's efforts at détente, however, pockets of the Cold War continued to plague the U.S.-Soviet relationship: Cuba and Central America in the Western Hemisphere; Afghanistan in South Asia; and the Cuban- and Soviet-supported civil wars in Angola and Mozambique in southern Africa, and in Ethiopia, Somalia, and Eritrea in the eastern horn of Africa. In East Asia, tension across the 38th parallel on the Korea Peninsula and across the Taiwan Strait with China continued as well.

But for the moment, I had laid such strategic concerns aside and become enmeshed in the management function of the State Department. It proved to be a frustrating, sobering, and essentially thankless experience. In the Department of State's modern lexicon, *management* has become the watchword—without management skills the diplomat is nothing. He or she may be the most perceptive observer of foreign political and economic developments, the most skillful negotiator, or the most persuasive interlocutor; but if management skills and experience are lacking, the chances of rising to the top of the profession today are presumed to be limited. Stripped to its essence, management is the process of employing the human and material resources at one's command in the most efficient manner possible to accomplish one's mission.

As was true for most Foreign Service officers of the Cold War generation whose experience was primarily in political or economic reporting and analysis (or the "substantive" work of the Foreign Service and the State Department), the first time I had to grapple seriously with "management" issues, that is, concern myself with the human and budgetary resources needed to accomplish my mission, was as an ambassador, some twenty-five years into my career. To be sure, before that as a deputy assistant secretary, I had occasionally defended the budget of the Bureau of East Asia and Pacific Affairs before the relevant congressional committees. Yet I had had nothing to do with the preparation of the budget, with issues of how to match the bureau's responsibilities with the resources needed to accomplish those tasks, or with the tough job of establishing priorities in an era of increasingly scarce resources. These chores were the responsibility of the bureau's executive office, which was staffed with administrative, personnel, and budgetary specialists, in consultation with the assistant secretary. Even in Malaysia, the embassy budget was prepared by the administrative section within guidelines established by the department and submitted to me only for pro forma approval.

For most of my career—and that of most of my contemporaries—budget issues were rarely a concern. The State Department and Foreign Service were growth industries. After World War II and during the Cold War, America's vastly expanded responsibilities spawned equally expanded bureaucracies and budgets to carry out our containment policy worldwide. Resources were not a problem, certainly not in the crucial Cold War battlegrounds where I had gotten most of my experience—NATO, the Congo, and Vietnam. But after Vietnam, in the face of burgeoning inflation and national debt, resources became ever scarcer as successive administrations of both political parties were increasingly forced to conduct foreign policy and programs with declining budgets (in real terms).

Meanwhile, the societal changes sweeping the country were also at work in the State Department and Foreign Service. Women and minorities demanded greater access to productive Foreign Service careers, while consular and administrative officers already in the Foreign Service grew progressively restive with their lack of access to the political and economic reporting and analysis positions that led to ambassadorships and other senior policy jobs in the department and in embassies abroad.

These pressures, combined with ever-tightening budgets, obliged the department to give greater attention to management skills and management experience; and management required administrative, as well as political and economic, skills and experience. Foreign Service officers, myself included, had no experience and generally no interest in relating policy and analysis to the resources needed to support the policy process. Thus, the management of resources in support of our diplomacy became as important as the conduct of diplomacy itself.

As the State Department changed from a growth to a declining industry and the competition for career-enhancing jobs—jobs that kept one moving up the career ladder—tightened, officers who had joined the Foreign Service to become diplomats found that their careers were more likely to prosper by becoming manager-diplomats. The article of faith of earlier years—that if Foreign Service officers went where the needs of the Service took them and they performed well, their careers would prosper—came into doubt. Officers began to pay close attention to the assignment process. Professional considerations were increasingly infected by careerism: Senior political or economic counselor jobs in large embassies abroad, formerly plum assignments, were being shunned in favor of deputy chief of mission jobs in even the smallest embassies because the latter were designated as "management" jobs—positions entailing supervision of all activities of the mission under the overall guidance of the ambassador. Such jobs were more likely to enhance one's promotion prospects than serving as a political or economic counselor—the core functions of diplomacy—in large posts such as Moscow or Manila.

In the State Department in Washington, to be a "manager" one had to become at least a deputy assistant secretary with supervision over more than one subordinate office. As budgets declined and job opportunities shrank, assistant secretaries resisted efforts to reduce the numbers of deputies in their bureaus because the workload was not shrinking correspondingly; and, more important, if such positions were not found for talented officers ready for promotion, they could fail to be promoted and thus get "selected out"—retired early for exceeding "time in grade" limits. The alternative to "substantive" management jobs was to seek out jobs in personnel, budget, or administration, or in the Office of Management Operations. Additional scarce resources were devoted to managing the department's difficult budgetary situation as officers became convinced that management was the path to a successful career, thereby putting even more constraints on the essential task of the department—diplomacy.

The Office of Management Operations (M/MO—its bureaucratic symbol: *M* for the under secretary of state for management and *MO* for management operations) was a logical outgrowth of this trend. With a small staff—about thirty professional and clerical employees—it worked directly for the under secretary for management. It was the management bureaucracy's bureaucracy, the management equivalent of the Executive Secretariat, the policy bureaucracy's bureaucracy. The office had been established several years before by then Under Secretary for Management Lawrence Eagleburger. A career Foreign Service officer and protégé of Henry Kissinger, Eagleburger had been frustrated by the unresponsiveness of the three large bureaus under his authority—personnel, administration, and the comptroller's office. He had determined that these bureaus, with their powerful vested interests and the resources at their command, could not be relied on for objective recommendations or for compromise solutions in the interest of the department as a whole. Eagleburger found he needed a staff directly answerable to him that was not responsible itself for large programs or for the expenditure of large sums of money, in order to get objective advice on management issues and to work deadlocked issues toward resolution or compromise. In other words, Management Operations, the title itself a meaningless euphemism or tautology, represented an admission of bureaucratic failure.

Ben Read, Eagleburger's successor in the Carter administration, used M/MO in the same way. Read, who had recruited me for M/MO, was a delight to work for. An intelligent, decent, and humane man, he was a champion of the new Foreign Service Act and its provisions aimed at bringing the Foreign Service into the modern world. However, he was no more able than his predecessors—or his successors—to make sense out of the department's organization or its management.

Almost without exception, my nearly three years' experience as director of the office resulted in a personal conviction that the existence of M/MO itself represented the bureaucracy's failure. A telling paradigm: One of my first tasks after becoming director of management operations was to cope with the widespread negative reaction to the department's decision to close seven consulates around the world in the face of budgetary and personnel constraints. Shortly after I arrived, I took an irate phone call from an American businesswoman in Brisbane, Australia, protesting the closure of our consulate there. I signed numerous letters to others, explaining why we were closing the seven posts, and my staff prepared briefing papers for the secretary of state, who received visits from unhappy mayors of European cities where U.S. consulates were being closed.

Three years later, as I left the job, we were dealing with the financial and personnel consequences of being forced by the Congress to reopen the same posts. Each consulate, it turned out, had a member of Congress opposed to its closing. The Congress included riders on the State Department's authorization and appropriation bills prohibiting any expenditures whatsoever until the posts were reopened, or earmarking an important sum that could only be spent on the posts' reopening. The department's judgments in deciding which consulates to close to save resources were based on considerations of workload and current need in the region, while congressional judgments were based on sentiment and domestic and foreign political pressures. This case in fact exemplifies why the State Department cannot be "managed" effectively the way a private corporation can. In the case of the seven consulates, the department spent more resources in closing and reopening costs than it would have in simply keeping them open in the first place.

Perhaps my greatest disillusionment as director for management operations came early in my tenure: Taking seriously my responsibility to assist the under secretary for management in allocating scarce resources in support of foreign policy priorities, I was pleased to discover shortly after my arrival on the scene that Secretary of State Cyrus Vance had presented a comprehensive review of the Carter administration's foreign policy priorities to the Senate Foreign Relations Committee. In my innocence, I convened a meeting of all of the department's principal resource managers, the executive directors of the bureaus, to discuss the allocation of the next year's State Department budget in accordance with the secretary of state's priorities. The meeting was a total fiasco. Those resource managers whose offices were not mentioned, or were given short shrift, in Vance's presentation flatly refused to use it as a basis for resource-allocation decisions on the grounds they had not been consulted on the preparation of the statement.

I also discovered that despite the increasingly tight budget environment, once an organizational unit had been established in the department—and the Cold War period had seen the establishment of many new such units—it was virtually impossible to abolish it. Recommendations to do so, to consolidate functions, merge positions, or reduce responsibilities arouse the most primitive instincts in the seasoned bureaucrat: instincts of bureaucratic self-preservation. Resource-allocation discussions, therefore, even at senior levels in the department, were for the most part futile exercises that affected only the margins of problems. Raising real issues—giving the secretary of state real choices—is avoided because the secretary does not desire the complication of issues that will seriously divide the staff and divert their attention from important policy issues and foreign crises. Only when these choices are made at the top political level, as they were in the Clinton administration, as part of the pressures to balance the federal budget, can real consolidation be achieved. Even then, the process involves day-to-day combat and rearguard actions to move it forward.

In any case, despite these—and other—disillusioning experiences, from the vantage point of management operations I was well placed to see how the department and the Foreign Service, as well as the political environment within which they carried out their tasks, had changed. When I arrived in Washington in March 1980, the department was awaiting final congressional action on the new comprehensive Foreign Service Act. The law was in fact passed that year and became the Foreign Service Act of 1980. In addition to a major revamping of the career service in ways that remained controversial even two decades later, the new act codified ways for dealing with many of the issues of social change that were affecting our society as a whole and that had their particular ramifications for the Foreign Service. For example, the act established the American Foreign Service Association (AFSA) as the legal bargaining agent for the Foreign Service and laid out the kinds of issues on which management is required to negotiate with AFSA. It legislated affirmative action programs for the Foreign Service, provided for the family liaison structure, and established pension rights for divorced spouses based on the length of time they had been married to their employee spouses and had accompanied them on assignments at home and abroad.

The Office of Management Operations, however, dealt less with personnel matters and more with organizational and resource matters. Reflecting the growing complexity of foreign affairs, the department's organization has become a jerry-built structure of overlapping and duplicative functions and bureaus. A classic organizational tension within the State Department had existed for many years between the geographic and the functional bureaus. The State Department's core organization for the conduct of foreign relations had long consisted of five geographic bureaus: Africa, American Republics (now Western Hemisphere), East Asia and the Pacific, Europe and Canada, and Near East and South Asia. The Bureau of African Affairs had been created in the 1950s, taken from the Near East and South Asia Bureau, becoming the fifth geographic bureau. South Asia has now also been taken out of the Near East and South Asia Bureau and made a sixth, separate bureau. Each bureau is divided into offices dealing with smaller groupings of countries within the regions, and those offices in turn are made up of country "desks" dealing with a single larger country or a group of small countries.

However, foreign affairs issues in today's world must be dealt with increasingly on a "functional" basis—that is, across geographic lines. Thus, beginning in the immediate post–World War II period, the State Department established Bureaus of Economic Affairs, now Economic and Business Affairs; International Organization Affairs, dealing with the United Nations and other international organizations; Consular Affairs, dealing with the whole range of citizen services—passports, visas, welfare and protection; and Administration, Political-Military Affairs, Public Affairs, Legislative Affairs, Intelligence and Research, and others. And, more recently, there has been a virtual explosion of functional bureaus, reflecting the complexity of today's world: Diplomatic Security; Equal Opportunity and Civil Rights; Foreign Missions; Human Rights and Humanitarian Affairs; Refugee Programs; International Communications and Information; International Narcotics Affairs; International Terrorism; and Oceans, Environment, and Technology. Some of these bureaus have been created by executive branch initiative, and some thrust upon the State Department by congressional initiative. Usually, the stimulus for creating a new bureau has been frustration on the part of some constituency that felt that the existing structure was not giving adequate attention to a growing set of issues. But another stimulus is defensive: The State Department has created new bureaus to deal more effectively with growing bureaucracies elsewhere in the federal government—Political-Military Affairs to handle issues with the Pentagon's "little State Department," the Bureau of International Security Affairs; Economic and Business Affairs to deal with the Departments of Commerce and Treasury and the Office of the Special Trade Representative; International Narcotics Affairs to deal with the burgeoning antinarcotics bureaucracy—the Department of Justice, the Drug Enforcement Agency, the intelligence community; Intelligence and Research to deal with the growing intelligence community; and others.

Each proposal to create a new bureau may make sense in itself, but the cumulative result is increasingly bureaucratic gridlock within the U.S. government as a whole. One of management operations' functions was to assist the under secretary for management in trying to make some sense out of this morass to induce greater work efficiency but also increasingly to conserve scarce budgetary and human resources.

Unfortunately, in the three years I was in the job, I can recall only frustration and failure. As we had said of the Vietnam negotiations, here, too, we thought of everything and it was rejected—or ignored. We did studies of the proliferation of functions, the overlapping and duplication of responsibilities, the accretion of supervisory layers, and so on. Almost no recommendation we made was accepted. My sobering conclusion was that the only criterion for success in management operations was to displease everyone equally. Almost every recommendation we made "broke someone's rice bowl"—invaded someone's turf, threatened someone's authority or prestige, and thus would require resolution by the secretary of state. The under secretary for management was reluctant to take up the secretary's valuable time with management issues because the secretary had enough difficult foreign policy issues to resolve with his senior officers without forcing on them difficult and unpopular resource decisions.

When the Reagan administration took over in January 1981, my staff and I saw an opportunity to persuade the new under secretary for management, Richard Kennedy, to make some changes before the new appointees in charge of the bureaus felt a need to protect their turf and while they still looked upon their responsibilities as inherited from their Democratic predecessors. Our optimism could not have been more misplaced. Kennedy, a crusty character with a volatile temper, looked at my staff and me as holdovers whose loyalties to the new administration were doubtful. He refused to entertain any recommendations until he knew the department better—a not unreasonable position to take. But by the time he "knew the department better," it was too late. As we had feared, the new assistant secretaries, once installed, resisted any suggestion that they could give up resources for higher-priority tasks elsewhere.

* * *

After I had served nearly three years as director for management operations, the department proposed me for appointment as U.S. ambassador to Côte d'Ivoire (Ivory Coast) in West Africa. During my three years in M/MO I had received a promotion to career minister after nearly thirteen years as a minister counselor. I was fifty-six, pleased with the promotion, and pleased to receive a second ambassadorial assignment. The U.S. mission in Abidjan, Côte d'Ivoire's capital, was much larger than that in Kuala Lumpur. It housed many regional functions that supported U.S. programs and activities in many countries of West and Central Africa. As it turned out, running the mission in Abidjan was indeed a management challenge!

Throughout the Cold War, Côte d'Ivoire had never been on the U.S. foreign policy radar screen. Our concerns in Africa had focused on the very real tensions in southern Africa: the continuing apartheid regime in South Africa; the transition in Southern Rhodesia (now Zimbabwe) from a minority white regime to a majority elected black government; and the civil wars in Mozambique and Angola. These last were former Portuguese colonies in which radical African nationalist movements supported by the Soviet Union and China, and bolstered by Cuban troops, sought to wrest control of those new countries from elements supported by the West, especially the United States and, in some cases, by South Africa.

Just north of the southern Africa cauldron lay Zaire, whose aging leader, Mobutu Sese Seko, played an important role in the region. He had, however, been in power far too long and over the years had been siphoning off his country's riches into his large Swiss bank accounts. The United States was unwilling to withdraw its support from Mobutu for fear Zaire would descend into chaos and complicate solutions for the rest of southern Africa.

The United States was also concerned about civil wars in Central and Eastern Africa—in Chad, Sudan, and the horn of Africa—where Muammar Qaddafi's Libya, Iran, and the Soviet Union supported radical elements and where important strategic U.S. interests were perceived to be at stake. In West Africa, we focused on the troubled situation in Nigeria, a country of over 100 million people and large oil reserves and revenues, beset by continual internal political turmoil and instability. Our other interest in West Africa was in tiny Liberia, adjacent to Côte d'Ivoire, where we had historical ties dating from when the country was created to receive thousands of emancipated American slaves after our Civil War and where we maintained large airfield and communications complexes. In addition, the Firestone rubber company had major holdings in Liberia.

For Kaity and me, Africa would be a totally new experience. Despite my involvement with the Congo crisis twenty years before while serving as Belgium-Luxembourg desk officer, we had never been to Africa. Kaity and I prepared ourselves for this new area in the customary ways of the Foreign Service: We attended the Foreign Service Institute's three-week course on sub-Saharan Africa and read everything we could on Africa in general and French West Africa and Côte d'Ivoire in particular. We had plenty of time. By 1983, the processing of new ambassadorial nominations was already becoming long and tortuous. Ten months elapsed between the time the Bureau of Personnel asked me in December 1982 if I would be willing to have my name put forward to the secretary of state as a nominee for Côte d'Ivoire until we actually arrived in Abidjan in October 1983.

Just getting the secretary of state's approval and then the White House's informal go-ahead took two months. Then the paperwork began in earnest—security forms and investigation; financial disclosure to ensure the avoidance of any conflicts of interest in the new assignment; checks with the Internal Revenue Service to ascertain any problems with unpaid taxes, audits, or other actions; and medical clearance. Then, as is the usual procedure, the nomination is submitted formally to the president, and the prospective candidate waits—and waits—and waits—for the formal nomination as the president's personal representative to the country in question. Up to this point, nothing can be taken for granted. If you pass all the paper hurdles, and your nomination is formally submitted to the White House personnel office, that estimable body may, since giving informal approval, have turned up a suitable political candidate to put up to the president alongside the career candidate.

President Reagan followed the agreeable custom of personally telephoning his nominees to inform them of his decision. It was a nice touch. In my case, it happened in June, six months after the process began. I was sitting in the sub-Saharan Africa class at the Foreign Service Institute after lunch listening to a lecture when a staff member sought me out to tell me that I had an important phone call from the White House. As it turned out, the closest telephone was two flights up and the elevator was not working! Happily, by the time I rushed up two flights of stairs, the White House operator had hung up, leaving her number. I thus had time to catch my breath before returning her call. When I did so, the president quickly came on the line, very pleasantly told me of his decision, and asked me if I would accept. I did, with alacrity. He thanked me, asked me to transmit his regards to my wife, and hung up. I was launched!

However, hurdles still lay ahead. Once the president's decision had been made, the State Department sought *agrément* from the Côte d'Ivoire government—assurance that I was acceptable to that government as the new U.S. ambassador. That took another month. Then the White House announced my nomination and sent it to the Senate for the confirmation process, but the nomination papers arrived just as that body began its summer recess. Since the recess exceeded thirty days, the nomination was sent back to the White House with the advice that it should be resubmitted after Labor Day—at which point Kaity and I left for Greece on vacation.

I finally appeared before the Senate Foreign Relations Committee for my confirmation hearing in mid-September. A number of nominees for African posts appeared together before Senator Nancy Kassebaum, chair of the Foreign Relations Committee's Subcommittee on Africa. Senator Kassebaum was the only senator present. As I recall, she asked us each one general question, gave us each her best wishes for a successful mission, and sent us on our way. Then came full Senate confirmation and the final White House paperwork—preparation and presidential signing of commissions, and so on—and finally, the swearing-in ceremony at the State Department. Daughter Margaret held the Bible. Kaity had remained in Greece waiting for the process to be completed.

After being sworn in and duly attested to, I was finally sent on my way following brief calls on the president and the secretary of state—largely "photo opportunities." The president presented me (as I am sure he did to all his departing ambassadors) with a set of gold cuff links with the presidential seal on the face and his signature engraved on the back. Secretary George Shultz, with whom I discussed briefly the possibility of a visit to West Africa, presented me with another set of cuff links with the State Department seal and a matching lapel pin for my wife. The Bureau of African Affairs had discouraged me from seeking appointments with the department's top officers—the secretary, the deputy secretary, and the under secretaries—reflecting its own bias that I should not waste senior officials' time on a post that was so marginal to the concerns of the bureau. Indeed, I was surprised that the secretary received me at all, since few of his under secretaries did. After these formalities, I flew to Paris for consultations with our embassy there. Kaity met me in Paris in late October, and we flew together to Abidjan.

Côte d'Ivoire was one of the few postcolonial success stories in Africa. Abidjan, its capital, is a big, modern city. As a former French colony, Côte d'Ivoire remained an important element in French foreign policy in general and French policy toward Africa in particular. Along with Senegal, Cameroon, and Gabon, Côte d'Ivoire represented a "jewel in the crown" of France's colonial and postcolonial policy in West and Central Africa. The French treasury fully backed the currency of former French West Africa, the CFA. Côte d'Ivoire was the world's largest producer of cocoa and the third or fourth largest producer of coffee. It also exported tropical hardwoods (although the reserves of these hardwoods were dwindling fast), pineapples, and other tropical products. It enjoyed a civilian, elected, constitutional, and parliamentary government, which had been dominated since independence in 1960 by one party headed by one man—Félix Houphouet-Boigny.

The American ambassador's residence in Abidjan was a pleasant, spacious villa on a small side street in Cocody, the "European" residential section. As in Kuala Lumpur, the residence was surrounded by a large garden with tropical trees and flowering plants (but about one-third the size of the Kuala Lumpur garden). We settled in quickly, met the embassy staff, and began our duties while I awaited the opportunity to present credentials to President Houphouet-Boigny.

After two or three weeks, Houphouet received me, along with several other new ambassadors. During this waiting period, I was able to begin my official functions, which included calling on ministers. At the appointed time, each ambassador was received formally in a brief, individual, televised ceremony at the presidential palace. The chief of protocol, Georges Ouegnin, formally presented each of us to the president, we handed the president our letters of credence and our predecessors' letters of recall, and we recited, in French, a brief, standard, prearranged sentence indicating that by these letters our respective heads of state were accrediting us to him as their personal representatives. Houphouet introduced his foreign minister, Simeon Ake, and principal officials of the presidency. Then we sat with the president and the foreign minister—still before the television cameras—for fifteen minutes of chitchat. During this time, we exchanged formal copies of prepared remarks, the texts of which appeared in the local press the following day, and then took our leave. We all became at that point officially the ambassadors of our respective governments to Côte d'Ivoire.

Houphouet-Boigny, a small, grandfatherly-appearing man, was then close to ninety years old (some said more). He was trained during the colonial period as an "African doctor"—permitted to minister to Africans' illnesses and deliver African babies. One of his ministers of state spoke with pride of having been delivered by Dr. Houphouet-Boigny.

Houphouet made his political reputation during the colonial era as a fighter for Africans' rights. He was elected to the French Parliament from Côte d'Ivoire before World War II and was manifestly proud that he had served as a member of six French governments. His strong political position at home derived originally from his successful fight, as a member of the French Parliament, against the French practice of forced labor in the colonies. When Côte d'Ivoire became independent, Houphouet-Boigny was already the dominant leader and the natural choice to become president. In addition to his reputation as a medical doctor and his parliamentary fight for Africans' labor rights, Houphouet was also chief of the largest and most prosperous tribe in Côte d'Ivoire, the Baoule. The Baoule occupied a large, fertile territory in the east central part of the country and owned large cocoa and other plantations, from which they—and their chief—derived huge wealth.

With this backing, Houphouet had run the country for a generation by the time we arrived, through a single political party, the Democratic Party of Côte d'Ivoire. He maintained power by a shrewd manipulation of political forces, by occasional strong-arm methods, and by his continuing close relationship with France. When we were there, France's expatriate colony in Côte d'Ivoire was larger than it had been at independence. French investments in Côte d'Ivoire were great and wide-ranging. In fact, France had the predominant foreign position in the country, carefully maintaining that position through its widespread influence with virtually every ministry in a position to admit—or block—foreign competition.

America's role in Côte d'Ivoire was important but secondary. We provided little aid because the country was too prosperous to meet our aid criteria, which focused at the time on supporting "basic human needs." Although there was some U.S. private investment there, the internal market was too small to be of great interest to our private sector; but the United States was one of the biggest markets for Côte d'Ivoire's cocoa and its coffee. As in Malaysia, we were accused of permitting—even manipulating—great swings in international market prices for these products.

For all these reasons, including the strategic ones discussed above, the United States gladly relied on France to give strong financial support to Côte d'Ivoire, thereby conserving scarce American resources for other areas where our interests were more directly engaged. Moreover, although both France and Côte d'Ivoire denied it, France was loath to see American influence in Côte d'Ivoire grow for fear that it would somehow undermine French interests. For their part, the Ivorians denied that Côte d'Ivoire was a French *chasse gardée*—a private hunting preserve—but the Ivorians found dealing with the French quite comfortable, while few Americans were fluent in Côte d'Ivoire's official language, French. Côte d'Ivoire was a potential engine of growth for a much larger market in the surrounding hinterland—hundreds of thousands of emigrant workers from neighboring Burkina Faso, Mali, Ghana, Guinea, and elsewhere worked in Côte d'Ivoire and sent home millions of dollars' worth of remittances per year. However, the poorer countries surrounding Côte d'Ivoire strongly resisted any formal efforts to make their economies more dependent on their wealthier neighbor than they already were.

The United States was also comfortable with Houphouet's moderate, pro-Western stance on most international issues. He supported U.S. efforts to find compromise on southern Africa and quietly worked behind the scenes to that effect. He supported our efforts to contain Libya's influence in Africa and was one of the few African leaders that had restored relations with Israel after the 1967 war with Egypt. He had broken relations with the Soviet Union because, as he put it publicly, he had found that the Soviet ambassador, who had presented credentials to him and professed to be interested in working for better Soviet-Ivorian relations, was going around the country speaking against him and trying to engineer his overthrow.

Houphouet had also chastised the Iranian chargé in Abidjan for displaying large banners with rabidly anti-American slogans in the garden of his residence on the occasion of Iran's national day.

Although the United States periodically threatened to reduce or cut off aid to countries that did not support U.S. positions in the United Nations and other international forums, we did little to help countries like Côte d'Ivoire, which by and large supported our positions. On one occasion when I sought some small, carefully tailored assistance for Côte d'Ivoire, I was summarily rebuffed by a deputy assistant secretary of state for African affairs with the cynical retort, "Bob, we'll worry about Côte d'Ivoire when it starts going down the drain!"

My tasks in Abidjan began in an auspicious atmosphere. Some months before I arrived, Houphouet had been to the United States, the first sub-Saharan African leader that Ronald Reagan invited to the White House on a state visit. Houphouet boasted that every U.S. president since Kennedy, except Jimmy Carter, had invited him to the White House, and he was well pleased with his reception by the Reagan administration.

As a consequence, it was relatively easy for me to get an appointment with Houphouet, and I tried not to abuse the privilege. In any case, my business was infrequent and usually related to updating him on our efforts to resolve crises elsewhere on the continent, mostly in southern Africa. Occasionally I accompanied a visitor from Washington to call on him: Assistant Secretary of State for African Affairs Chester Crocker, who was actively pursuing the Reagan administration's "constructive engagement" policy in southern Africa, briefed

Houphouet on the progress of his efforts once or twice while I was there. Hank Cohen, then deputy director of intelligence and research in the State Department and later Crocker's successor as assistant secretary for Africa, briefed Houphouet on intelligence developments in the area. Both Crocker and Cohen spoke excellent French.

My staff and I had more business with the Foreign Ministry, much of which related to global issues on the United Nations' agenda. Because Abidjan had many amenities lacking elsewhere in the region, including good airline connections, our embassy was also the site of various U.S. regional conferences. I recall once hosting a regional conference on security, which Ronald Spiers, a Foreign Service colleague and then under secretary of state for management, attended with Oliver North, of the National Security Council staff in the White House and later renown in the Iran-Contra Affair.

We had other visitors. Mayor Marion Barry of Washington, D.C., while en route to a world conference of mayors in Monrovia, was guest of honor at an embassy lunch. A number of U.S. officials stayed with us on official visits to Côte d'Ivoire, including Loret Miller Ruppe, head of the Peace Corps, and Gregory Newell, assistant secretary of state for international organization (UN) affairs. Newell was accompanied by Alan Keyes, a deputy to Jeane Kirkpatrick, U.S. ambassador to the United Nations.[1] All were routine visits on routine matters of consultation.

I can recall only one occasion when Houphouet urgently tried to find me. It was a Sunday morning and Kaity and I were at the beach. When we returned that afternoon, I found messages everywhere that the president of the republic was looking for me. I called him immediately. The weekend edition of the *Fraternité Matin,* the government-controlled morning newspaper, had had a banner headline and an editorial strongly critical of President Reagan, labeling him "Killer of the United Nations!" The issue, now long forgotten, presumably had something to do with U.S. dissatisfaction with the United Nations' overblown bureaucracy and a threat to withhold funds. Houphouet wanted me to assure our president that the editorial did not represent the policy of his government and that he had reprimanded the editor for straying from his policy. He asked me to come to see him the following morning to hear a further explanation of his views. I assured him I would convey his message to the president promptly, and we had a pleasant discussion the following morning.

Among my more enjoyable occupations was travel throughout the country, sometimes by invitation to visit the home region of a minister, sometimes to attend an official ceremony organized by the Ivorian government, and sometimes to preside over a ceremony inaugurating a village school, clinic, or other local project financed by our small self-help aid program or by our local AID Regional Housing and Urban Development Office. On occasion, we traveled on our own to see the country.

During one ceremony inaugurating a U.S.-financed village school some 30 miles outside Abidjan, I was inducted into membership into a local tribe in the presence of the tribal chieftain, the king of Bonua. The king wrote me later, stating his intention to send me, as now a "member of the family," one of his sons so that I could find him a job. I replied, suggesting that the king's son send us a résumé of his training and experience. It never came.

On another occasion, as the guest of a minister of state, I visited a village in west-central Côte d'Ivoire, where I was presented with a live goat, a local robe, and a heavy iron bracelet as a symbol of village power. Protocol required that I either share the goat with my hosts and eat it on the spot, or take it home. Fortunately, I was traveling with some staff members, and we were able to truss up the goat and carry it back to Abidjan, some 125 miles away, in an embassy station wagon. I awarded the goat to the driver once we got home and asked him to share it with my driver and his family.

On yet another occasion I was invited to be the guest of honor at a ceremony inaugurating a new U.S.-financed drainage system for the town of Vavoua, the capital seat of the Bete tribe in central Côte d'Ivoire. After I made a brief speech stressing the cooperation between the United States and Côte d'Ivoire on such projects, I was presented by the mayor of Vavoua with an object wrapped in a colorful beach towel. The mayor whispered in my ear that the gift was a mask that had belonged to a well-known local masked dancer who had recently died, and that he had kept the mask wrapped so as not to upset the audience, which had revered the late dancer.

This information made my wife and me uncomfortable. Later at lunch under a big tent, I asked the mayor if I should really accept something that had meant so much to the local populace. He assured me that the mask had been *désacralisée*—deconsecrated—and therefore it was perfectly all right for me to take it. I did so, but still with some discomfort! I later tried to offer it to the Smithsonian's African Museum, but they declined it.

Africa is a wondrous, deeply mysterious, and beautiful continent, but also deeply troubling and troubled. Côte d'Ivoire shares this beauty and mystery: its people are gentle and graceful, with great personal dignity and warmth. The *paysage lagunaire,* the lagoon-dotted landscape along the coast, is surrounded by graceful coconut palms and villages of wooden huts and shops. In contrast, the savanna landscape to the north—the open, mildly rolling countryside—is dotted with baobab trees and other savanna vegetation. Both landscapes had their attraction and their individual character.

With my tenure in Abidjan nearing an end after almost three years, I knew that my Foreign Service odyssey through the Cold War was also winding down, even as the Cold War neared its end. I therefore threw my hat into the ring for the vice presidency of the National Defense University (NDU), a job traditionally held by a senior Foreign Service officer. Although a colleague had already been selected for the job before I knew whether it would be available, he was suddenly asked to go as ambassador to Honduras, and the job was mine. After a round of farewell calls and farewell dinners, we were on our way—with no regrets and many pleasant memories of our brief time in Africa.

Fort Lesley J. McNair, where the National Defense University is located, is the oldest active U.S. Army base in the United States. It enjoys a beautiful site in southwest Washington, D.C., on the point of land where the Anacostia and Potomac Rivers and the Washington Channel all converge. Fort McNair has played its own role in the nation's history. It was overrun when the British attacked Washington during the War of 1812, and Mary Seurat, a coconspirator in the Lincoln assassination, was hanged there after the Civil War.

As vice president of NDU, I was assigned quarters on the post—Quarters 15 on "Generals' Row," a group of fine old Georgian-style houses built in 1903 and 1904 for majors and captains. The houses ran in a row along the east bank of the Washington Channel across from Hains Point and alongside the parade ground. It was indeed an enjoyable place to live for three years, flanked on one side by the Washington Channel, whose boat traffic was a constant source of interest, and on the other side by the wide-open green space of a compact nine-hole golf course and the parade ground, the site of frequent military parades, tennis matches, and other diverting activities.

In August 1986, when I arrived to take over my duties at NDU, the Cold War's Iron Curtain was cracking in earnest. Mikhail Gorbachev's policies of glasnost and perestroika were in full swing in Moscow. The Soviet satellites in Eastern Europe were wriggling loose from the Soviet Union's stranglehold, and masses of refugees from those countries were flooding into West Germany and other countries of Western Europe. The Reagan administration was softening its attitude toward the "evil empire" and cautiously exploring the beginnings of a new relationship. Truly, fresh winds were blowing through a weakened and dispirited Cold War.

The National Defense University was playing its own small part in this effort. Under the Pentagon's guidance, NDU was cultivating academic relationships with its Soviet and Chinese counterparts. Students from the National War College and the Industrial College of the Armed Forces (ICAF) could now choose to visit the Soviet Union or East European countries during their regularly scheduled spring tours abroad. Gradually, War College commandants and eventually NDU presidents and vice presidents began to exchange visits with their Soviet and Chinese counterparts.

Before I arrived, NDU's president had traveled to Beijing with a small delegation of officers and staff as the guests of the Chinese National Defense University. In 1988, I was asked to lead a joint delegation, with the commandant of the National War College, Rear Admiral John Addams as coleader, of National War College and ICAF students, again as guests of the Chinese National Defense University and the Peoples' Liberation Army. It was my first visit to China and a fitting end to my Cold War odyssey. In addition to being taken on the traditional sightseeing tours of the Forbidden City, other historical points of interest in Beijing, and the Great Wall nearby, we held discussions with the president of China's National Defense University, General Zhang Zhen, and his senior staff, and I gave a lecture to the student body on the mutually reinforcing roles of force and diplomacy in the conduct of foreign affairs. We also visited Xian—site of the now-famous terra-cotta Chinese soldiers arrayed in the trenches where they had lain buried and unknown for centuries—and Nanjing, Shanghai, and Guangzhou (Canton) in southeastern China.

In addition to sightseeing tours in each of these cities, as in Beijing, discussions with members of "think tanks" sought to dispel mutual misconceptions and misunderstandings of Chinese and American military intentions, capabilities, strategies, and tactics. As might have been expected, our Chinese interlocutors showed great apprehension and mistrust about U.S. intentions regarding Taiwan, as well as the U.S.-Japan security treaty. They kept pointing to our obligations under the Shanghai Communiqué to regard Taiwan as part of China and not to build up Taiwanese military forces. They also declared that they had every right to occupy Taiwan by force without "outside interference" because Taiwan was a Chinese "internal affair." In fact, one Chinese scholar insisted that because Taiwan was a part of China (and not a separate country), China's long-standing pledge not to be the first to use nuclear weapons against another country did not apply to Taiwan.

For our part, we reminded our Chinese counterparts of their own obligations under the Shanghai Communiqué to resolve the Taiwan issue peacefully. On the U.S.-Japan security treaty, the Chinese professed to see it as directed against China and not, as we claimed, an element of stability in the western Pacific.

We left China with many impressions and, in any case, better informed. The following year, 1989, the president of China's National Defense University, still General Zhang Zhen, accompanied by a sizable delegation, was the guest of Lieutenant General Bradley Hosmer, president of our National Defense University. In his upper seventies at the time, General Zhang Zhen was a "long march" veteran of Mao Zedong's victorious campaign against Chiang Kai-shek's nationalist forces in the late 1940s and a close associate of Deng Xiaoping.

Our discussions with General Zhang Zhen and his party in Washington reflected Chinese concern at developments in the Soviet Union—developments they were persuaded were provoked by the United States and that might presage similar American efforts against their own regime in Beijing. Their underlying strategic concern was that the United States and the new Soviet Union might patch up their differences and present a united front against China.

Shortly before I left the National Defense University, I participated in hosting a similar visit of senior Soviet military officials, including Marshal Sergey Akromeyev, the counterpart to Admiral William Crowe, then chairman of our Joint Chiefs of Staff. In some respects, Soviet-U.S. high-level military contacts were a mirror image of their Chinese-U.S. counterparts: The Soviets feared that the United States and China might take advantage of a Soviet Union now beset by great internal turmoil and weakness in order to gang up against it.

At the time, in the late 1980s, the Reagan administration viewed Gorbachev cautiously, not certain what he was up to. It was difficult for me, too, whose entire Foreign Service experience had taken place in the environment of the Cold War, to absorb these changes. Like most Americans, I welcomed them but was not sure whether they signaled the sea change that became evident later on. Gorbachev viewed himself as a Communist, but one who had to find solutions to the Soviet Union's increasingly difficult economic position and political unrest—the legacy of the Soviet Union's Afghanistan quagmire and the pressure put on the Soviet Union by the Reagan administration's determined military buildup, especially its effort to launch the costly, if unfulfilled, Strategic Defense Initiative, dubbed Star Wars.

The administration was only too conscious that Soviet nuclear missiles were still aimed at the United States and that major conventional forces still faced each other across the central front in Germany. Many Americans feared that Gorbachev was trying to lull us into a false sense of security only to catch us off guard in some unpredictable way.

After three years, I left the National Defense University for a final two-year assignment as diplomat-in-residence at the Elliott School of International Affairs at George Washington University, the last stop in my Foreign Service career.

My service had spanned the administrations of nine presidents—from Truman to Bush—and eleven secretaries of state—from Acheson to Baker. When I retired in 1991, I was sixty-three and had served the State Department and Foreign Service for almost forty years. The new State Department leaders under James Baker were understandably focusing on younger men and women for senior appointments, and it was time to go, with many satisfactions and no regrets.

While I was at the Elliott School, immersed in its academic atmosphere, it was becoming clear that the Soviet empire was in a state of dismemberment, that the Soviet Union itself was in a state of collapse, and that the United States was emerging as the world's sole remaining superpower. Americans were quick to brag that the United States had won the Cold War and the Soviet Union had lost it. However, this apparently clear outcome, as well as the self-satisfaction toward it displayed by most Americans, obscured more complex questions about the Cold War, and more particularly about the U.S. role in Vietnam, that will undoubtedly be treated by historians and political scientists for years to come.

I now return to where I began this account of my personal odyssey through the Cold War: The fruits of America's major post–World War II foreign policies—the rebuilding of Europe and Japan, the dissolution of Europe's colonial empires, and the dismantling of the Soviet empire—had remained manifest; and America remained stronger and more prosperous than ever. Could anyone really have asked for more in terms of career satisfaction?

In 1993, two years after I retired from the Foreign Service, Kaity and I returned to Vietnam as tourists. For Kaity it was some twenty-eight years after she and the children were evacuated from Saigon in 1965; for me, some nineteen years after my last visit in 1974. I was engaged as a lecturer aboard the *Ocean Pearl*, an American cruise ship making the first cruise to Vietnam since President George H. W. Bush had eased the trade and financial embargoes against it sufficiently to allow American ships to visit and American tourists to spend money there.

From Singapore, the *Pearl* crossed the South China Sea and sailed upriver from Cap St. Jacques, or Vung Tau, to Saigon (now called Ho Chi Minh City), where it docked for some twenty-four hours. It then put in up the coast successively at Nhatrang, Da Nang (from where we were bused over the beautiful *Col des Nuages*—Pass of the Clouds—to the old imperial capital of Hue), then, for our first time, on to Haiphong and Hanoi, and finally to the hauntingly beautiful Halong Bay, northeast of Haiphong. Haiphong, Hanoi, and Halong Bay had all been out of bounds in Communist North Vietnam during the war.

Returning to Vietnam was a nostalgic experience. We had lived in Saigon for almost three eventful years, our children had gone to school there, and we had made many friends. It was home, as much as a Foreign Service tour can make it home. We had vacationed at the run-down but atmospheric Hotel Nautique in Nhatrang and had spent long weekends with friends in Hue on two or three occasions. We returned this time with George and Kitty Calfo, whom we had met in Saigon thirty years before and who had joined us on the cruise.

In Saigon we sought out our familiar haunts of yesteryear: the houses we had lived in, the children's schools, the *Cercle Sportif* where the children had learned to swim and I had played regularly in a tennis foursome, the old embassy building where I had worked and been injured by a car-bombing in 1965, a month before I left Vietnam. We walked the streets of downtown Saigon, down Catinat, or Tu Do, the main commercial street; Nguyen Hue and Le Loi (all since renamed), commercial avenues nearby. We visited the Hotels Continental, Caravelle, and Majestic, centers of Saigon social life in the old days. We went to the top of the Caravelle to see the view, wrote and mailed postcards from the Majestic, and had coffee at Givral's as in the old days. We even took a *cyclopousse,* the three-wheeled pedicabs that could still be found everywhere. We visited the cathedral and the old post office, still landmarks of the city.

Also, with our cruise tour group, we visited the Saigon Museum, drove by the "new" American embassy building—where the helicopters had landed on the roof to evacuate Americans and a number of Vietnamese in 1975—and toured the presidential palace. Visiting the palace felt eerie. It had been left the way North Vietnamese troops found it when their tanks had crashed through the wrought-iron gates surrounding it in April 1975. In the basement, Nguyen Van Thieu's old military command post still existed: One could see the army cots, the field telephones, the wall maps showing the positions of South Vietnamese and enemy forces. Upstairs, curious foreign tourists and Vietnamese peered at Thieu's conference room, state dining room, and other official flotsam and jetsam of the past. However, we could not bring ourselves to visit the Cu Chi tunnels just outside town—now a favorite tourist attraction.

The elaborate Cu Chi tunnel complex was the underground headquarters of the Viet Cong throughout the war—facilities that the mighty U.S. military establishment never succeeded in locating and destroying, despite the fact that they were right under its nose.

The city itself had changed very little in twenty years, in contrast to the booming, mushrooming cities almost everywhere else in Southeast Asia—Singapore, Kuala Lumpur, Bangkok. Very little new construction could be seen—the war had absorbed every resource, every bit of energy. Saigon was only shabbier and junkier: The manicured grassy strips and parks lining the streets from the French colonial era, and which still existed in the 1960s and early 1970s, had been replaced by hastily erected stalls of corrugated metal selling food and household items, or housing bicycle and motorcycle repair shops.

The *Cercle Sportif* was still there as a "workers athletic club," but the tennis courts and surrounding grass areas were badly maintained and run-down, and what had been the clubhouse kitchen looked like the black hole of Calcutta.

Unlike the streets of modern cities elsewhere in the region (and throughout the world), Saigon's were jammed with thousands upon thousands of bicycles, pedicabs, motor scooters, three-wheeled putt-putt conveyances, and old trucks and buses. Except for the shiny new taxicabs, it was as if Saigon had been caught in a time warp, left behind the rest of the world by a sad trick of fate: Having realized the dream of a millennium—an independent, unified Vietnam victorious over its enemies, including the world's greatest superpower, it was now alone, exhausted, and adrift in a crumbling global communist system. By 1993, Vietnam's mentor and principal supporter, the Soviet Union, had collapsed, its empire a shambles. Deprived of its principal source of aid, Vietnam was now obliged to seek a restoration of relations with the United States, to invite foreign investment, even to modify its communist principles, at least to accommodate "market socialism," in order to attract capitalist investment from the West.

In the streets and from our tour guides we found no evidence of hostility to us as Americans. On the contrary, everyone was friendly—sometimes aggressively so in an effort to sell us trinkets, such as toy helicopters made from crushed Budweiser beer cans, or to beg money with outstretched hands. We saw what seemed an inordinate number of maimed people, including children, with missing hands, arms, legs, or eyes, sometimes all of these, many panhandling or selling trinkets to tourists.

It was hard to avoid the thought in 1993 that Vietnam's victorious but aging leadership must have wondered in the end if it had chosen the wrong path to independence, unity, and development—communism and thirty years of warfare—in contrast to its neighbors, which had achieved their independence much earlier and with much less bloodshed. It was equally hard to avoid wondering whether all the trauma inflicted on our own society by the war had not been misplaced as well: The worst had happened—the enemy had won—and yet the security of the United States had not been undermined—nor had that of Southeast Asia. The only domino that had fallen was the Soviet Union and its communist empire.

As we walked the streets of Saigon in 1993, perhaps the only clear conclusions we could come to were that the Cold War, fortunately, was over; that those who had chosen opposite sides in that war, whether in Europe, Asia, or Africa, could now be friends again—or at least stop being enemies; and that the United States continued to grow and prosper at home.

Notes

PART I: PREPARATION AND APPRENTICESHIP

One. Prelude to Service

1. Among them were John Gunther Dean, who later served as ambassador to Cambodia, Lebanon, Denmark, Thailand, and India; Thomas Shoesmith, who capped his career as ambassador to Malaysia after serving as minister in Tokyo, consul general in Hong Kong, and deputy assistant secretary of state for East Asian and Pacific affairs; and Ted Cheney, who was tragically killed in a plane crash while serving as economic counselor in Manila. John Brademas, another classmate, left the program for a Rhodes scholarship at Oxford and distinguished himself as a longtime U.S. representative from South Bend, Indiana, and later as president of New York University.

2. Included among them were Jane Abell Coon, who later became a deputy assistant secretary of state for Near East and South Asian affairs, and then ambassador to Bangladesh; and William Edmondson, who served as ambassador to South Africa and later as deputy inspector general of the Foreign Service. (I later succeeded Bill Edmondson as president of Diplomatic and Consular Officers, Retired [DACOR] and the DACOR Bacon House Foundation.)

Two. From NATO to the Congo

1. Dean Acheson's memoir, *Present at the Creation: My Years in the State Department* (New York: W. W. Norton, 1987), describes the real sense of crisis besetting the young alliance at the time. See pt. III, secs. C and D, 491–724.

2. In the ensuing years, Ed and Peggy Martin became lifelong friends.

3. See U.S. Department of State, *Foreign Relations of the United States, 1952–1954* (hereinafter *FRUS*), vol. V, *Western European Security* (Washington, D.C.: Department of State, 1983), pt. I, 107–79, 349–51.

4. Acheson, *Present at the Creation,* 718–20.

5. Ibid., 721.

6. Townsend Hoopes, *The Devil and John Foster Dulles* (Boston: Little, Brown, 1973), 3–9.

7. Hoopes, *Devil and John Foster Dulles,* 134–60, gives a graphic account of the atmosphere in the department at the time.

8. *FRUS,* 1952–1954, vol. V, 853–54.

9. Hoopes, *Devil and John Foster Dulles,* 246–50.

10. Stanley Karnow's *Paris in the Fifties* (New York: Times Books, 1997) captures the flavor of the times and France's twin agonies of Indochina and Algeria.

11. Acheson, *Present at the Creation,* describes the genesis of the Executive Secretariat (129, 213) and its institutionalization (257).

12. Sadly, both Jim Carson's and Bob McKinnon's careers were cut short prematurely. Carson died during assignment as DCM in Haiti, McKinnon while serving in Africa.

13. See *FRUS,* 1958–1960, vol. XV, *South and Southeast Asia,* for documents relating to this visit, June 18–19, 1958.

14. *FRUS,* 1958–1960, vol. VI, *Cuba,* 429–30.

15. *FRUS,* 1958–1960, vol. VI, 424, 430.

16. See Dean Rusk as told to Richard Rusk, *As I Saw It,* ed. Daniel S. Papp (New York: W. W. Norton, 1990), 530–31, for an account of the decision to establish the Operations Center.

17. For accounts and documentation of the 1959 Geneva Foreign Ministers Meeting on Berlin, see U.S. Department of State, *Foreign Ministers Meeting, May–August 1959, Geneva* (Washington, D.C.: Department of State Publication 6882, September 1959); and Jack M. Schick, *The Berlin Crisis, 1958–1962* (Philadelphia: University of Pennsylvania Press, 1971).

18. Dwight D. Eisenhower, *The White House Years: Waging Peace, 1956–61* (Garden City, N.Y.: Doubleday, 1963–65), 485.

19. For accounts of the president's trip, see Eisenhower, *White House Years,* 485–513; and Merriman Smith, *A President's Odyssey* (New York: Harper, 1961). For more recent accounts of Eisenhower's visits to India and Pakistan, see Dennis Kux, *India and the United States: Estranged Democracies, 1941–1991* (Washington, D.C.: National Defense University Press, 1993), 164–168; and Kux, *The United States and Pakistan, 1947–2000: Disenchanted Allies* (Washington, D.C.: Woodrow Wilson Center Press; Baltimore: Johns Hopkins University Press, 2001), 106–11.

20. This account of the "U-2 summit" and its background draws heavily on Michael R. Beschloss, *May-Day: Eisenhower, Khrushchev, and the U-2 Affair* (New York: Harper & Row, 1986).

21. *FRUS,* 1958–1960, vol. XIV, *Africa,* 381–83.

22. Ibid., 474.

23. Ibid., 446–47.

24. Ibid., 473–74.

25. See, for example, Madeleine G. Kalb, *The Congo Cables: The Cold War in Africa—From Eisenhower to Kennedy* (New York: Macmillan, 1982), 25. This account draws heavily on Kalb's book.

26. At the time of the Congo crisis in the early 1960s, the State Department's organization was much simpler than it is today. There was no Bureau of Political-Military Affairs, no Refugee Bureau, no Bureau for International Terrorism, and no elaborate management empire to control the allocation of resources in a systematic way.

27. Cargo later headed the State Department's Policy Planning Staff under Secre-

tary of State William Rogers, then went as ambassador to Nepal. Sisco went on to serve as assistant secretary of state for Near East and South Asian affairs and under secretary for political affairs. Vance served as ambassador to Zaire, and McBride, as ambassador to Zaire and later, Mexico. All were career Foreign Service officers.

28. For a detailed account of Lumumba's death and CIA's alleged role therein, see Kalb, *Congo Cables,* chap. 8.

29. *FRUS,* 1961–1963, vol. XX, *Congo Crisis,* 79–81.

30. Ibid., 135.

31. Ibid., 146.

32. Ibid., 157

33. Ibid., 341.

34. Ibid., 345–46.

35. Ibid., 353.

36. Ibid., 355

PART II: VIETNAM

Three. The Cold War Turned Hot

1. For a historical account of US-Vietnamese relations, see Robert Hopkins Miller, *The United States and Vietnam, 1787–1941* (Washington, D.C.: National Defense University Press, 1990).

2. "Free world" was a convenient catchall Cold War term used liberally in the United States at the time to describe the rest of the world not dominated by communist regimes and, more particularly, the Western or pro-Western nations allied to or friendly with the United States. Its simplistic terminology ignored the vast differences among governments and peoples, including their state of economic development and the vast differences in their attitudes toward the United States, the "leader of the free world," and the Soviet Union, the leader of the communist world.

3. Eisenhower used the phrase "a row of falling dominoes" to describe the situation in Southeast Asia in a press conference on April 7, 1954. See Hoopes, *Devil and John Foster Dulles,* 214.

4. Acheson, *Present at the Creation,* 671–78.

5. Ibid., 677.

6. See, for example, Rusk, *As I Saw It,* sec. V. For other possible policy choices open to successive presidents, see Robert H. Miller, "Vietnam: Folly, Quagmire, or Inevitability?" *Studies in Conflict and Terrorism* 15 (1992): 99–123.

7. Stanley Karnow, *Vietnam: A History* (New York: Viking Press, 1983), 268.

8. Anthony Lake and Peter Tarnoff served as staff assistants to successive ambassadors. Richard Holbrooke, who had been assigned in the Mekong Delta in a junior AID position, made sure that he came to Saigon often enough to get the ear of high-level mission officers. Eventually, when Jimmy Carter was elected president in 1976, Lake, Tarnoff, and Holbrooke attached themselves to Carter's foreign policy team and served

in senior positions in the State Department under Secretary of State Cyrus Vance: Lake as director of the Policy Planning Council, Holbrooke as assistant secretary of state for East Asia and the Pacific, and Tarnoff as executive secretary. Later, during the Clinton administration, Lake became Clinton's national security adviser, Tarnoff became under secretary of state for political affairs, and Holbrooke became ambassador to Germany. Then, as assistant secretary of state for Europe and Canada, Holbrooke was widely credited with hammering out the Dayton Accords that restored peace in Bosnia and a later agreement providing for the withdrawal of Serbian forces from Kosovo. Thereafter, he became U.S. permanent representative to the United Nations.

Although they left the Foreign Service at different times and under different circumstances, the three tied themselves to one or more top Democratic political figures like Cyrus Vance and Averell Harriman. All five were also close to Philip Habib, the senior Foreign Service officer whose own remarkable career took off with Vietnam and carried him to top positions of influence with successive secretaries of state and presidents. Habib, like his political seniors, recognized the talents and ambitions of these young men and helped to promote their fortunes along the way.

Negroponte and Wisner stayed with the career Foreign Service. Their rise through the ranks, if not meteoric, was far more rapid than normal, and they did well under both Democratic and Republican administrations. During the Reagan-Bush years, Negroponte, who had been on Henry Kissinger's NSC staff during the Nixon presidency, served as ambassador to Honduras, assistant secretary of state, deputy national security adviser to General Colin Powell, and later, ambassador to Mexico. Wisner served as ambassador to Zambia, Egypt, and the Philippines. Both continued to prosper in the Clinton administration: Negroponte as ambassador to the Philippines and Wisner first as deputy under secretary of defense (under Secretary of Defense Les Aspin, whom he knew from Vietnam), under secretary of state, and then as ambassador to India. President George W. Bush named Negroponte ambassador to the United Nations.

9. For a detailed account of this program, see William A. Buckingham Jr., *Operation Ranch Hand: The Air Force and Herbicides in Southeast Asia, 1961–1971* (Washington, DC: Office of Air Force History, United States Air Force, 1982). For background on the evolution of policy regarding chemical defoliation and crop destruction, as well as the evaluation of the early test operations, see *FRUS,* 1961–1963, vol. II, *Vietnam, 1962,* especially chaps. 7 and 9, and vol. III, *Vietnam, January–August 1963.*

10. *FRUS,* 1961–1963, vol. III, docs. 58, 63, 96, 98, 110, and 242.

11. For a detailed account of the battle of Ap Bac and its impact on U.S. policy and actions in Vietnam, see Neil Sheehan, *A Bright Shining Lie: John Paul Vann and America in Vietnam* (New York: Random House, 1988), Book 3.

12. *FRUS,* 1961–1963, vol. III, doc. 42.

13. Ibid., doc. 66.

14. Ibid., doc. 100.

15. Ibid., doc. 120.

16. Ibid., doc. 19.

17. Ibid., doc. 45.

18. Nolting had received routine home-leave-and-return orders in mid-April (*FRUS,* 1961–1963, vol. III, doc. 91).

19. For an embassy assessment of the elections, which took place on September 27, 1963, see *FRUS,* 1961–1963, vol. IV, *Vietnam, August–December 1963,* doc. 155.

20. A colleague, Kenneth Rogers, who was consul at the time, recounts that Tri Quang arrived at the embassy entrance surrounded by twenty or so soldiers with their guns at the ready. Tri Quang was greeted by Rogers, who told him to hold onto his (Rogers's) belt. Rogers then backed into the embassy without touching the monk but with him holding on. Rogers wished neither to provoke the South Vietnamese authorities by actively escorting him into the embassy, nor to embarrass the U.S. government by such an action.

21. See *FRUS,* 1961–1963, vol. III, doc. 281, together with footnote 1, for the text of the first of numerous instructions to Lodge that ended with the coup of November 1, 1963, against Diem. Footnote 1 briefly describes the still-controversial process by which that first instruction was (or was not) coordinated at the highest levels of the U.S. government. See also Anne Blair, *Lodge in Vietnam: A Patriot Abroad* (New Haven, Conn.: Yale University Press, 1995), and Francis X. Winters, *The Year of the Hare: America in Vietnam, January 25, 1963–February 15, 1964* (Athens and London: University of Georgia Press, 1997), for assessments of Lodge's ambassadorships in Vietnam.

22. *FRUS,* 1961–1963, vol. IV, doc. 12.

23. See *FRUS,* 1961–1963, vol. IV, doc. 83, for an account of the meeting with the president.

24. See *FRUS,* 1961–1963, vol. IV, doc. 73, for the mission's instructions.

25. See *FRUS,* 1961–1963, vol. IV, doc. 136, for a summary of embassy views. As footnote 2 to that document indicates, MACV did not agree with the embassy's views and sent in its own independent assessment.

26. See *FRUS,* 1961–1963, vol. III, docs. 175 and 179, respectively, for Washington's earlier instructions and Trueheart's reply.

27. See, for example, *FRUS,* 1961–1963, vol. IV, doc. 92.

28. *FRUS,* 1961–1963, vol. IV, doc. 102.

29. Ibid., doc. 266.

30. *Ibid.,* doc. 338. See also Blair, *Lodge in Vietnam,* 104–5, 114–15, for discussion of "neutralism" in South Vietnam; and Winters, *Year of the Hare,* 79, 86, regarding Ngo Dinh Nhu's contacts with Hanoi.

31. Blair, *Lodge in Vietnam,* 114–15.

32. See Blair, *Lodge in Vietnam,* 138–40, for an account of Lodge's resignation.

33. See, for example, *FRUS,* 1964–1968, vol. II, *Vietnam, January–June 1965,* docs. 153 and 252.

34. See William Prochnau, *Once upon a Distant War: Young War Correspondents and the Early Vietnam Battles* (New York: Times Books, 1995), for an in-depth account of the press in Vietnam during that period.

35. An account of Taylor's consultations appears in H. R. McMaster, *Dereliction of Duty: Lyndon Johnson, Robert McNamara, the Joint Chiefs of Staff, and the Lies That Led to*

Vietnam (New York: HarperCollins, 1997), 189–94. I attended none of the meetings described therein.

Four. The Home-Front War

1. State Department Records, East Asia Bureau (hereinafter SDR), Unger memo to VNCC members, 11/5/65, Boxes 75D167 and 74D362.

2. SDR, Miller memo to VNCC members, 10/20/65, Box 71D88.

3. SDR, Miller memo to Unger, 10/25/65.

4. SDR, Unger memo to VNCC members, 4/19/66.

5. SDR, Miller memo to Unger, 8/24/66, Boxes 70D233, 70D45 and 70D212.

6. SDR, Unger memo to Komer, 8/24/66.

7. SDR, Komer memo to Unger, 8/31/66.

8. SDR, Miller memo to Unger, 10/3/66.

9. *FRUS,* 1964–1968, vol. IV, *Vietnam, 1966,* doc. 147.

10. SDR, Unger memo through Bundy to Ball, 3/15/66, Box 75D167, 74D362.

11. *FRUS,* 1964–1968, vol. IV, doc. 177.

12. Ibid., doc. 188.

13. SDR, Miller memo to Cooper, 9/14/66, Boxes 70D233, 70D45 and 70D212.

14. *FRUS,* 1964–1968, vol. IV, doc. 236.

15. SDR, Miller memo to Unger, 3/7/67, Box 72D207. I have no idea whether my memo went any further than Unger's desk. However, William Bundy, in the fifth volume of his five-volume unpublished study of U.S. government decision making on Vietnam, discusses the significance of the change of government in Indonesia. He asserts that by March 1966—one year before my memo—"there was no doubt that Suharto, Malik, and their cohorts had come out on top." Bundy quotes George Kennan, also in the spring of 1966, as judging that the Indonesian events had "much reduced . . . [the] stakes for which the United States was acting in Vietnam." Bundy concludes: "It is an extension that I rejected at the time, but it will be one of the might-have-beens to explore. . . ." Bundy argues that "during the fall and winter of 1965–66, no such long-term conclusions could even be attempted. . . . Hence, the immediate significance of Indonesia was not great, nor was it ever argued in Washington discussions that the possible fall of Sukarno made a difference that reached into American policy discussions concerning Vietnam. Short-sighted or not, this was the historic fact. For the time being, all that could be seen was that China's calculations had gone astray, but not that she had suffered what was necessarily a lasting or serious defeat."

16. SDR, Unger memo to Harriman, 4/17/67, Box 70D202.

17. SDR, Bundy memo to Rusk, drafted by Miller, 9/13/67, Box 7D207.

Five. Peace Talks in Paris

1. See Raymond Seitz, *Over Here* (London: Weidenfeld and Nicolson, 1998), pt. V. Seitz, a Foreign Service colleague who capped his career as ambassador to the Court of

Saint James's in London, has written an entertaining and insightful account of British attitudes toward Europe and the United States.

2. Karnow, *Vietnam: A History,* 536.

3. Ibid., 575–76.

4. The account of Thieu's special adviser and ambassador to Washington, Bui Diem (Bui Diem with David Chanoff, *In the Jaws of History* [Boston: Houghton Mifflin, 1987]) gives an interesting Vietnamese insider's version of these events.

5. When I was serving in Malaysia some years later, An called me from France and upbraided me for my staff's decision to allow one of his sons, who had arrived in East Malaysia (Sabah) by boat as a refugee, to be sent to France rather than to the United States, where his prospects would have been much brighter.

6. SDR, Paris Peace Talks Files (hereinafter PPTF), Group B, Box 20 of 27, Miller memo, 11/12/68.

7. SDR, PPTF, Group B, Box 20 of 27. See, for example, memo of conversation between Harriman and Lam, 11/13/68.

8. SDR, PPTF, Group B, Box 20 of 27, Miller memo, 11/15/68.

9. SDR, PPTF, Group B, Box 15 of 27, USDEL [U.S. delegation] Paris Tel [telegram] 24014, 11/17/68.

10. SDR, PPTF, Group B, Box 15 of 27, USDEL Paris Tel 24559, 11/27/68.

11. Henry Kissinger, *White House Years* (Boston: Little, Brown, 1979), 234.

12. SDR, PPTF, Group B, Box 15 of 27, Miller memo to Harriman, 12/27/68.

13. Kissinger, *White House Years,* 257–58.

14. SDR, PPTF, Group B, Box 15 of 27, USDEL Paris Tel 434, 1/12/69.

15. Ibid., Miller memo of conversation, 1/16/69.

16. Ibid., Toumayan memo of conversation, 1/17/69.

17. Ibid., USDEL Paris Tel 781, 1/18/69.

18. Ibid., USDEL Paris Tel 788, 1/18/69.

19. Kissinger, *White House Years,* 52.

20. Ibid., 52–53.

21. Ibid., 29.

22. SDR, PPTF, Group B, Box 14 of 27, USDEL Amembassy [American Embassy] Paris, "Chronology of Plenary Sessions," 5/6/70.

23. Ibid.

24. Sheehan, *Bright Shining Lie,* uses Vann's flawed character as a paradigm for what he sees as the flawed U.S. policy in Vietnam.

25. SDR, PPTF, Group B, Box 14, USDEL Amembassy Paris, "Chronology of Plenary Sessions," 5/6/70.

26. See Allan E. Goodman, *The Lost Peace: America's Search for a Negotiated Settlement of the Vietnam War* (Stanford, Calif.: Hoover Institution Press, 1978), for a detailed account and analysis of the U.S. search for an elusive peace in Vietnam from 1962 to 1975.

27. Kissinger, *White House Years,* 278.

28. Ibid., 444.
29. Ibid., 448.
30. Ibid., 308.
31. Ibid., 282.
32. Rusk, *As I Saw It,* 497.

Six. The Fighting Ends

1. In later years Iklé went on to become an under secretary of defense in the Reagan presidency. Wolfowitz ultimately had a distinguished career as assistant secretary of state for East Asian and Pacific affairs, ambassador to Indonesia, and under secretary of defense for policy during the Reagan-Bush years. During the Clinton years he left government to become dean of the Johns Hopkins University's School of Advanced International Studies and later served the George W. Bush administration as deputy secretary of defense.

2. This background is based on memoranda from SDR, MBFR, Box 74D473: Kissinger memo to secretaries of state and defense, 7/10/73, subject: Conducting MBFR and Security Conference Negotiations; Dean memo to Rush, 7/24/73, subject: Increase in Personnel for D/MBFR; Rogers memo to the President, 7/27/72, subject: Conducting MBFR and European Security Conference Negotiations; Iklé memo to Rogers, 8/8/73, subject: Backstopping for MBFR; Dean memo to Rush, 8/17/73; Pickering memo to Rush, 8/21/73, subject: Position Reallocation Decisions; Pickering memo to Rush, 8/24/73, subject: Backstopping MBFR; Dean memo to Rush, 8/24/73, subject: Your Forthcoming Discussion with Dr. Kissinger—Need for Decisions on MBFR; Pickering memo for the record, 9/11/73, subject: Staffing MBFR.

3. For an interesting, if unorthodox, interpretation of why Vietnam became a Cold War battleground far out of proportion to its intrinsic importance, see Winters, *Year of the Hare.*

4. In the third volume of his memoirs, *Years of Renewal* (New York: Simon & Schuster, 1999), 483, Henry Kissinger cites Bullington's report as evidence supporting his contention that the Democratic-controlled Congress was responsible for the United States' failure to live up to its commitments to South Vietnam.

5. A colleague, Francis Terry McNamara, who was then consul general in Can Tho in the Mekong Delta, has written a gripping account of his escape down the Bas Sac River using two small naval vessels that were able to carry to safety all American and many Vietnamese and third-country employees (*Escape with Honor: My Last Hours in Vietnam* [Washington, D.C., and London: Brassey's, 1997]).

6. Kissinger, *Years of Renewal,* 536–46, gives an account of these meetings. William Colby, a key participant in these meetings in the White House Situation Room, in the opening chapter of *Lost Victory: A Firsthand Account of America's Sixteen-Year Involvement in Vietnam* (Chicago: Contemporary Books, 1989), also captures the somber atmosphere of gloom and inevitability that pervaded the Ford administration's deliberations on Vietnam in the final days.

7. U.S. Congress, Senate Judiciary Committee, "Indochina Evacuation and Refugee Problems, Part I: Operation Babylift & Humanitarian Needs" (Washington, D.C.: Government Printing Office, 1975).

8. Ibid.

9. Stone eventually went to Cyprus as ambassador.

10. SDR, Box 78D268, Memo from Habib and Lord [Winston Lord, Director of Policy Planning] to the Secretary, 5/6/75.

11. Ibid.

12. In *Years of Renewal,* Kissinger devotes an entire chapter to the *Mayaguez* incident: chap. 18, "Anatomy of a Crisis: The *Mayaguez,*" 547–75. In it he recounts his irritation with Zurhellen and with the entire bureaucracy beneath him for sitting on the information (which was not the case). It turns out that his other accusation, that the bureaucracy knew that the Cambodians had stopped other ships a few days before stopping the *Mayaguez* but had not bothered to inform him, is true. As often happens in the bureaucracy, the desk concerned with the earlier incident had not informed those dealing with Southeast Asia. Even if it had, I'm not sure we would have considered it important enough to alert the secretary, nor am I sure he would have wanted to know. Kissinger also gives an account of the NSC's deliberations in this chapter. See also Ralph Wetterhahn, *The Last Battle: The* Mayaguez *Incident and the End of the Vietnam War* (New York: Carroll & Graff Publishers, 2001) for a recent account focusing largely on military operations and issues.

13. See Paul F. Gardner, *Shared Hopes, Separate Fears: Fifty Years of U.S.-Indonesian Relations* (Boulder, Colo.: Westview Press, 1997).

14. Sullivan was a former ambassador to Laos and later U.S. ambassador to Iran when the embassy in Tehran was stormed some months before the taking of hostages.

PART III: BEYOND VIETNAM

Seven. Aftermath

1. For a careful, detailed study of U.S.-Malaysian relations, see Pamela Sodhy's *The U.S.-Malaysian Nexus: Themes in Superpower–Small State Relations* (Kuala Lumpur, Malaysia: Institute of Strategic and International Studies [ISIS], 1991).

2. See Barry Wain's *The Refused: The Agony of the Indochina Refugees* (New York: Simon & Schuster, 1981) for a vivid account of the Indochina refugee drama in Southeast Asia at the time.

3. See Sodhy, *U.S.-Malaysian Nexus,* chap. VIII, for a more detailed account of Hussein Onn's visit to Washington.

4. See Wain, *The Refused,* 20–35, for an account of the *Hai Hong* episode.

5. Wain, *The Refused,* 196–97.

6. See Karnow, *Vietnam: A History,* 58–59, and Steven Hurst, *The Carter Administration and Vietnam* (Basingstoke, UK: Macmillan; New York: St. Martin's Press, 1996), Introduction.

7. Jane C. Loeffler's *The Architecture of Diplomacy: Building America's Embassies* (New York: Princeton Architectural Press, 1998) includes the Kuala Lumpur embassy building on 235, 242, 244–46, and fig. 127. See also Carleton Knight III, "The U.S. Chancery in Malaysia: Neither Fortress nor Hut," *Architecture* (July 1986), 62–68.

Eight. Last Assignments, Retirement, and a Return to Vietnam

1. Keyes, a career Foreign Service officer, later ran repeatedly, if unsuccessfully, for public office in Maryland and for the Republican nomination for president.

Bibliography

UNPUBLISHED WORKS

Bundy, William P. Unpublished study on Vietnam decision making. 5 vols.

U.S. State Department, East Asia Bureau. Records. Boxes 75D167, 74D362, 71D88, 70D233, 70D45, 70D212, 70D207, 72D207, 78D268.

———. Paris Peace Talks Files. Group B. 27 Boxes.

———. MBFR, Box 74D473.

PUBLISHED WORKS

Acheson, Dean. *Present at the Creation: My Years in the State Department.* New York: W. W. Norton, 1987.

Beschloss, Michael R. *May-Day: Eisenhower, Khrushchev, and the U-2 Affair.* New York: Harper & Row, 1986.

Bird, Kai. *The Color of Truth: McGeorge Bundy and William Bundy—A Biography.* New York: Simon & Schuster, 1998.

Blair, Anne. *Lodge in Vietnam: A Patriot Abroad.* New Haven, Conn.: Yale University Press, 1995.

Boykin, John. *Cursed Is the Peacemaker: The American Diplomat versus the Israeli General, Beirut 1982.* Belmont, Calif: Applegate Press, 2002.

Buckingham, William A., Jr. *Operation Ranch Hand: The Air Force and Herbicides in Southeast Asia, 1961–1971.* Washington, D.C.: Office of Air Force History, United States Air Force, 1982.

Bui Diem, with David Chanoff. *In the Jaws of History.* Boston: Houghton Mifflin, 1987.

Colby, William, with James McCargar. *Lost Victory: A Firsthand Account of America's Sixteen-Year Involvement in Vietnam.* Chicago: Contemporary Books, 1989.

Eisenhower, Dwight D. *The White House Years: Waging Peace, 1956–61.* Garden City, N.Y.: Doubleday, 1963–65.

Gardner, Paul. *Shared Hopes, Separate Fears: Fifty Years of U.S.-Indonesian Relations.* Boulder, Colo.: Westview Press, 1997.

Goodman, Allan E. *The Lost Peace: America's Search for a Negotiated Settlement of the Vietnam War*. Stanford, Calif.: Hoover Institution Press, 1978.

Hoopes, Townsend. *The Devil and John Foster Dulles.* Boston: Little, Brown, 1973.

Hurst, Steven. *The Carter Administration and Vietnam.* Basingstoke, UK: Macmillan; and New York: St. Martin's Press, 1996.

Johnson, U. Alexis, with Jeff Olivarius McAllister. *The Right Hand of Power: The Memoirs of an American Diplomat.* Englewood Cliffs, N.J.: Prentice-Hall, 1984.

Kalb, Madeleine. *The Congo Cables: The Cold War in Africa—From Eisenhower to Kennedy.* New York: Macmillan, 1982.

Karnow, Stanley. *Paris in the Fifties.* New York: Times Books, 1997.

———. *Vietnam: A History.* New York: Viking Press, 1983.

Kissinger, Henry. *White House Years.* Boston: Little, Brown, 1979.

———. *Years of Renewal.* New York: Simon & Schuster, 1999.

Knight, Carleton III. "The U.S. Chancery in Malaysia: Neither Fortress nor Hut." *Architecture* (July 1986): 62–68.

Kux, Dennis. *India and the United States: Estranged Democracies, 1941–1991.* Washington, D.C.: National Defense University Press, 1993.

———. *The United States and Pakistan, 1947–2000: Disenchanted Allies.* Washington, D.C.: Woodrow Wilson Center Press; Baltimore: Johns Hopkins University Press, 2001.

Lodge, Henry Cabot. *The Storm Has Many Eyes: A Personal Narrative.* New York: W. W. Norton, 1973.

Loeffler, Jane C. *The Architecture of Diplomacy: Building America's Embassies.* New York: Princeton Architectural Press, 1998.

McMaster, H. R. *Dereliction of Duty: Lyndon Johnson, Robert McNamara, the Joint Chiefs of Staff and the Lies That Led to VietnamE-.* New York: HarperCollins, 1997.

McNamara, Francis Terry. *Escape with Honor: My Last Hours in Vietnam.* Washington, D.C.: Brassey's, 1997.

McNamara, Robert S., with Brian VanDeMark. *In Retrospect: The Tragedy and Lessons of Vietnam.* New York: Times Books, Random House, 1995.

Miller, Robert H. *The United States and Vietnam, 1787–1941.* Washington, D.C., and London: National Defense University Press, 1990.

———. "Vietnam: Folly, Quagmire, or Inevitability?" *Studies in Conflict and Terrorism* 15 (1992).

Nguyen Cao Ky, with Marvin J. Wolf. *Buddha's Child: My Fight to Save Vietnam.* New York: St. Martin's Press, 2002.

Nolting, Frederick E. *From Trust to Tragedy: The Political Memoirs of Frederick Nolting, Kennedy's Ambassador to Diem's Vietnam.* New York: Praeger, 1988.

Prochnau, William. *Once upon a Distant War: Young War Correspondents and the Early Vietnam Battles.* New York: Times Books, 1995.

Rusk, Dean, as told to Richard Rusk. *As I Saw It.* Edited by Daniel S. Papp. New York: W. W. Norton, 1990.

Schick, Jack M. *The Berlin Crisis, 1958–1962.* Philadelphia: University of Pennsylvania Press, 1971.

Seitz, Raymond. *Over Here.* London: Weidenfeld and Nicolson, 1998.

Sheehan, Neil. *A Bright Shining Lie: John Paul Vann and America in Vietnam.* New York: Random House, 1988.

Smith, Merriman. *A President's Odyssey.* New York: Harper, 1961.

Sodhy, Pamela. *The U.S.-Malaysian Nexus: Themes in Superpower–Small State Relations.* Kuala Lumpur, Malaysia: Institute of Strategic and International Studies [ISIS], 1991.

U.S. Congress, Senate Judiciary Committee. "Indochina Evacuation and Refugee Problems, Part I: Operation Babylift & Humanitarian Needs." Washington, D.C.: Government Printing Office, 1975.

U.S. Department of State. *Foreign Ministers Meeting, May–August 1959, Geneva.* Department of State Publication 6882, September 1959.

———. *Foreign Relations of the United States (FRUS).* Washington, D.C.: Department of State, 1983–1994.

———. *FRUS.* 1952–1954. Vol. V, *Western European Security, Part I,* 1983.

———. *FRUS.* 1958–1960. Vol. VI, *Cuba,* 1991.

———. *FRUS.* 1958–1960. Vol. XIV, *Africa,* 1992.

———. *FRUS.* 1958–1960. Vol. XV, *South and Southeast Asia,* 1992.

———. *FRUS.* 1961–1963. Vol. II, *Vietnam, 1962,* 1990.

———. *FRUS.* 1961–1963. Vol. III, *Vietnam, January–August 1963,* 1991.

———. *FRUS.* 1961–1963. Vol. IV, *Vietnam, August–December 1963,* 1991.

———. *FRUS.* 1961–1963. Vol. XX, *Congo Crisis,* 1994.

———. *FRUS.* 1964–1968. Vol. IV, *Vietnam, 1966,* 1992.

Wain, Barry. *The Refused: The Agony of the Indochina Refugees.* New York: Simon & Schuster, 1981.

Wetterhahn, Ralph. *The Last Battle: The* Mayaguez *Incident and the End of the Vietnam War.* New York: Carroll & Graff Publishers, 2001.

Winters, Francis X. *The Year of the Hare: America in Vietnam, January 25, 1963–February 15, 1964.* Athens and London: University of Georgia Press, 1997.

Index